Performing the Past

A Study of Israeli Settlement Museums

ဆ ▪ ૦ઙ

Everyday Communication: Case Studies of Behavior in Context
Wendy Leeds-Hurwitz & Stuart J. Sigman, Series Editors

Performing the Past

A Study of Israeli Settlement Museums

ഇ ▪ ര

Tamar Katriel
University of Haifa

LEA LAWRENCE ERLBAUM ASSOCIATES, PUBLISHERS
1997 Mahwah, New Jersey   London

Lawrence Erlbaum Associates, Inc., Publishers
10 Industrial Avenue
Mahwah, New Jersey 07430

Cover design by Mairav Salomon-Dekel

Library of Congress Cataloging-in-Publication Data

Katriel, Tamar
Performing the past : a study of Israeli settlement museums /
Tamar Katriel.
p. cm.
Includes bibliographical references and index.
ISBN 0-8058-1657-7. —ISBN 0-8058-1658-5
1.Kibbutzim—Museums. 2.Historical museums—Is-
rael–Yif'at. 3. Historical museums—Israel—Ein Shemer. 4.
Museums—Educational aspects—Israel. 5. Communication
and culture—Israel. I. Title.
HX742.A3K38 1997
307.77'6'095694—dc21 96-6601
CIP

Printed in the United States of America
10 9 8 7 6 5 4 3 2 1

Contents

ℬ ∎ ℛ

Editors' Preface

ℰ ∎ ℛ

The editorial mission of the "Everyday Communication" series is to provide a forum for scholarship addressing the relationship between communication and context. As editors we have not confined our work to a single definition or framework for the study of "context," and indeed across the several books currently in print no one level or approach to this has predominated. The monographs already published have demonstrated that there is no single object to be labeled "context," and that relevant contexts are both fluid and of varying sizes.

Tamar Katriel's *Performing the Past: A Study of Israeli Settlement Museums* interweaves many levels and types of context, and thus provides readers with a rich perspective on communication performances within and about Israel's pioneer museums. Katriel examines tour guides as they set about hosting visitors to one or the other of two such museums. At its most basic level, her analysis focuses on the interactional unfolding of each tour guide's narrative during particular tours—how the physicality of each museum enters into the performance, how accommodations to the various audiences (Jews vs. Arabs, religious vs. nonreligious Jews) are embedded in each story, and what the guides envision they are accomplishing by their work.

But each tour performance is not only contextualized by the particular museum being presented and the particular kibbutz in which it is located. Katriel shows us that the tour performances invoke a master narrative about Israeli settlement, the multiple waves of immigrants to this land, and the relationship between Jewish and Arab inhabitants. This master narrative is accepted by some and rejected by others, but all participants in the museums' tours are positioned in relationship to it. The various discursive accommodations made to Mizrahi Jews (those from the Middle East and North Africa), religious Jews, and Arabs in the context of guided tours represent the ongoing struggle for identity, power, and self-determination of each of these groups on the larger Israeli political and cultural scene. Thus, this master narrative is not confined to discourse within or about particular settlement museums, but indeed has influenced the ideas forming the larger struggle for Israeli identity and Arab–Jewish relationships in Israel.

Based on 4 years of ethnographic visits to the two museums, Katriel's work incorporates an analysis of 30 hours of audiotape and 30 hours of videotape data. The analysis is initially constructed as a Hymesian ethnography of communication performance, emphasizing the connection between the visual forms (the material objects being displayed in each museum) and the verbal behavior (the interpretive stories told by the guides) that constitute the tour event. The study ultimately develops into a meditation on how people construct their past, and convey it among themselves and to others—their peers, their neighbors, and the next generations. Recognizing that the struggle to maintain and communicate an identity is not limited to local history museums, in her conclusion Katriel situates the two museums in a broader context of the Israeli museum scene and the still larger discourse in the media and in modern fiction, where ideas about identity are continually debated and refined.

Because the negotiation of identity and place is a political as well as a communicative act, and because Katriel both describes and critiques the museum performances which are local instances of this ongoing national negotiation, this study is likely to gain considerable attention. It contributes significantly to the national (and international) conversation over how the varying claims regarding control of the land and attachment to place are being addressed and negotiated in various cultural contexts.

In brief, Katriel offers a cultural analysis of one type of communication performance; this analysis contextualizes the museum tours through consideration of their immediate interactional circumstances and of the history of the participants' ongoing and contentious relations with each other.

Wendy Leeds-Hurwitz
Stuart J. Sigman

Acknowledgments

ℰ **■** ℭ

I owe a great deal to a great many people who have accompanied my work on this project in a variety of ways. My deepest gratitude goes to the museum guides and curators at Yifat and Ein Shemer for their warm hospitality, their interest in my work, and their willingness to contribute to it despite the inevitable intrusiveness this sometimes entailed. I dedicate this book to them.

Many colleagues, too many to mention by name (both in Israel and abroad), have responded to oral or written versions of parts of this project. I have greatly benefited from their insightful comments. The many conversations I have had with Barbara Kirshenblatt-Gimblett, who has encouraged this study from its very inception, have been particularly important to my thinking on issues related to museums and heritage. She has also read and commented extensively on an earlier draft of the manuscript. I am also greatly indebted to Don Handelman for volunteering to read the manuscript and for important suggestions he made, some of which were incorporated into its final version. Rivki Ribak, my son, Hagai, and my partner, Jacob, read the first draft of the manuscript. Tamar Rapoport and Brenda Danet have read the close-to-final draft. I especially appreciate their willingness to do so at these crucial stages in the writing process, and their many helpful comments. The series editors, Wendy Leeds-Hurwitz and Stuart Sigman, deserve my special gratitude for their interest in my work, their valuable comments, and their patience. Of course, I remain responsible for the use I have made of all these responses to my work.

I owe a debt of gratitude to Shimon Zafrir for his help with the videotaping that formed part of my data base, and to Yair Gil for generously volunteering to do the photography work included in this book.

I would like to acknowledge a grant I received from the Basic Science Fund of the Israel Academy of Sciences and Humanities, which enabled me to do the kind of data collection this study required. I am also extremely grateful to the Institute for Advanced Studies at the Hebrew University in Jerusalem for a 6 month fellowship I received as a member of the research group on "Visual Culture in Modern Jewish Societies," headed by Ezra Mendelson and Richard Cohen, in the spring and summer of 1996. This fellowship gave me an ideal scholarly environment in which to complete the book.

Tamar Katriel

ఴ ▪ ಐ

The living utterance, having taken meaning and shape at a particular historical moment in a socially specific environment, cannot fail to brush up against thousands of living dialogic threads, woven by socio-ideological consciousness around the given object of an utterance; it cannot fail to become an active participant in social dialogue. After all, the utterance arises out of this dialogue as a continuation of it and as a rejoinder to it—it does not approach the object from the sidelines.
—Bakhtin (1981, pp. 276–277)

ఴ ▪ ಐ

Chapter 1

By Way of Introduction

80 ▪ 08

HERE IT ALL BEGAN: TALES OF ORIGIN

Driving along a country road in the Jezreel valley, some 15 minutes from the village where we were living at the time, I spotted the sign of "the museum for the beginning of settlement" in *kibbutz* Yifat. It was the fall of 1980 and we had recently returned from a 2-year stay in the United States. I thought it would be a good idea to take the kids there on one of our Saturday morning excursions; it was high time they learned about their own roots after all the sightseeing we had done in the American West. A couple of weeks later, we drove up the hill and found ourselves at the Yifat museum. There were very few people there on that crisp Saturday morning, and the valley lay before us in all its splendor. The leaves of the olive trees that spread over the slope of the hill shone and shimmered in the mellow sun and the light wind of early autumn. I took a deep breath and felt that yes, we're back home.

My 8-year-old daughter's hand held fast to mine; we walked into the walled enclave of the museum itself and began to move along the somewhat cluttered display of agricultural tools that hung on the walls or lay on the ground. The kids climbed the old tractors, we peeped into the reconstructed pioneers' tent, entered the communal dining room and pretended to eat from the tin plates on the rough wooden tables. The babies' cabin with the small cots covered by a mosquito net and several earthen pots caught my daughter's fancy. We stopped at some of the enlarged pictures of pioneers that were scattered on the walls, helping me to put some faces on the fragments of pioneering tales I was trying to recount to the kids. There were very few explanatory labels and no other means of verbally mediating the display. The elderly man who had greeted us on our arrival said that the guides were off duty on Saturday and went back to the far

1

corner of the museum from which he had emerged, apparently interrupting some work he was doing there. We had never seen some of the tools and household implements before; others looked vaguely familiar, and a few matched implements the kids could still remember from grandma's kitchen and grandpa's basement. For us adults, there was something both touching and amusing about this blend of strange and familiar objects, and we walked around the museum for a while, fingering artifacts, identifying some and guessing at others. We spent about an hour in the museum, moving around playfully at our will, half recalling and half making up stories that would help the kids give meaning to what we were seeing. And when we were ready to leave, my daughter stopped short in her tracks and asked for the third time: "But what kind of museum is this?" Intercepting her older brother's impatient look, I tried once again: "They call it the museum of the beginning of settlement. It's about the people who came to Israel many years ago and were the first ones to settle the land. We call them pioneers." Again she pondered for a moment and finally a smile spread over her face. "Ah, I know, you mean Adam and Eve."

Museums, I realized, are open texts. Both the inexplicable magic of the place and the memory of my daughter's struggle to make sense of it have stayed with me. Less than 10 years later, I came back to the Yifat museum with a group of students who were participating in my seminar on communication and material culture. I had arranged for us to be taken on a guided tour of the museum, thinking that it would be a good place to explore the interface between verbal and material culture. The museum had not changed much, although there seemed to be a few more labels. It was a weekday and the museum director at the time, an old-timer who introduced himself as Binyamin, took us around and held us in his spell for some 3 hours with tales of pioneering and with stories about the making of the museum. This time, the museum came alive for me in a new way and we all felt we could not disentangle the artifacts on display from the stories Binyamin wove around them. Words and objects became intertwined in a way that both enhanced and constrained our movement within the museum context and our reading of the museum setting.

It was this point of semiotic interest and the lure of the recounted stories that originally drew me to the museum. As a discursive site, it seemed to invite rhetorical analysis and criticism. Following several more visits, I obtained the permission of several guides to make the Yifat museum my research field. The museum became increasingly attractive to me as a public site in which cultural meanings were constructed and communicated through both visual display and verbal mediation. I soon realized that its study would require serious attention to the ideological and political dimensions of the museum-making enterprise as well. To get a better sense of the presentational strategies and ideological dilemmas associated with the telling and retelling of the socialist Zionist settlement story in the late 1980s, I decided to enrich my study by including another museum, and after some deliberation chose The Old Courtyard in Ein-Shemer as my second research site. I had originally come to the museum to reaffirm my sense of belonging and teach my children about their roots, as I had unreflectively come to label the foundation mythology of early Zionist settlement of Israel. At an early point in my ethnographic journey, I was only dimly aware of the complexity of the museum's project of reconstructing the past and nurturing cultural roots. The poignancy of later museum encounters would bring it forth.

This complexity became epitomized for me in a phrase repeatedly used by the old-timer guide from Yifat museum, Sarah, a vivacious woman in her late 70s. Born to an Orthodox Jewish family in pre-state Palestine, she ran away from home at age 16 to join a young *kibbutz*. She is a living embodiment of the pioneering spirit and the communal life and speaks about both with great relish. I see her standing in the observation post, which is situated at the entrance to the Yifat museum, her eyes gleaming, and with a sweep of her hand, she embraces the flourishing valley at her feet and says to her audience with a pride and passion I cannot hope to emulate: "You see, here it all began!" Most of her listeners are captivated by the warmth in her voice, as I was, and to most of them, this statement does not sound at all problematic. Yet this does not mean it would be easy for any of them to specify what the *here* or the *it* signifies, or in what sense they together might signal a beginning. This statement thus seems both to point to and to gloss over the narrative complexities and ambiguities I have come to detect in settlement museum displays and narrations. In a sense, the rest of my fieldwork was devoted to tracing and problematizing the trajectories and resonances of meaning encapsulated in Sarah's statement, and in the museum narrative that it prefaced.

THE LESSON OF THE THREE STORIES: STORYTELLING AS A POETICS OF INDIRECTION

It was getting dark outside. The days were shorter now that our summer of intensive fieldwork in the Yifat and Ein Shemer museums was coming to its close. We were beginning to gather the video taping equipment, which this time included some lighting fixtures, when our guide, Ronen, motioned us to wait and said there was one more thing he wanted to say to the camera. It was something he didn't get to say to the young women he had just finished guiding through the museum, an afterthought. We might want to use it in making our video, he counseled. He seemed much more full of energy than we were even though this had been a particularly lengthy tour of The Old Courtyard—it lasted 2½ rather than the 1 to 1½ hours devoted to most settlement museum tours—and it came at the end of a long day's work.

In the course of this tour, Ronen had addressed a group of young women soldiers who were undergoing training as guides in one of the field schools sponsored by the Society for the Protection of Nature. He had himself worked in such a field school for several years in the past, and throughout the tour, he treated them as would-be colleagues, sharing not only the museum story but also his personal and professional thoughts about the heritage enterprise. Since my arrival in the Ein Shemer museum, he had been a central informant for me, very sympathetic to the research focus on the performances of tour guides. So we had many good discussions and I had more audio and video tapes of tours he had led through the museum than of any other guide. In fact, I had decided not to make any more tapes of him in the interest of diversification when he told me that I should make a point of coming to observe the tour with the women soldiers on that particular afternoon; it would be worth it. It did turn out to be quite an interesting tour, allowing me a direct glimpse of some of the processes whereby tour guide lore becomes articulated and transmitted in a semi-formal fashion. But what I most vividly remember of that afternoon were the words he spoke after the soldier girls were gone, summarizing to himself, to us, to posterity, what it meant to him to be telling and re-telling the Israeli settlement story.

I glanced pleadingly at Shimon, the graduate student who was a video professional and was in charge of the taping, because he seemed to be in a bit of a hurry. Shimon relented and we stopped our packing. He repositioned the lighting so that it would catch Ronen's face. Ronen was still wearing a *rubashka*, the Russian peasant shirt that was originally adopted by the Zionist pioneers and was recently re-adopted by some of the settlement museum guides as an emblem of pioneering. He was now seated upright at one of the tables in the museum's reconstructed dining room display, and was almost indistinguishable from the several mannequins of early pioneers that were dispersed in various standing and sitting positions around him. Thus, in an earnest tone of voice, his eyes fixed straight on me with but a glimmer of a smile, he added this post-performance addendum for our records:

> Good. In conclusion we'll tell a story with an educational lesson. Okay? Actually, what are we all making such an effort for? ... Our idea is that one has to deepen one's roots in this country, in this land, in this people, and therefore all this reconstruction of The Old Courtyard. In fact, it is an attempt to take this place and use it as an educational tool. It [the museum] is not an end in itself, and the educational tool—the experience, the story, the impression, the actual feeling—is the attempt to touch the roots of things, perhaps to reach those roots. Now, every educational process usually tries to build up

some frameworks—social and personal, psychological—in the child, in any-body who is being educated, with the hope that in the future he will reach some level of integration, socialization, something like that. And in this connection I want to tell a short story. First of all, I have a friend in Karkur [a nearby village] who has a beautiful private house, and at the entrance to the house, along the path and at the entrance, he has lots and lots of flower pots. And one day he came to ask my advice. He said to me: "Ronen, listen, I have this problem. I have this friend from Hadera [a nearby town], and he comes every once in a while to visit me, every month or two, with his family, and every time he comes into our house, he shows great concern and appreciation for our flower pots. And he goes and checks them, feels them with his fingers, examines their color, then he pulls them out, takes a look at the roots, to see if they're strong enough, and puts them back in. And each time after his visit, it's a catastrophe 'til the plants recover. It's a problem, what can one do with it?"

I couldn't really come up with an answer for him, but this is story number one. Story number two took place in 1921. In 1921 Churchill came to the land of Israel; he was then Minister of the Colonies, and he wrote a document they called "The First White Paper." He stayed in Jerusalem then, the Arabs came to him, headed by the Mufti; the Jews came, and they had to discuss what should be done with this country. On that occasion they detached the Eastern Bank of the Jordan, what is today known as the Kingdom of Jordan, in 1921, and gave it to Hussein's father. And on that occasion the first Hebrew city, Tel Aviv, wanted to do him [Churchill] a great honor, and Dizengoff [the Mayor] invited Churchill to see Tel Aviv, and Churchill's secretary said: "Okay, we're coming to Tel Aviv tomorrow." Oh, all the dignitaries of Tel Aviv, and Dizengoff among them [said]: "Quick, quick, what do we do? We have to organize a reception. He will come in his "dilidjans" [fancy car at that time], and there's to be the avenue, children with small flags, and a stage, and he'll give his greetings, and speeches." A Garden City [Tel Aviv] it was then called. Okay, they mobilized all the employees at the municipality and built a stage. They brought in trees, lots of trees, date trees, and dug holes in the ground, it was round about Maze Street. Then they pressed down the earth and made pavements. The next morning, Churchill was to arrive. But that night the weather turned very stormy, a great wind blew from the sea, hit the trees and they all fell flat. In the morning, when all the municipal workers arrived at 8:00, they saw the disaster. There was nothing they could do, and at nine o'clock the trumpets sounded and Churchill's "dilidjans" came in. All the children of Tel Aviv were standing and waving their flags, Dizengoff and all the municipality people were seated on the honorary stage, and he [Churchill] gave a speech and a greeting, and promised help and support, and they shook hands, and were photographed, and everything was fine. The ceremony began to disband and then they saw Churchill bend over towards Dizengoff. Later, the guys at the municipality asked him [Dizengoff]: "At the end there, what did he [Churchill] whisper in your ear?" And that's what he told him: "Listen, by us in England, when we line our avenues with trees, we plant them with deep roots so that they can hold on to the soil, and so that what happened to you doesn't happen to us, that every passing wind can uproot them. If the roots aren't deep, the whole tree, everything on top, will not hold on. Take our advice, from the British." That is story number two.

And now story number three. During the third *aliyah* [third immigration wave, 1919–1923], a Jew came, Asherke was his name, to *kibbutz* Tel Yosef in the valley, the Jezreel Valley. He had prepared himself to be an orchard worker [*pardesan*]; from ideological motivation he wanted to be an orchard-worker, and he was the orchard worker of Tel Yosef. Twenty years he was an orchard worker, and when the state was established, in 1948, in the early 1950s they were organizing the state and in the Ministry of Agriculture they asked, "Who is an expert on orchards?" They said "Asherke in Tel Yosef, he is the most experienced orchard worker in the country." They went to Asherke, and said to him, "You'll be the Ministry of Agriculture *madrich* [consultant] for orchard workers." But he said, "I don't want to be a consultant. I came to the land of Israel to be an orchard worker, all my life I've been an orchard worker, and all my life I'll remain one. I don't want any of this, all I want is to work in the orchard in Tel Yosef." But he was ready to compromise and said: "If there are specific cases that you cannot solve, call me, I am prepared to help you." In brief, one day they call him: "Come to Yavniel. There's a problem with an orchard plot, something terrible, nobody knows what to do. Nobody managed to do anything there, no advice seems to help—Asherke!" Fine, he went to Yavniel, and there, you know there's this slope going down to the valley, Yavniel's cultivation plots are partly on the slope and partly in the valley, the Yavniel Valley. He arrives in Yavniel, they get out of the car and onto the carriage and get to the plot. They mount the slope very slowly, come to the orchard plot and wring their hands. What do they see? Somebody, a farmer, planted an orchard on the slope, and the winter rains eroded all the soil from underneath the roots, and the trees were standing like that with the roots dangling in the air, no soil underneath, all the soil was down in the valley. The trees were altogether dry, fruit was out of the question. "Asherke, what do we do?" And the person [Asherke] turns round and round and says, "Listen, I don't know exactly what to do. I have no school solution for you, but, listen, the problem here is the altitude. You have to take into account that the soil will erode because if all the soil erodes from in between the roots then the tree will die. You have to plow according to the altitude of the mountain, and at the more distant spots, too, you have to plow deep enough and close enough [to the roots] but not get too close to them so that you don't hit the roots with the plow. Because also if you cut the roots with the plow then the tree will die. And so, if you do your plowing properly, and you plow according to the altitude, then the soil will not erode. The soil will be loose and the trees will stay in good shape and so the orchard will survive and not die. I think this is the solution," so said Asherke. This is the third story.

And our lesson, our educational lesson after 3 years of operating this Courtyard, is the lesson of the three stories. We don't know exactly if the educational goal we set out for ourselves as a means of cultivating our roots, our roots in this country, if it has been attained. But it's clear to us that it's no good to take out the roots all the time and see how they're doing and that we should plant them deep enough so that the soil can stick to them. And if we're doing this pedagogical work, this educational plowing, so on the one hand we should make our furrows deep, but we should also take care not to get too close so we don't cut the children's roots. At the same time we should not avoid plowing altogether or else the soil will erode and will not remain in its proper place. And then if we do all this perhaps there's a chance we'll achieve something with this educational tool, this Old Courtyard, and that's the idea for which this place was established (Ronen, Ein Shemer. 10.15.91)[1]

The flavor and texture of Ronen's stylized postperformance account are in many ways emblematic of the kind of museum discourse my study focuses on. In particular, the concatenation of apparently unrelated stories loosely linked through a common metaphor or overarching theme is a narrative strategy employed by all the museum guides I have observed as a matter of routine. And, as we shall see, many of these stories were metonymic in nature, providing narrative anchors that point to some aspect of the Zionist master-narrative that dominates the museum message through the concrete materiality of the items on display. This is, in a way, a poetics of indirection, replacing the pathos of Zionist preaching with the lightheartedness of everyday stories and folkloric tales. I couldn't help thinking that there was an echo of the Jewish sermon (drasha) and its use of the parable (mashal) about these performances.[2] The somewhat fragmentary, associative pattern of this style is particularly adaptable to the guided tour's movement along the museum display where every item stands on its own, inviting narrative elaboration in its own right but in a way that loosely connects it, through a shared moral lesson, to what came before and to what comes after. It is in the guide's act of performance that the threads of this narrative collage come together as they did in Ronen's recounting. What Ronen's postperformance seemed especially to dramatize was the contingency and fluidity of his performative acts. Despite the relative fixity of the museum's material display, the verbal interpretations attending them are essentially improvisational, and the guide can choose different stops and different stories as he or she moves along the tour route. So that just as Ronen's move from an informal chat with some of the visitors to the framework of the guided tour

---

[1]For each excerpt segment taken form a guided tour, I indicate the name (or pseudonym) of the speaker, the location of the museum (Yifat or Ein Shemer), and the date, following the American convention of month, day, year (thus, 10.8.91 would be October 8, 1991).

[2]Ufaz (1986) discussed the extensive employment of the form of the midrash by second-generation kibbutz ideologues, some of whom were directly associated with the settlement museum-making project. For an interesting recent discussion of a contemporary version of Jewish sermonizing within the framework of an anthropological study, see Shokeid (1995).

itself was clearly noticeable, so was the pronounced stylization of his verbal performance as he spoke to the camera.

A few years later, after I had included the vignette with Ronen as a way of introducing my study, I found a slightly different version of Ronen's three-part tale of roots in a book by Tsur (1995), one of the most influential contemporary leaders and ideologues of the kibbutz movement. My guess is that Ronen must have heard these stories from Tsur in one of his many public appearances as the kibbutz movement's arch-sermonizer and storyteller. Throughout the research, I would observe a free-flowing traffic of tales between published texts and oral narration (including Tsur's own 1981 popular collection of *kibbutz* tales), between one guide and another, one museum and another. Artful adaptation punctuated by occasional improvisation was the name of the game, and even though some tales were individually stamped (as in talk about "Binyamin's stories," for example) they were considered a publicly shared form of "cultural capital" (Bourdieu, 1984) to be drawn on by individual members, much like proverbs.

Ronen's stories bring out the overall character of settlement museum discourse, which is the focus of my study. Indeed, unlike most other contemporary secular discourses in mainstream Israeli educational settings, heritage museum discourse is explicitly and unabashedly saturated with ideological assertions. This is particularly notable in an era in which Zionist and post-Zionist scholars are engaged in an open public debate over the interpretation and standing of the Zionist project and its history (Cohen, 1995a; Kimmerling, 1995; Pappe, 1995; Ram, 1995b; Shapira, 1995). The post-Zionists' call for the legitimation of alternative views of Israeli history, such as the Palestinian version of the Jewish settlement story or the narrative that gives voice to the immigration experience of Middle Eastern and North African [*Mizrahi*] Jews, has no overt trace in the discourse of settlement museums. Whereas many contemporary scholars are engaged in either an attack or a defense of the hegemonic version of the Israeli nation-building story as it has been traditionally told in official histories and school texts, settlement museums appear to be unproblematically engaged in cultivating a singular idiom of place and roots that replicates this familiar tale. This idiom seems undisturbed by the historiographical debate raging in intellectual circles and its wider ramifications in the public sphere, although, as I indicate throughout this study (and especially in chapters 5 and 6), its very emergence and significance hinge on the existence of wider cultural and ideological rifts. Indeed, in trying to make sense of the museums' discourse, one does not need to look deeply for hidden ideological resonances—they are there in the tour guides' stories and the commentaries appended to them for anyone to hear and take note of, framing and motivating the museum-making enterprise as a whole. Ronen's stories about roots thus give expression to the cultural valorization of tree planting as an act of rootedness, both literal and metaphorical.[3]

The problem that Ronen's stories jointly suggest relates to the inevitable tension between ideological talk and the mundane texture of a taken-for-granted cultural experience that grounds it. Zionism as ideological assertion and Zionism as a lived sense of belonging to place and community are two very different things; so is the un-selfconscious experience of rootedness as compared to the active, deliberate cultivation of cultural roots. Yearning for the former, the Zionist pioneers were consumed by the latter. This paradox of having to consciously cultivate a sense of affiliation where it should have been a cultural given became even more pronounced in the lives of later generations of native-born Israelis. For them, a sense of place was an essential cultural experience, and the rhetoric of roots only threatened to undermine its existential force. The more markedly ideological these assertions became—as they did in the context of settlement museums—the more potentially destabilizing they seemed to be, and the more riddled with self-doubts. These self-doubts were related to the problematic present and, more specifically, to the sensitive and ideologically charged task of intergenerational transmission.

Thus, the uncertainty and tentativeness that surround this metaphorical planting project—with its aura of place making and self-formation—comes through in the three stories Ronen told us. So little can be taken for granted, and endless questions accompany every step of the enterprise: Are the roots deep enough? Are the trees planted in proper agricultural manner? Are the plants getting enough attention, or too much? And beyond these specific queries concerning actual as well as metaphorical roots, there lurks the major question of how a consciously held ideological position of place making can be transformed into the unself-conscious structure of feeling associated with rootedness and nativeness that the pioneers were actively and paradoxically trying to produce. Isn't there a danger that all this roots talk will result in undue meddling with cultural roots in the manner of the obsessive plant lover in Ronen's story?

An educational activity I observed in the Yifat museum at an early stage of the research brought home to me the paradoxical undercurrent attending the explicit search for cultural roots to whose problematic nature Ronen's story pointed. This activity was designed by a well-intentioned guide as part of a tour she gave to a group of young grade-school children. The children were wearing what passed as pioneers' clothes and the session began with

---

[3]The uses of the past and the role of collective memory in the symbolic construction of communities and national identities have been recurrent themes in both sociological, anthropological and historical research in recent years. See, for example, Appadurai (1981); Bodnar (1992); Brow (1990); Halbwachs (1980); Handler (1988); Hobsbawm and Ranger (1984); Johnson et al. (1982); Kammen (1991); Lowenthal (1985); Lumley (1988); Middleton and Edwards (1990); Nora (1989); Rosaldo (1989); Silberman (1989); Wallace (1981). For studies specifically concerned with the Israeli context, see Azaryahu (1993); Ben-Yehuda (1995); Bruner and Gorfain (1984); Dominguez (1989); Liebman and Don-Yehia (1983); Zerubavel (1995). Previous articles related to the present project include Katriel (1993a, 1993b, 1994a, 1994b).

an old-timers' song called "We Shall All Be Pioneers" that the children all sang with gusto, led by the guide. Thus seated at the tables of the communal dining room, they were invited to momentarily pretend to be the pioneers of yesteryear. Then the guide began to tell them pioneering stories associated with the dining room and the objects it housed. At one juncture, the guide pointed to a glass case placed against the wall that contained some musical instruments, books, and other possessions she said the pioneers had brought with them when they came to the land of Israel from Europe. In order to help the children to imaginatively identify with the early pioneers' immigration experience, she asked them what they would have taken along in a suitcase were they to emigrate to another country. The children took a while to respond, pondering—probably for the first time in their young lives—what it would be like for them to emigrate, or as some of them specifically phrased it, to leave Israel. The guide called on each of the 20-some children to state the objects of affection he or she would choose to take along—some spoke of favorite toys, musical instruments, or pictures, but most of these pragmatic kids said they would take along all the money they had. Like other imaginative role-playing activities, this one was enthusiastically greeted and felt to be a highly successful moment of playfulness along the tour route. As an outside observer, however, I could not help noting that through this activity, the museum's rhetoric of identfication had actually engendered an imaginary experience of uprooting, conjuring the possibility of dislocation for these youngsters whose sense of place and roots had never before been questioned. I felt the children's roots may have been poked too hard, all the more so because of the effectiveness of the experientially based pedagogy employed.

A second-generation guide in another museum once vividly articulated what appears to be the rationale for the proliferation of this kind of museum discourse. Speaking to a group of students I had brought with me, he repeated the routine statement that heritage museums have been established in order to re-assert Zionist and patriotic values, cultivate young Israelis' rootedness, and combat their growing disposition to emigrate to other countries. The reference to emigration is a significant statement as emigration of Israeli-born youngsters is held to signal the ultimate failure of the Zionist project of the Jews' return to the land of Israel. He concluded by explicitly addressing the tension between overt ideology and lived practice that attends the deployment of settlement museum discourse, saying, "Our parents made a mistake. They thought it was enough to give us orange juice to drink and we'd come out Zionists. But Zionism has to be spoken, loudly."

In this view, museum encounters are expected to work like some kind of ideological inoculation, reinvoking adherence to the master–narrative of Zionist revival that is a centerpiece of Israeli mainstream ideology. This master–narrative, of which a variety of localized versions exist both in and out of the museum walls, runs as follows: After 2,000 years of dispersal in which Jews maintained their distinctive religion and culture in the face of persecution and suffering, they returned to their Biblical, promised land to build a new kind of Jewish society grounded in a new type of Jewish person. The accomplishment of this enterprise is signaled by the establishment of the state of Israel, which involved many sacrifices and heroic deeds associated with both settlement activities and military battles.

This master narrative is central to the discourse of settlement museums. The remainder of this book is concerned with the ways in which this particular discourse is positioned in relation to the master narrative of the Zionist project, both reiterating it and re-negotiating some of its contours. Museums can thus be said to partake of the larger cultural struggle in Israeli society over conceptions of shared history and ways of speaking about the past. This is true of the role of museums as guardians of collective memory in other societies as well.[4]

Thus, following some introductory comments in chapter 2 about the ethnographic approach I have utilized in my study of settlement museum discourse, chapter 3 offers an overview of the interpretive texture of tour-guide performances in actual museum encounters in two such museums. Second, even though settlement museums participate in the production and reproduction of the Zionist master narrative, each museum encounter is a truly contingent communicative performance. The self-enclosed, mythic version of the Jewish settlement narrative these museums promote is routinely reiterated in actual museum encounters. At times, it may be subverted, when the tour guides' and/or the visitors' social positioning shapes their relationship to the hegemonic version of the museum story in particular ways. Thus, across various tour performances, there are generational differences in the ways in which tours are performed and in the ways guides position themselves vis-à-vis the museum story (chapter 4). Also, as situated and contingent communicative performances, museum tours allow for a degree of linguistic accommodation and thematic improvisation, taking account of visitors' presumed background in terms of ethnic, religious, and national affiliation in shaping the way the tour is conducted (chapter 5). There is, however, a hegemonic quality to the master narrative invoked in the museum context, and to the entire cultural production enterprise

---

[4]In the past decade or so, museums have attracted a great deal of attention in both social science and historical research. This scholarly interest has also given rise to the separate field of museology. Additional relevant titles, which comprise but a selected list, are: Ames (1992); Azoulay (1993, 1994); Bennett (1988); Bronner (1989); Cannizzo (1991); Clifford (1988); Dorst (1989); Falk and Dierking (1992); Gable, Handler, & Lawson (1992); Gover (1993); Handler and Saxton (1988); Hewson (1987); Hooper-Greenhill (1989, 1992, 1995); Horne (1984); Karp and Lavine (1991); Karp, Mullen Kraemer, and Lavine (1992);Kavanagh (1991); Leon & Rosenzweig (1989); Macdonald & Silverstone (1990; Maier (1988); Pearce (1990, 1994); Price and Price (1995); Stone & Molyneaux (1994); Vergo (1989).

engaged in by the museum personnel, such that oppositional voices are largely muted. These alternative or oppositional voices are heard in other heritage museums and most clearly in literary works and theatrical plays, as discussed in chapter 6. This chapter therefore concludes by contextualizing settlement museums in relation to the larger Israeli heritage museum scene, of which settlement museums are one subgenre, as well as in relation to some other domains of cultural production in contemporary Israel.

Chapter 2

Studying Museums as Performative Arenas

$\wp$ ∎ $\curvearrowleft$

THE FIELDWORK

Two pioneer settlement museums, both located in *kibbutzim,* served as the main research sites for this study. One is the Museum for the Beginning of Pioneer Settlement in the Land of Israel in *kibbutz* Yifat, and is located in the Western Jezreel Valley. The other is The Old Courtyard in *kibbutz* Ein Shemer, which is located in the Sharon coastal plain. These two museums count among the most successful of the more than 80 heritage museums and sites that were established in Israel in the 1970s and 1980s to commemorate the nation-building, prestate era.[1] They are located about an hour's drive apart. The Jezreel valley is a prominent symbol of early pioneering mythology. The site of one of the earliest and most heroic settlement efforts in the early 1920s, it involved the drying of the Jezreel Valley swamps and the establishment of the first cooperative and collective settlements (Naor, 1993). The story of *kibbutz* Ein Shemer, the focus of The Old Courtyard site-museum, exemplifies the tale of a typical collective settlement in the

---

[1]When I began my study, the number of settlement museums cited in official talks, such as those given in professional gatherings of settlement museum professionals, was 60 (nationwide). At the time of this writing, the number usually cited is 80. There is some ambiguity in terms of what counts as a museum because some of them are outgrowths of temporary exhibits and some are attached to local archives. There is also some ambiguity as to which heritage museums count as settlement museums in this context. Thus, one of the clandestine immigration museums is quite a prominent participant in the settlement museum division due to its director's dynamic personality and contacts whereas the other is not and is actually counted among military museums as it includes naval history as well. The category of Heritage Museums and Sites would probably best describe the scope of these museums. See museum guides by Inbar and Schiller (1990) and Rosovsky and Ungerleider-Mayerson (1989).

coastal plane in the late 1920s and early 1930s and the communal ideology it espoused. Both museums, thus, commemorate a critical period in the formation of the Israeli Socialist-Zionist ethos—the 1920s and 1930s—the era around which a good part of Israeli early settlement mythology is spun. Both cultivate a composite Zionist symbolism of territorial return and national renewal that capitalizes on the values of agricultural labor and communal living as these were shaped in what are known as the second and third Jewish immigration waves to Palestine (1904 to 1914 and 1919 to 1924, respectively).[2]

The museum for early settlement in *kibbutz* Yifat was established in 1972 as the first Israeli museum of its kind and grew out of an agricultural exhibit that was assembled to celebrate the anniversary of the *kibbutz*. All my informants credited its establishment to the late Oded Artzi and spoke of him admiringly as the enthusiastic originator of the museum project, or in native terms, *meshuga ladavar* (enthusiast, literally someone who is nuts over the cause). He was a passionate collector of old agricultural tools and implements, and with the help of some other *kibbutz* members whom he managed to infect with his passion, he scoured the whole country for discarded tractors and old tools.[3]

The preservationist mission of the museum founder, encoded in the material display of tools of agricultural production, matches an educational ideology of the Israeli Socialist-Zionist movement that emphasizes the special role of agricultural labor in the nation-building era. I was told several times that Odedi, as he is affectionately known, had brought back the idea of the heritage museum from his visits to such museums in the United States.[4] It is clear, however, that both the ideological orientation and the mode of display he adopted echo earlier attempts at museum-making in prestate years, notably the Museum for Agriculture established in Jerusalem in 1920 and the Museum for Home Products established in Tel Aviv in 1925

---

[2]The history of Jewish settlement in Palestine has been a topic of considerable research as well as a heated debate among sociologists and historians who are divided as to whether the Zionist project should be viewed primarily in terms of a nation-building or a colonialist agenda. Some of this debate commanded a good deal of public attention through extensive press coverage in the past 2 years. For some recent studies concerned with aspects of settlement history, or the controversy surrounding it, see Ben-Avram and Nir (1995); Kellerman (1993, 1996); Kimmerling (1983, 1995); Pappe (1995); Penslar (1995); Ram (1995b); Shafir (1989); Shapira (1995); Sternhell (1995).

[3]As Azoulay (1993) pointed out, the mythic figure of *hameshuga ladavar* as a mover and shaker who is single handedly responsible for the construction of a museum serves to blur the collective nature of this cultural project.

[4]Lowenthal (1982, 1989), who has studied pioneer museums in North America, pointed out that the pioneer landscape is one of many realms of modern nostalgia in American popular imagination, and attempted to clarify its distinctive cultural meanings and popular appeal for contemporary Americans. He characterized pioneer landscapes as the most elusive and evanescent of places, a landscape of transformation, and argued that it is the essentially fleeting nature of the pioneering experience that endows it with its special force and unique allure.

(see Kol-Inbar, 1992). Interestingly, this localized tradition of material display, which had its roots in the Agricultural Fair held in Tel Aviv in 1919, has never been alluded to by any of my informants during the research.

The untimely death in 1986 of Odedi was a hard blow to the museum enterprise. But he left a legacy of love for the many agricultural implements he had arduously collected and the many stories associated with them. Although he was well known as a gifted storyteller and greatly enjoyed telling and retelling the tales of the valley, he saw the most enduring testimony of the pioneers' project not in the visions they spun or the ideological statements they made but in the materiality of the tools on display. For him the tools were the concrete traces of human deeds, ideas actualized in action. They are not like ideas written down in a book, which are lost after the reading ends. This view points to a culturally inflected interpretation of the meaning of museum making, grounded in a distrust for words and a preference for ideological expression in an idiom of deeds. This dichotomous view of words set against deeds is, I believe, central to the construction of Israeli culture (see Katriel, 1986; Katriel & Shenhar, 1990). In this context, rather paradoxically, the museum performs its social role by providing an arena for the utterance of words that valorize the deeds to which the display objects serve as testimony. The story of pioneering finds its articulation within the museum frame through the verbal interpretations given to these objects, however. Whereas the pioneers' pragmatic deeds—such as drying the swamps and establishing agricultural settlements—have been at the heart of the Israeli action-oriented idiom of place making, museum-sponsored acts of speaking sustain the meaning and value of these history-making foundational endeavors. The museum performs its ideological work through a contemporary version of making history, that is crucially shaped by the art of speaking and storytelling, as well as the aesthetics of visual display.

The museum was initially designed to cover the whole saga of Jewish settlement in Palestine following the collection of agricultural tools from around the country by Odedi and his companions. This ambition is reflected in its name, which neither temporally nor spatially demarcates its scope with any degree of accuracy. In recent years, the museum has undergone a far-reaching process of rethinking, resulting in an expansion and rearrangement of its displays and the introduction of new activities and a modified interpretative line. Nowadays it presents a more modest claim, although this is not reflected in a change of title, and purports to encompass the Zionist settlement history of the Western Jezreel Valley only, even though it still contains several display items from other parts of the country as well as a few items from other places (a threshing machine from Egypt, a plow for rice fields from Japan) that somehow found their way into the museum and are felt to be too impressive to give up. This ambiguity in the museum's scope goes largely unacknowledged, but it definitely gives it a different flavor from that of the Ein Shemer museum, which traces the particular local history of the *kibbutz*. Yifat's more generalized orientation is probably not quite incidental, as this *kibbutz* was established in 1952 as a result of a split from *kibbutz* Gvat due to the larger ideological battle over attitudes toward the Soviet Union that cut at the heart of the *kibbutz* movement.[5] Thus, although the museum is generally referred to as the Yifat museum, it essentially tells a generic tale of Zionist settlement that is not significantly different from the ones recounted in other settlement museums.

As described earlier, I initially selected this particular museum as my main research site because of my longtime acquaintance with it as a resident of the area. My interest in it was further kindled by the fact that, unlike other settlement museums I had visited, it was jointly run at the time by three old-timer guides, Sarah, Yehudit, and Binyamin, who was also museum director. Several younger people worked in the museum on a part-time basis and some worked as occasional guides (*madrichim nishlafim*), offering expert knowledge when this was necessary (e.g., designing special activities for kids, interpreting in a foreign language). This flexible organization of work in the museum had a distinctively *kibbutz* flavor to it—the division of labor was rather loose and involved both interpretive activities and maintenance tasks. A weekly work schedule (called *sidur avoda*, following *kibbutz* parlance) was adjusted on a daily basis as necessary. Individuals' preferences and capabilities in both guiding and maintenance activities were taken into account, and the successful performance of the museum's work in offering satisfying educational experiences and keeping the site in shape was viewed as a collective project and accomplishment (a similar mode of operation could be observed in Ein Shemer).

The display and interpretive lines were set out by its late founder, Odedi. Neither Odedi nor any of the people involved with the museum at the time my research began had any professional background in museology or a related field, nor were any of them professional historians. They were all *kibbutz* members and relied heavily on the authenticity of the display, on their firsthand experience and love of the place, on occasional coaching by historians and experienced teacher-guides, and on their ability to generate audience identification with the museum through their narrative performances. There was nevertheless a good deal of discussion and debate over how to go about their museum making in terms of their felt need to improve on the current display, to interpret it more persuasively, and to draw more

---

[5]This battle left quite a number of *kibbutzim*, and even families within them, split up and hurting. This split is still considered by *kibbutz* members as one of the most traumatic memories of *kibbutz* history, although I never heard it discussed either in official museum discourse or in private conversations I had with various people during my fieldwork. Indeed, some of the local stories of early days I was told explicitly related to the times in Gvat and were simply subsumed under the heading of Stories of the Valley.

visitors to it. They often expressed concern for the future of the museum (given Odedi's untimely death) and a hope that the importance of the museum would be recognized by the kibbutz and the regional authorities; in particular, they hoped that younger people would become involved in the running of the museum (a move requiring their release from other work places on the kibbutz), and that more public funding would be allocated to its further development despite the severe financial crisis facing the kibbutz movement at the time. It was in this context of institutional flux that my fieldwork was set. I subsequently became a witness to the museum's continued growth and renewal following the appointment of a young, resourceful, and energetic director, Avner, who was the son of one of the founding families of the kibbutz. Although a social worker by training, he took a post-graduate course in museology shortly after entering his new job. He also made a point of sending the two second-generation guides who joined the museum during his tenure to a special in-service training program for settlement museum personnel run by the Society for Historic Preservation.

From the very start of my field research, the guides shared with me their problems and deliberations even though I did not presume to have any specialized knowledge about museum making or about local history. I felt my positioning was that of an insider-outsider. In broad cultural terms, I was an insider, falling neatly into the visitor category of settlement museum patronage—middle class and Ashkenazi (i.e., of Jewish-European heritage). But insofar as my interest was in the distinctive professional culture of museum personnel, I was an outsider. I always felt welcome when I came, which was as often as I could possibly manage given my teaching schedule, but my frequent visits never seemed frequent enough. There was always a wonderful guided tour I had missed, a group I should have seen, a new activity they had to show me. I was often referred to as "our regular visitor," and my visits became a blend of actual observations of guided tours, ongoing conversations about guided tours I had not been able to observe, and deliberations about the how-to of museum work. I was also invited to nonroutine events that the museum sponsored on its grounds over the years of the research. There were special storytelling sessions and sing-alongs, seasonal festivals, the celebration of the museum's 20th anniversary, the ceremony in which the museum received the regional award in official recognition of its contribution to the Jezreel Valley, the opening of a special temporary exhibit of Passover Haggadahs (ritual texts) published by various kibbutzim, Binyamin's 80th birthday party, then his retirement party, later Sarah's 80th birthday celebration, and others.

While the recordings I made of actual museum guiding practices (30 hours of audio and 30 hours of videotaping) form the core of the analysis of museum discourse, my sense of the museum as a cultural site was greatly informed by the many observations I made of everyday life in the museum over 4 years (1989 to 1993) and by many conversations surrounding the practices I observed. What the guides felt was memorable about their experiences—and worth recounting to me—or the points of disagreement they chose to air with me; all of these gave me inroads into their understanding of their role in a way that their performances in and of themselves could never provide.

The opportunity to follow the many changes that were introduced into the museum's visual and verbal interpretation over the years was particularly valuable, as such processes tend to be accompanied by discussion, planning, and debate and thus are unusually self-reflective. Another such opportunity arose in conjunction with the editing of a 54-minute instructional video based on the over 30 hours of guided tours taped with the help of a graduate student, Shimon Zafrir, a professional videographer. The video was designed to serve as an instructional aid in the in-service training of museum guides in the Israeli heritage industry, currently undergoing a process of increasing professionalization. The production and evaluation of the video formed the basis of the student's M.A. project, which I directed (Zafrir, 1992). After an initial stage of rough editing, we showed the video to 10 groups of (mainly) heritage-museum personnel and solicited their responses to it in a focus-group format. Although these discussions certainly contributed to the final editing process, they also became opportunities for the expression of attitudes toward the museum message and format, and thus became an additional source of self-reflexive data on the part of museum makers and workers. The video has been repeatedly used in lectures and workshops for museum workers and teachers in various parts of the country, including the Israeli branch of the International Museum Association, and in-service training courses recently established by the Society for Historic Preservation. No less important, perhaps, the museums themselves have recycled various segments of the videotaped materials to form self-portraits for celebratory occasions such as the aforementioned birthday parties or anniversaries. The experience of sitting among a crowd of visitors in a celebratory mood and seeing what I considered to be my field materials blown up on a large screen in front of us (at times even myself as interviewer) was a bit startling as the line betwen research site and research text, documentation and commemoration, became momentarily blurred.

Although I conducted most of my fieldwork between the years 1989 and 1993, my involvement in the world of museum professionals through occasional visiting, lecturing, and workshops continues to this day. Through these activities, I have come to know many bright and committed museum people and have benefited greatly from the opportunities they gave me to hear their views. These exchanges gained added importance for me as I began to present them with my own interpretations of the settlement-museum-making enterprise. It came to feel especially problematic when I developed the critical angle in my reading of settlement museum discourse, notably in discussing the suppressed narratives it entails, especially in relation to the Palestinian version of the Israeli past (further discussed in chapter 5). Somewhat to my surprise, my interlocutors never responded with antagonism to the discussion of politically sensitive issues, even when this occurred explicitly and publicly (e.g., in a public lecture to a nationwide group of museum personnel later published by their official association [Zemer, 1993], in a radio program which involved a dialogue between the director of the Yifat museum and me). Issues I raised often seemed to touch on concerns they had themselves harbored. At other times, I felt the guides found my concerns utterly irrelevant to their project—for example, when they responded to my queries about the history of earlier Arab settlements in the area by reminding me that their job was to tell the Jewish settlement tale, not the Palestinian one. Their most skeptical responses were to my suggestion—following some examples from abroad—that the museum could be turned from a temple into a forum by incorporating a more multivocal presentation of the past. Although Israeli heritage museums generally support pluralism, and different museums are expected to present at least partly competing versions of the past, most museum personnel consider a multivocal presentation within the context of one and the same museum to be highly problematic, even self-defeating.

Following a period of participant observation and recording in various situations, I decided to conduct formal interviews with several guides in Yifat and Ein Shemer. I wanted a better sense of the guides' personal backgrounds and professional attitudes. I also sought to clarify specific points of museum practices I had observed. The interviews only partly met my expectations. In the final analysis, I learned most from the many hours we had spent together, the personal ties we had established, the free-flowing exchanges, and the informal discussions directly related to their work as I observed it, or as we watched it on video. I became very attached to the old-timer guides who—through their unspoken example—taught me no less about the struggles, triumphs, and sometimes the pains of aging than about museum interpretation. To me, the whole museum project, in its defiance of the temporal, gained a special poignancy because of them.

It was probably because of the old-timer guides that I came to consider the museum in *kibbutz* Yifat as my main ethnographic site and invested most of the time and energy there. I initially decided to extend my fieldwork to the Ein Shemer museum precisely because their guides were all second- and third-generation *kibbutz* members, even though the museum story they told related to roughly the same period as the story recounted in Yifat. The young guides there credit the initial preservation of the early settlement site in Ein Shemer—the stone house and the stone wall surrounding the courtyard—to an old-timer who would not allow anyone to tamper with it. None of the old-timers, however, was involved in the day-to-day operation of the museum. I was intrigued by the possibility of making an intergenerational comparison of how the museum story gets told, and later went back to Yifat to collect some data related to the performances of second-generation guides who joined the old-timers there. The weight I have given to the old-timers' interpretations and to the issue of intergenerational comparison in effect dates my own work because the old-timers' role in the museum's narrative project has consistently decreased over the past few years. At the time of this writing, Binyamin is no longer able to work in the museum (a painful renunciation for him), Sarah is working on a part-time basis, and Yehudit divides her time between the museum and the *kibbutz* archive, with an emphasis on the latter. Along with the change in personnel came changes in the nature and organization of the material display against which the old-timers told their stories. Although my descriptions relate to the way the museum looked during the main part of my fieldwork, I discuss changes in the display when I find them relevant to my overall account.

The Old Courtyard in Ein Shemer was established 15 years after the Yifat museum, in 1987, and seems to represent a more self-conscious, even professional approach to museum making. The guides there openly conceded that they were building, inter alia, on the experience of the Yifat people with whom they were on friendly relations. Like them, they explicitly treated their verbal performances as a major aspect of what the museum offers to its visitors even though theirs did not necessarily carry the testimonial flavor that the old-timer guides in Yifat could inject into their own performances.

The Yifat museum is somewhat removed from the center of the *kibbutz*. Located close to the local school on top of a hill that overlooks the main section of the *kibbutz*, it can be reached by a side road. In contrast, the Ein Shemer museum is located right at the entrance to the *kibbutz*, close to the central dining room. It is in view of anybody who visits the *kibbutz* and seems to be more directly enmeshed in its members' lives. The person most frequently credited with the founding of the Ein Shemer museum spoke proudly in an interview with me about the deep personal investment each *kibbutz* member felt in the museum. In attempting to demonstrate the extent to which it was a collective enterprise, he told of the many ways in which *kibbutz* members contributed to the collection, restoration, and preservation of the museum structure and display, how individuals chipped in, and how whole school classes undertook parts of the reconstruction project. No such stories came forth in Yifat. Although the *kibbutz* community there seemed to appreciate the museum, they were less involved in its construction and operation at the time and identified less with the guides' recollections of the original museum-building project. In both cases, however, the small group of regular guides and some additional occasional guides whose regular employment was in some other vocation on the *kibbutz* carried the main responsibility as custodians of the collective past.

Viewing the two museums in relation to one another provides a more nuanced picture of the communicative and performative practices employed in each. My fieldwork in Ein Shemer followed the lines of the work I had done in Yifat, but took place only in 1990 and 1991. Nor have I made sporadic returns there as often as I have done (and still do) to Yifat. My work in Ein Shemer served mainly for comparison with Yifat at specific junctures in my analysis. The data I collected were sufficient for this purpose. I, therefore, do not purport to offer a balanced or fully comparative view of these two sites. I have learned a great deal from the people in Ein Shemer; the candid discussions I held with various members of the dynamic staff have significantly affected my thinking about settlement museum making. Thus, drawing on the actual and symbolic affinities as well as the differences between these two museums, I try to weave an analytic tale that encompasses lessons from both in the pages to come.

Finally, a few words about the way the material is presented. I deliberated whether to identify the particular museums I studied and the tour guides whose words I cite and interpret. Should I follow the standard social science tradition of scholarly presentation, which requires that names of places and people be changed so that their identity can be protected? Or should I follow the tradition of scholarly presentation associated with artistic performances (as in the field of folklore), where correctly identifying individual performers and the places they come from pays a tribute to the quality of their performance and acknowledges their authorship? I have consulted with several of the guides on this matter and met with mixed responses, so I opted for a mixed solution. I have retained the actual names of the museums and their locations; I have used the correct first names of the old-timer guides, which was the solution they had preferred, and I changed the names of the younger guides, some of whom did not wish to be identified by name. All the cited excerpts are taken from field recordings, audio and video; I translated all of them, hopefully retaining some flavor of the original Hebrew; excerpts appear throughout the text. Given the particular focus of my study on museum discourse as ideological assertion and verbal performance, I have chosen to present a broad range of obviously selected and inevitably edited versions of the publicly situated discourse I was studying. I have indicated textual leaps with.... and have added contextual information between brackets [....]. Despite the many limitations associated with any attempt to render faithfully the texture of a performative occasion in written form, and despite the multiple translations involved in presenting these materials, I hope to have captured at least some of their richness.

MUSEUM ENCOUNTERS AS COMMUNICATIVE EVENTS

Performing the Museum Story

As I have begun to suggest, there is a historical metanarrative in Israeli society, and there is a struggle over it; this metanarrative can be framed in terms of the tension between the Zionist perspective and promise at Israel's founding and the country's current sociopolitical climate. I view settlement museum encounters as cultural sites in and through which this tension is articulated and negotiated.

The defining dimension of museum encounters is the setting itself, which combines the edifying and imaginative thrust of verbal expositions and narrations with the concreteness, authenticity, and authority associated with the material display. The objects serve as mnemonic devices, which trigger stories grounded either in individuals' memories or, more commonly, in the collective fund of museum tales shared by the guides.[6] The museum experience involves both visual and kinetic components in that the guides construct and organize their verbal interpretation as they take their visitors along the museum path, controlling the pace and rhythm of their movement along the visual display.

The museums tend to alternate classificatory displays—agricultural tools in one corner, kitchen implements in another—and mimetic displays in the form of reconstructed settings of pioneering life such as the babies' nursery or the communal shower along the museum route, thereby introducing variety into the visitors' experience. Classificatory displays seem to support a relatively removed, analytic stance involving a knowledgeable discernment of differences within a larger category of objects—for example, different kinds of plows—whereas mimetic forms encourage an experience of immersion, especially when visitors enter a reconstructed enclosure such as the dining room display.

The basic museological move of decontextualization, which consists of removing objects (and the stories about them) from their natural life contexts of production, consumption, and use, and re-contextualizing them in the museum setting is an ideologically driven as well as a value-conferring gesture (Clifford, 1988; Kirshenblatt-Gimblett, 1991). Indeed, the transfer of objects and meanings into a museum involves their removal from the culture's ongoing stream of life, signaling their state of obsolescence even while marking their presence in the public eye. An oft-repeated statement by museum guides suggests that this museological move speaks for itself, that the tools tell the story. But the reality of settlement museum presentation

---

[6]See Stewart (1993) for her elaboration of the notion of narrated objects in relation to souvenirs and nostalgia.

is that the testimonial presence of the various tools they put on display does not in itself tell the museum story. So that even as they may pose as incidental ventriloquists for the stories told by the tools and implements, the guides are quite aware that much of the museum experience offered to visitors hinges on the interpretive performances they provide, on the stories they themselves tell.

Settlement museum tours are temporally bounded performances and are verbally constructed in a modular fashion. They alternate descriptions of particular visual items, providing standardized factual information about them—where the object came from, how old it is, who made or used it—technical accounts of work processes, and narrative segments. Woven around undistinguished, mundane objects of the recent past, these narrative segments carry the main burden of enhancing the site, of making it appear more interesting than it is in and of itself. Ronen, the second-generation guide from Ein Shemer cited in the previous chapter, articulated this special difficulty in talking to a group of girl soldiers who were training to be teacher-guides both on nature trails and in historical sites:

> A nature guide finds it difficult to explain how people lived in a particular place, to convey the feeling, to bring the site to life, that's the problem. He gets to a site ... and he has to take a deserted place, a quiet place, with walls and stones, with buildings, and after the kids had walked around it with you, it is expected suddenly to come to life, what we call *making the walls speak*. That's our job. That's the problem ... How to make an ankle-high site into towers floating in the air. (Ronen, Ein Shemer, 10.18.91)

The guide here clearly underscores the constructive and imaginative dimensions of museum interpretation. He sees himself as a ventriloquist whose job is to "make the walls speak," to animate what would otherwise be a lifeless site. The narrative segments inserted into museum interpretation constitute the performative backbone of the tour and can be viewed as embedded performances, dramatic moments set apart from the encompassing expository discourse that serve to transform it from a lowly "ankle-high" site into a fantasy of "towers floating in the air." The tour guides were, indeed, quite explicit about the importance of the anecdotal material they injected into their talk, and tended to think of a tour in terms of the chain of narrative segments they chose to link together, with the rest of the verbal material acting as significant factual substance (which goes under the heading of "history"), but as experientially secondary stuff: "History they can learn at school," I have heard again and again. "Here they come for the experience." And the museum experience they want to provide is produced mainly by what the guides often term *folklore*, the little stories that tell visitors what the museum is really about.

The view of tour guides as speakers who select, arrange, and deliver culturally and situationally appropriate messages, and of guided tours as communicative events, is clearly commensurate with an ethnography of speaking perspective for the study of language in use.[7] My analysis is thus grounded in Hymes' (1981) and Bauman's (1977, 1986) ethnographic approach to the study of verbal performance as a distinctive mode of language use that sets up an interpretative frame (Goffman, 1974) within which the messages communicated are to be understood and appreciated. Bauman (1977) formulated this view:

> Fundamentally, performance as a mode of spoken verbal communication consists in the assumption of responsibility to an audience for a display of communicative competence. This competence rests on the knowledge and ability to speak in socially appropriate ways. Performance involves on the part of the performer an assumption of accountability to an audience for the way in which communication is carried out, above and beyond its referential content. From the point of view of the audience, the act of expression on the part of the performer is thus marked as subject to evaluation for the way it is done, for the relative skill and effectiveness of the performer's display of competence. Additionally, it is marked as available for the enhancement of experience, through the present enjoyment of the intrinsic qualities of the act of expression itself. Performance thus calls forth special attention to and heightened awareness of the act of expression and gives license to the audience to regard the act of expression and the performer with special intensity. (p.11).

I would further propose that Briggs' (1988) analysis of the discourse about the past enacted by elderly and middle-aged men in the New Mexican village he studied can help to illuminate settlement museum discourse. Briggs distinguished different types of what he called "historical discourse" that are differentiated by occasion and participant roles along generational lines. Generational affiliation, as we shall see in chapter 4, is an important dimension of settlement museum presentation, too, but the main participant roles of guide versus visitors cut across generational lines, indexing less rigid knowledge-as-power relations than those found in Briggs' study. In the case of settlement museums, what counts is familiarity with the museum

---

[7]See Hymes (1962, 1972, 1974). In Hymes' perspective, which draws on a Burkian approach to rhetorical action (e.g., Burke, 1969), the analysis of culturally focal speech events is a central strategy for the exploration of the social dimensions of speaking on the one hand and of the discursive dimensions of social life on the other. Settlement museum encounters are, indeed, speech events in the sense discusses by Hymes, and can be profitably studied in terms of the SPEAKING framework he proposed for the study of events that are defined and dominated by verbal activities. In this framework, the categories involved are those of Setting, Participants, Ends (both individual and communal goals), Act sequence, Key (or tone), Instrumentalities (or communication media and channels), Norms (for both production and interpretation), and Genres.

story and with the role the guide is supposed to play as provider of information and pleasure. This gives him or her institutionalized control over the encounter, both in terms of speaking rights and in terms of topic selection and regulation. As we shall see, this controlling position is sometimes challenged by visitors who seek to play a more active role in the museum encounter, but it is usually the guides' voice that predominates. The guides clearly operate within an ideological and performative arena in which they hold a privileged position.

Briggs (1988) furthermore traced the structuring of historical discourse as a verbal performance through the use of evocative signs that carry special meanings within the particular story-telling context in which they are embedded. These signs are multifunctional in that they both refer to elements of the world of bygone days, invoke a great deal of additional information associated with them, and mark the performance discursively as a particular kind of ideologically infused talk.[8] In Briggs' study, such pivotal signs are verbal and form part of the shared culture of village members. They include:

> references to goats and sheep, threshing, moccasins, hard work, bringing fuelwood, and homegrown tobacco. These topics and the terms used to describe them recur frequently in collective recollections. Beyond their referential value, these expressions possess an unusual degree of pragmatic force; this fact emerges in their ability to bring to mind a great deal of information about bygone days and their role in structuring this kind of discourse. (p. 82)

Similar pivotal and evocative signs appear in the settlement museum discourse I studied, where their effectiveness lies in the materiality of the objects on display, not only in the force of the linguistic expressions used by the guide. In this case, the evocative signs include such terms and images as the plow, the first furrow, the first tractor, the family tent, the communal kitchen and dining-room, the communal shower, water, and so forth. These signs invoke a whole range of cultural meanings and values associated with the pioneering era, and many of them can be traced back to the symbol system representing the *kibbutz* as it has become crystallized in the early Jewish settlement literature of the 1930s and 1940s (Keshet, 1995). The museum, in fact, rematerializes this symbol system, which provides narrative building blocks grounded in the concrete objects around which the tour is constructed. These signs have a significant structuring role, especially in conjunction with what Briggs (1988) called "pedagogical discourse," that is,

---

[8]Briggs (1988) referred to these signs as triplex signs or multiplex signs claiming that "the power of these expressions for structuring collective recollections and conveying the speaker's meaning emerges from their multifunctionality" (p. 80).

narrative acts addressed by the elderly to younger participants in intergen-erational exchanges. These narrative acts serve as directions given by seasoned travelers to those who set out on their first journey. The small sets of evocative signs included in them

> provide "students" with a tool for grasping the way that pedagogical discourse is structured in the absence of a fixed narrative structure or content ... such signs occur as key expressions in all examples of the genre. Familiarity with these signs provides younger participants with a vital tool for grasping what an elder is telling them about the past and how she or he is doing so. (p. 91)

Although Briggs' discussion focused on verbal performance, he was also aware of the importance of the visual component in acts of personal and collective remembering. Thus, he told us how the Mexicano elders took him to the sites they narrated about so as to help him visualize and better understand their tales.

In settlement museums, of course, the verbal and visual components intertwine. A loose set of focal objects and key expressions is made familiar through multiple and repeated exposures to them—in the selection of objects for inclusion in the display, in the guide's oral interpretation, in the slide or video presentation that is used to either preface or sum up the tour. Moreover, these visual and verbal images are familiar to many visitors from prior exposure to the Zionist story and symbolism, most conspicuously through schooling and other educational practices. For those unfamiliar with this symbolism, such as young children or cultural outsiders (including newcomers to the land), the structuring of the guide's oral performance through his or her use of key terms and stories—supported by the visual display—serves as a powerful way to initiate them into the Zionist story of settlement.

It seems to me that much of the learning new guides do as they apprentice themselves to more experienced guides relates to their growing ability to use these objects, verbal expressions, and images selectively and differentially in constructing situationally appropriate versions of the museum story, taking into account the time frame allowed for the particular tour and the nature of the audience addressed.

Other strategies of narrative organization identified by Briggs (1988) in the pedagogical discourse of the Mexicano elders are also relevant to the analysis of museum discourse. One such strategy is what Briggs called the "antes frame," which involves the use of verbal signals to indicate that a particular stretch of discourse is concerned with, and seeks to invoke, an image of bygone days. In the case of heritage museums, such framing is embedded into their institutional definition as sites of memory (Nora, 1989), but is also signaled through a variety of visual and verbal means. What settlement museum guides and Mexicano elders share in their verbal structuring of their tales is a nostalgic, back-and-forth movement between past and present, between *antes* and *ahora*, between pioneering days and nowadays.

Notably, the performance perspective that has been developed within an ethnography of speaking framework and applied to this study differs from Schechner's (1985) and Snow's (1993) analyses of performance in restored historical sites such as Plymouth Plantation. The latter emphasize the theatricality of the sites. Although elements of role playing and play acting can be observed in the Israeli settlement museum context—guides make use of a period garment, children dress up in pioneer clothes—they are much less central to the overall production of the museum experience than the guides' storytelling activities. A discussion of these elements will be incorporated into my analysis when appropriate, but it should be stressed that settlement museum encounters are not so much pieces of environmental theater in the sense discussed by Schechner and Snow as they are storytelling sessions of the kind explored so insightfully by Bauman (1977, 1986), Briggs (1988), Bauman and Briggs (1990), and Fine and Speer (1992).

The Tour Guide as Cultural Broker

As noted, a statement frequently heard in settlement museums is that "the tools tell the story." But as the few available studies on guided tours and my own observations suggest, the objects' testimonial presence and aura of authenticity notwithstanding, the museum's story and message are in fact conveyed no less centrally through written labels and tour guides' verbal interpretations than through visitors' direct visual encounters with the objects on display. The crucial role played by the tour guides' oral mediation of the material display in settlement museums invites a closer consideration of the tour guide role and its performative idiom.

Cohen (1985) provided a helpful synthesis of the rather small number of sociological studies that explore the tourist guide role and its origins and structure as well as the dynamics of change associated with it. Tracing the origins of the role of the modern tourist guide, he noted that it involves both a practical-geographical and a spiritual dimension. It thus combines and expands elements of the role of the *pathfinder* (one who shows the way along an unfamiliar route and points out objects of interest) and elements of the *mentor* role (one who directs a person on matters of proper conduct). Cohen pointed out that the confluence of these two antecedent roles in the modern role of the professional tourist guide "is neatly expressed in the Hebrew term for the role, *moreh-derech*, i.e., 'teacher of the way'" (p. 9). He further suggested that tourist guides' activities fall into two complementary spheres: the leadership sphere and the mediatory sphere. It is in the sphere of cultural mediation that the role of the settlement museum guide finds its quintessential expression. The museum guide serves as cultural broker assigned to interpret and enhance the sight for visitors who come from a variety of cultural backgrounds.

According to Cohen (1985), the communicative component of the guide role is given primacy both in the guides' formal training (when such exists) and in their understanding of their role. He distinguished four components of the guides' communicative role. The first involves the selection of objects of interest to be pointed out along the tour route, which implies the structuring of visitors' attention both as to what they will and as to what they will not see. The second involves the provision of information about the sights. This takes a particular shape, as Cohen noted:

> Despite the academic veneer and the frequently dry presentation of the information—such as the recitation of dates, numbers and events connected with a given site—the information imparted is rarely purely neutral; rather it frequently reflects the information policy of the tourist establishment or of the official tourist authorities, intended either to impart or maintain a desired touristic image of the host setting, or to engender in the visitors some wider social and political impressions, as part of a national propaganda campaign. (p. 15)

In other words, the dissemination of information cannot be really divorced from the third component proposed in this scheme, which refers to the interpretation of the sight, and which is "the distinctive communicative function of the tourist guide" (Cohen, 1985, p. 15).

The art of interpretation is a well-recognized component of the working of heritage sites. Tilden (1957), for example, provided a well-known formulation of what he called the philosophy of heritage interpretation in the American context. In its transcultural form, tour-guide interpretation involves the translation of the sight to visitors, thereby reducing its cultural strangeness, an activity that requires not only familiarity with the visited sight but also knowledge of the audience's cultural background. In the case of settlement museums, the distance that needs to be bridged by the guides' interpretive activities is always a temporal distance and sometimes a cultural one as well. Indeed, as is discussed in the forthcoming chapters, settlement museum visitors cannot be neatly allocated to either the category of cultural insiders or outsiders. Rather, they occupy a range of positions vis-à-vis the museum story whose dynamics and implications for the structuring of the guided tour I intend to explore.

Fabrication is the fourth element of tourist guides' communicative practices that Cohen (1985) mentioned. Fabrication refers to the ever-present temptation guides face to indulge in invention or even deception in order to enhance the sight (even while making claims to its authenticity). This kind of temptation may be especially felt in the case of relatively minor tourist sites such as settlement museums, which house mundane objects of the recent past and depend on the guides' verbal enhancement to attain the status of attractions.

This communication-centered view of the tourist guide role as a cultural broker fits in well with standard analyses of the rhetorical dimensions of speaking, and has been addressed more systematically in terms of a perform-ance-oriented ethnography of communication framework in Fine and Speer's (1985) work.

Cohen's (1985) discussion of the tourist guide role addresses the culture of tourism as a transcultural field of activity but it is, at the same time, receptive to the notion that the tour guide role may be subject to cultural coloration. Indeed, he referred to Katz's (1985) study of the localized Israeli version of the tourist guide, referred to as the teacher-guide (*madrich*) role, to make this point. Because, I believe, the settlement museum-guide role has at least been partly modeled on the image of the Israeli teacher-guide, the analysis of this role is worth recapturing in some detail. As Katz pointed out, the Israeli teacher-guide role is associated with the ethos of *tiyulim* (roughly, *hiking*), special walks designed to promote an emotional attach-ment to the land of Israel through the cultivation of a knowledge of its landscapes, its fauna and flora, as well as its history (Katriel, 1995). This body of knowledge is known as *yedi'at ha'aretz* (knowledge of the land). The ethos of *yedi'at ha'aretz* has been central to Israeli native culture and has been sustained by formal and informal educational ideologies and practices upheld by the official school system, as well as by a variety of nonprofit agencies such as the Society for the Protection of Nature. This means, as Katz (1985) said, that "every week thousands of Israelis take part in organized walks, *tiyulim*, which may last a few hours or several days. The declared purpose of these *tiyulim* is that walking along open air routes is a good way of learning about *yedi'at ha'aretz*; i.e., knowledge of one's native country, the translation of the German term, *Heimatkunde*" (p. 50). These *tiyulim* are led by teacher-guides who combine the functioning of youth movement leaders and regular teachers, serving as mediators between the hikers and the physical and cultural landscapes they encounter.

In recent years, more and more of these *tiyulim* have come to incorporate stops in various heritage museums as part of their itinerary, thus combining walks along open-air routes with site visitations. Special programs sponsored by the Ministry of Education have also encouraged the turning of heritage museums into preferred destinations for the large numbers of school trips undertaken by Israeli school classes each year. During these museum visits, the guiding function usually shifts from the teacher-guide, who is responsible for the tour as a whole, to the local museum guides, who are considered experts in their own domain. This shift of personnel, however, is marked by a continuity of role and style that stems from the standard arrangement whereby the museum visit is an integral component of a more extended trip, and, significantly from the fact that, as noted, regular tour guides as well as museum guides tend to interpret their role with reference to the same teacher-guide model. Indeed, quite a number of the museum guides I have observed had previously worked for the Society for the Protection of Nature or a comparable organization, and a couple of them were combining such employment with their museum work at the time of the research.

Katz (1985) explained the emergence of the teacher-guide role as an outcome of a unique combination of the very particular social and ideological circumstances of Israel's prestate, nation-building era when newcomers to the land required the teacher-guides' mediation in affiliating themselves to the new environment. He noted that the renewed demand for *tiyulim* and *yedi'at h'aretz* in the 1970s and 1980s (and similarly, I would add, the establishment of settlement museums during those years) have their ideological underpinnings in the Zionist project of "strengthening the feeling of belonging to both the Israeli collectivity and territory" (p. 69). The concern with the concrete and symbolic aspects of the immediate locale as an end in itself is a unique feature of both *yedi'at ha'aretz* lore and settlement museum presentations. Speaking of the rhetoric of place inscribed in written materials and hiking practices, Katz made a comment that is equally true for museum displays: "This particularization is aimed at emphasizing or even glorifying the uniqueness of what is encountered in the surroundings by a potential reader, or along a special route by a potential walker" (p. 62). This tendency toward particularization is only one of the unique features of teacher-guiding mentioned by Katz; the others are similarly characteristic of settlement museum guides' discourse. The most central discursive strategy employed by Israeli teacher-guides and settlement museum guides alike is referred to by Katz as the "deneutralization of contents." He wrote:

> Information and interpretations are selected primarily in order to arouse feelings of belonging to the place and to evoke collective experiences of identification with symbolic heroes, groups and localities. Thus, archaeological relics or historical events are intentionally loaded with national meanings. This is, for example, in contrast to the process which modern secular educational systems have undergone. There, the more the instructional contents are based on scientific research, the more emotionally neutralized they become. (p. 63)

This harks back to my earlier comments concerning the ideologically saturated nature of settlement museum discourse and to its role in providing visitors an experience rather than mere information. These ideological underpinnings are closely linked to the ritual role played by tour guide performances in the process of sight sacralization as discussed by MacCannell (1989). If the sociocultural practice of *tiyulim* is a form of secular pilgrimage that is part of the civil religion of modern Israel (Liebman & Don-Yehia, 1983), then settlement museums are indeed prime pilgrimage sites and museum guides take after the Israeli teacher-guide who is "some kind of civil religion mentor ... an encourager of faith" (Katz, 1985, p. 69). It is against the background of these culturally specific professional role expectations that contemporary settlement museum guides must negotiate their situated enactments of their guiding role. Fine and Speer's (1985) illuminating study of touristic encounters in a Texas Historic Home, the only study I am aware of that similarly employs a discourse-centered perspective in studying the tour-guide role, points to some features of tour-guide discourse that seem to cut across specific cultural contexts, forming part of a transcultural culture of tourism. Working within a tour-ism-as-pilgrimage metaphor, Fine and Speer described the guided tours they observed as involving the ritual transformation of "an unimposing cottage on a quiet street into an important, sacred historical sight in the community" (p. 76). Their analysis specifies the verbal correlates of the five stages of the sight sacralization process as it has been delineated by MacCannell (pp. 43–48). These include the naming of a sight as such, its framing as physically and socially separate from its environment, its elevation and enshrinement as worthy of cultural attention, and its reproduction through both mechanical and social means (such as promotional materials and activities).

Indeed, the view of touristic encounters as verbal performative occasions oriented to the sacralization of touristic sites invites a systematic elaboration of a discourse-centered perspective in the study of the tour guide role. Such a perspective informs the ethnographic account of Israeli settlement museums presented in the following chapters.

In the next chapter, I offer two composite tours that I have woven together out of my observational materials—one in the Yifat museum and the other in the Ein Shemer museum. These tours will not be reconstructions of specific tours I have observed during my fieldwork, but rather collages I have created in such a way as to bring together different cumulative observations of museum practices. Thus, in constructing these written representations of the museum tour, I re-enact on paper the strategy of imaginative tour construction that approximates the one employed by the guides themselves. Indeed, the old-timer guides in Yifat often jokingly nudged me to give them a hand in their guiding tasks when several groups arrived in the museum simultaneously, saying I probably "know it all by heart," given the long hours I had spent listening to them. I told them my time would come, and here it has. I invite the reader to my own version of two guided tours, first in Yifat museum and then in Ein Shemer.

Chapter 3

The Tools Tell the Story:
Narrative Trajectories
in Settlement Museum Tours

ೞ ∎ ಇ

THE VALLEY IS A DREAM: THE MUSEUM
FOR PIONEER SETTLEMENT IN YIFAT

The Museum and Its Story

A short, winding country road takes us up the hill to the Museum for Pioneering Settlement at the entrance to *kibbutz* Yifat. Because it is not a site museum, its location does not incorporate architectural traces of the past but was rather designed to encompass the view of the legendary Jezreel Valley that surrounds it, all lush and green. The path leading to the museum entrance is flanked by well-preserved, rust-coated ploughs and other medium-sized agricultural tools that are elegantly placed amid the bushes and trees, and opens up to an expansive lawn whose edge serves as a vantage point from which to view the surrounding area, a small olive grove and the splendor of the valley lying at its feet. It is here that the museum visit is usually launched. For some visitors, the first encounter with the Yifat museum comes actually through the attractive tourist brochure the museum has produced to market itself. This brochure is a beautifully laid-out collage of photographs depicting different corners of the museum display with an accompanying explanatory text. On top of its front page, there is the museum's emblem that consists of an enlarged reproduction of one of a set of well-known silhouettes produced in the early pioneering days that depicts a group of dancing pioneers. In the middle is a picture of an old wooden cart filled with wooden barrels and underneath it is the slogan used by the Valley Tourism Association that reads The Valley is a Dream (after a song dating from pioneering days). Both the picture and the slogan are powerful emblems of nostalgia utilized in other contexts as well—they're also found in postcards, annual calendars and on T-shirts sold at the museum kiosk. The dream quality of the valley now refers more to what it was than to what it could become, as it did in the early days of Jewish settlement. The text in this brochure—unlike the one that appeared in the less colorful and more verbose brochure it has replaced—is given both in Hebrew and in English (but no Arabic). The English version reads:

> The museum of pioneer Settlement in Kibbutz Yifat affords a magnificent view of the Jezreel Valley, the Kfar Baruch lake, and the Nazareth Hills. This is the area where the first pioneers settled during the second and third aliyah periods (1904–1923).
>
> The museum depicts in dramatic form how the new immigrants and their descendants realized their dream of settling the land. Visitors will obtain a realistic perspective of this exciting period. You can hear the clanging of the machinery, see the old water pump, visit the dining room, children's house and family tents. As you walk around you will be able to understand the context in which the first pioneers lived: the daily struggle to survive and to put down roots—both literally and figuratively; the ideological debates about living arrangements and child rearing methods; the encounter between European and Mediterranean mentalities; the argument over intensive and extensive agriculture; field crops versus plantations; the communal clothing store; and all the other problems that faced these early stalwarts.

This is clearly the discourse of tourism marketing. It highlights the visual experience the museum holds in store, the drama of the story it tells, the authenticity of the objects on display, and the participatory potential of the visit. Following these general exhortatory remarks, the brochure then proceeds to specify the various displays found in the museum and the different kinds of activities it offers. Being a recently compiled version of the brochure, it speaks in more inclusive terms than one might expect, referring not to pioneers (*halutzim*)—the small and select group of ideologically driven newcomers to the land—but to new immigrants (in Hebrew, the term used is *rishonim* rather than *mehagrim*, which would be the more precise translation of *immigrants*).

Many of the visitors to the museum, however, do not read the brochure before they actually arrive there, and their first encounter with the museum, its setting and history, takes place on the museum grounds in the context of the guided tour itself. The guided tour usually opens with an overview of the valley, its natural topography, its history of sparse Arab settlement, and its contemporary Jewish settlement map:

This is the longest valley in the country. It starts at the feet of the Carmel and ends in the Jordan river. It's divided into two parts, a western part from Afula to the Carmel and an Eastern part from Afula to the Jordan. The soil here is wonderful soil that the rains brought from the mountains and therefore it is so fertile.... The settlements you see here are Third Wave settlements (you know that in immigration we had waves—first, second, third and fourth)—[pointing and naming settlements] Ramat David, Sarid, Gvat...Nahalal was settled in 1921; they arrived in 1920 but could not begin settlement, can anybody guess why? [Child's voice]: Swamps.

The swamps, very good, there was quite a swamp in their area so they waited a whole year until they dried up a particular area and could begin settlement....There were different kinds of swamps and the pioneers worked very hard to dry them by digging canals and by planting all kinds of trees. (Binyamin, Yifat, 8.1.89)

This opening statement, which is given at various levels of elaboration, does far more than orient visitors to their physical and geographical environment. It first of all underscores the uniqueness of the site in terms of the landscape surrounding it. At the same time, it also encapsulates a whole settlement mythology about the swampy Jezreel valley, which was shunned by the Arab inhabitants of the area for many years until the Jewish settlers arrived in the early 1920s and, ignoring the risk of malaria, proceeded to dry up the swamps and make it into the rich agricultural land that it now is (for a controversy related to this mythology, see Bar-Gal, 1993; Bar-Gal & Shamai, 1983). The museum thus spills into the landscape, constructing its celebratory tale with reference to the visual argument the scenery provides. By spatially and narratively locating the museum in its past and present landscapes, the museum tour is thus framed as a story of continuity and accomplishment. Museum stories told throughout the tour of humble beginnings, times of hardship and heroic strivings are all to be heard against the celebratory preface provided by the guide at the observation point. These stories are both framed and fleshed out by the visually compelling splendor of the meticulously cultivated valley below.

The museum itself is made up of two very large shed-like constructions in which the displays are organized. In the first shed, the display objects are set out along the outer wall and in the open-air central area, which serves as a kind of inner courtyard. A large-lettered welcoming sign is hung at the very entrance to the Yifat museum. It accompanies a blown-up photograph of a workgroup of early pioneers, and reads (both in Hebrew and in English), "This is the story of the young people who heard the call of history and rose to the challenge, paving the way to the future of the country."

History is here a protagonist, but at the same time the pioneers are doers—note the building metaphor—the human agents who move history in its course.

Clearly, every museum tour involves descriptive attention to a considerable number of objects, but some of them tend to trigger particularly elaborate and/or evocative acts of narration. There are those objects that all the guides tend to tell stories about, and I make these the focus of my analysis. One should not forget, however, that each guide has an individual fund of self-selected and self-invested stories as well, and these contribute to the formation of individual styles within the museum's wider interpretive repertoire. The more personalized, expressive dimensions of museum narration are attended to in the next chapter.

Object and Frame Narratives

The narratives typically employed as part of tour guides' interpretations can be distinguished into two broad categories. The first involves what I have dubbed *object narratives*, that is, stories concerned with the uses of museum objects in the past and the meanings they held for the people who used them. The second involves *frame narratives*, which are stories concerned with the museum-making enterprise—for example, how objects were discovered and acquired, and the particular value they carried as museum items. Throughout the museum tour, stories concerned with the exploits of the original founding fathers, who dried the swamps and built the place, are interspersed with and echoed by stories about the adventuresome and committed activity of establishing the museum that was undertaken by their offspring. Particular emphasis is placed on the drama contained in the hunt for relevant, authentic objects, which are often rescued from demise (Thompson, 1979). The result, then, is a composite tale of double-layered acts of making place and making history, the original myth of foundation nested within a secondary heroics of historical preservation. This mutually reinforcing effect of object and frame narratives is quite notable. In fact, by foregrounding the process by which the display is assembled and organized, the frame narratives may also destabilize the museum tale and its representational claim to be showing the past the way it was then. Speaking of how the museum display was put together highlights its constructed nature, injecting moments of reflexivity into the story of the past. But more often than not, these moments, too, become incorporated into the museum's mythologizing agenda, so that, taken together, these tales about museum objects and about museum making anchor a cultural experience in and through which there emerges a localized sense of the Israeli pioneering past. Thus, much like the historical discourse of bygone days in the New Mexican village studied by Briggs, settlement museum discourse stands as "a communicative resource, providing a setting and an expressive pattern for discussions that transform both past and present" (Briggs, 1988, p. 99).

Some of the museum stories mark broader narrative strokes, providing prefaces to the tour as a whole. These encompassing narratives frame the localized stories relating to the nature and significance of particular objects that make up the bulk of the guided tour. One such preface, for example, delineates the broad historical background of Zionism, and was told (in Hebrew) to a group of Arab school teachers who were apparently judged to require such an explicit rendition of the museum's master narrative:

> ... At the end of the last century the Jews understand that the return to the land of Israel, a national revival in the land of Israel, has to begin from the land, from agriculture. This is the basis for the nation's existence...The Jews who arrived in Israel understood that they had to go back to the land, from which Jews had been cut off. In the diaspora they were not farmers, except for some exceptional cases...They come here and they have no idea of how to go about it, but they have a strong will and understand that this is the way to do it...(Raviv, Yifat, 10.13.91).

Another type of preface falls under the category of frame narratives. It tells the story of the making of the museum to a group of teenagers:

> What I want to tell you now is that this museum, we can say, was created some 18–20 years ago. The rare and fantastic collection of tools you'll see inside is a collection of tools that were no longer in use for more than 40 years. Because we simply made so much progress that these tools now appear to us outdated. They were out of use. You will soon see how we make progress, and that's why we brought you here to show you, and to show all the many visitors we get from all over the country, also grown-ups, elderly people, they all come here to see how we started to build our beautiful land of Israel, how we started to settle in this land, how we dried the swamps.... (Sarah, Yifat, 10.9.91)

Yet another common category of narratives, which frame the museum tale by recounting the story of the making of the museum itself (rather than the experiences and exploits of the founders of the *kibbutz*), is associated with the specific image of the Yifat museum founder, Oded Artzi, and with his extraordinary project of assembling the agricultural tools that make up the collection of the museum today. These stories became so much part of the framing of the museum that tape recordings of the museum founder's tales about his collecting exploits were printed in a special booklet produced in celebration of the museum's 20th anniversary. These frame narratives were frequently used by the guides, most notably by the old-timer guide Binyamin, who had been an active partner to Odedi's collecting efforts, and thus could turn these museum-making tales into personal experience narratives and—more often than not—into self-aggrandizing gestures:

Here you see this *mekalteret* [agricultural instrument] that has this duck-like legs and is very special. There's no other specimen of this kind anywhere. The precise distance between the legs determines the quality of the instrument.... Now, it was lying around in Zichron in the house of a *moshav* [noncommunal settlement] farmer, and this guy I'm telling you about, Oded Artzi, he negotiated with him over this tool for many years, 3 years the negotiation went on. He [the farmer] always told him, "I can't give you this tool because when I see this tool it makes me remember the past, so I can't give it to you." And he [Oded] was extremely disappointed. I was working at *yedi'at ha'aretz* [an educational division of the *kibbutz* movement that organizes trips as leisure and enrichment activities] at the time, and when I came home, he [Oded] told me, "Binyamin, come join me and work with me in the museum." I wasn't particularly attracted to the idea, a history of just 100 years is nothing, it's not such an exciting history, but finally I started out, and the bug got into me, and I went to work with him. And he [Oded] told me the story of the *mekalteret* , and I said, "I'll get it for you within a day." And he says, "How?" And I said, "I want you to give me the authority to take care of this [military parlance]." And he says, "You have it." So I went and called the guy and his wife answered the telephone. I didn't know who it was but I asked, "Who is it?" And she says, "Jacob's wife." I say to her, "I need Jacob, not you." She says, "He's not here." I say, "Oy vey, how come he's gone, he told us to come and take the plow." So she says, "Listen, if he told you then come and take it." And he [Oded] stands next to me and mutters, "No, he never said anything like that." And I said, "Stop being a vegetarian, if you want to get it, that's the only way." And I say to him, "Come, we'll get a truck and go there right away." The wife wanted to give us cold water to drink, like I just gave you, but I said, "There's no time, we must go," because I was afraid that he [the husband] will turn up all of a sudden. But this tool, let me tell you, if it wasn't here, it would have been lost. (Binyamin, Yifat, 6.22.89)

This story establishes a twofold lineage—the provenance of the agricultural implement and Binyamin's own position as participant in the early stages of museum making even though it sounds more like an updated version of the Israeli tall tales genre known as the *chizbat* of the *Palmach* than a factual report.[1] Indeed, the image of Odedi as the local enthusiast (*meshuga ladavar*), who—in the spirit of a military conqueror—will stop at nothing in his drive to accomplish his goal of collecting appropriate items for the museum display—which was in this case overtaken by Binyamin as the daring and cunning hunter of tools—is conjured up again and again by the various tour guides, often by way of introducing the museum story. This frame narrative anchors a sense of cultural continuity as the pioneers' exploits in the past and the museum makers' exploits in the present join into

---

[1]The *Palmach* refers to prestate military underground units, whose tall tale tradition was investigated by Oring (1981).

one larger endeavor—the project of initially building the place, and then that of continuing this act of creation through a commemorative agenda. In both cases, a sense of urgency and a single-minded devotion—in the spirit of "the end justifies the means"—were mobilized by those who were crazy enough to undertake the place-making project against all odds. And it is this contagious spirit of boundless commitment and fruitful endeavor that is hoped to color the visitors' reconstructions of the pioneering experience as they move along the museum route.

Arabs in Settlement Museum Lore

Following a chronological logic of narration, according to which the museum story begins with the arrival of Jewish settlers in Palestine and their initial adoption of the agricultural tools and methods they encountered among the Arabs, the tour starts at the Traditional Agriculture Corner. This corner consists of traditional farming implements, some of which are hung

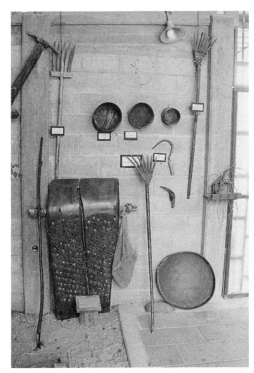

FIG. 3.1. The Traditional Agriculture Corner at the entrance of the Yifat museum. The threshing machine (left) and the sieve (bottom right) are leaning against the wall. The measures (by volume) for dry substances (*seot*) are arranged above them.

on the outer wall and some of which are placed on the ground alongside it. The tool display is punctuated by large photographs that depict scenes from traditional agricultural settings, such as a man ploughing with a pair of oxen, or sowing seeds by hand. Some of the objects on display are labeled in Hebrew and English, but no information is given beyond rudimentary naming of the objects. Even though many of them originated in Arab villages and are presented as part of local Arab agricultural methods, their Arabic names are not given either in Arabic or in Hebrew letters. The stories behind the objects, and the operational details associated with their production and use, as well as their Arabic names, are often given in the tour guides' verbal interpretations, however.

Given the transformative nature of the Jews' decision to return to agricultural work, this section of the museum tour carries a good deal of narrative weight. It tells stories that are as much about Arabs as they are about Jews, as much about the lure and authenticity of old ways as about the need to overcome them in the interest of progress. Thus, even though most of the stories that are repeatedly told by the various tour guides refer to the specific objects on display, they carry ideological resonances that serve to explicate and animate particular material objects by narratively embedding them within a meaningful human and social context.

Take, for example, the story of the sieve that is used to separate out the grain after the threshing has taken place. It falls under the larger category of Arab customs stories that introduce the taste of bygone days through depictions of technologically primitive agriculture. The sieve story is one of the most frequently recounted tales that introduces the theme of Arab culture into the museum's narrative texture, combining fascination with the exotic and a patronizing attitude of members of a more progressive culture. A typical version of it reads as follows:

> But there's a very nice story among the Bedouins. They tell that this sieve was used by the women to separate the wheat, and they would make the virgins sit outside the tent, next to it, moving the sieve with their arms from side to side [demonstrating movement], look at this, what does it look like, very sexy, isn't it? They are sitting next to the tent, separating out the wheat, and all the men working in the field say, "This one or that one is smashing, I'll go to her father and take her from him." But the married women, they worked inside the tent, they did not go out. They were not allowed to go out so that no one can cast any suspicion on them.... (Sarah, Yifat, 11.5.91)

Embedding the sieve within a broader context of culturally encoded forms of social conduct, this story offers a glimpse of what is, to most visitors, an alternative set of attitudes and practices concerning male–female relations and familial roles. As a narrated object, the sieve becomes an opportunity for a momentary act of self-definition constructed polemically around the exoticism of the Arab as a cultural Other. When Binyamin tells this and other stories related to the implements of the traditional agriculture corner, he makes a point of mentioning the Arab names of the tools, taking particular satisfaction in introducing them to Arab city dwellers who are no longer familiar with their forefathers' farming ways (as occurred several times with Arab students in the university groups I brought to the museum). The pride he takes in acquainting young Arabs with their own cultural heritage is linguistically reflected in his speech by the recounting of many Arabic tales, the injection of Arabic words and proverbs as well as by the occasional thickening of his "oriental" accent as a dramaturgical device. However, there was more than a linguistic point to his comment to me one day when he said, "The story of this museum can't be told in one language only. It must be told in both Hebrew and Arabic."

Another way in which this bilingual conception of the museum story was expressed in Binyamin's performances involved the adoption (some would say appropriation) of Arab tales as a way of conveying key aspects of the museum message. This narrative appropriation, which not only takes liberty with Arab tales but also implies that they are best suited to articulate the meanings and values the museum seeks to enhance, became part of the performative repertoire of younger guides as well. An example of this strategy, given in Binyamin's personalized style, was the story of the thirsty Sheikh, who was defeated in a tribal war over water sources, but was then revived by a girl who gave him water to drink:

> The Sheikh of this [Bedouin] tribe was going home, sad and beaten. He went back and his mouth was full of white foam because he was very thirsty. And he passed by the encampment, and suddenly a girl walked towards him with a bowl of water and gives him a drink. And he was so thirsty that he was ready to swallow the water all at once. But he could not drink because on top of the water were pieces of straw. He had to blow on it all the time, move the straw aside, drink some of the water and take a pause. After he finishes drinking, and was not thirsty anymore, he tells the girl, "Sister "—he doesn't say *girl* or *chick*—he says to her, "sister, how come everything is so neat around you and yet you give me a bowl of water all dirty with pieces of straw?" So she tells him, "I saved your life, because if you had drunk the water all at once you would have gotten a stroke."
>
> [Child's question, "What's a stroke?" Guide, "What's a stroke? It's a heart attack."]
>
> [Guide continues] " … or you could have gotten some other attack and fallen down, and I didn't want you to die here." The moment she said this he looked into her eyes and fell in love with her, love at first sight. And he came home, and when he was home he gathered all his dignitaries and sent a delegation to the girl's parents. And the girl's parents spoke well of their daughter, and while they were speaking it turned out that he [i.e., the Sheikh] wants to marry this girl. Now, the most important thing is that among the

Bedouins one can marry four wives, [turning to some boys] you know this, boys? By us it's not permitted, you marry one woman and that's it."

[Child's voice, "So you divorce the woman."]

"Divorce, well …" I asked the Sheikh, "Why didn't you marry [another woman]?" He said, "That was my first love, I love her and I'll take no other woman." So that's what happens when you fight over water. Therefore, when you come home, there's one thing you should remember, when you see your parents washing their cars [with a water hose], you should stop them. Why? Because they're wasting water. Say to them, "Take a bucket of water and a rag and clean up the cars." We shouldn't waste water, there's not enough of it. (Binyamin, Yifat, 8.1.89)

This adaptation of an Arab tale was told to a group of grade-school children around the reconstructed well in the museum's inner yard in the context of discussing problems of the water shortage, which are problems shared by Jewish and Arab agriculturists alike. Once, when I asked Binyamin what he most wanted kids to take home with them from the museum, he promptly said, "The idea that you shouldn't waste water." Handling water properly is spoken of in terms that make it symbolic of a good and balanced relationship between human beings and their natural environment, and through this bit of Arab folklore, this sense of graceful balance is extended to the domain of human relationships as well.

Some of the display practices and other tales associated with the artifacts located in the Traditional Agriculture Corner convey a much more problematic picture of Arab-Jewish contacts in pioneering days. This aspect of the museum's representational idiom is discussed in chapter 5, which considers settlement museums as a culturally contested arena.

Agricultural Progress and the Spirit of Nostalgia

A good portion of the agricultural display is devoted to various stages and forms in the technological development of plows, tractors, and similar tools and machines. However, whereas the linear "grammar" of the display—from the more primitive to the more modern tool in any given category—suggests a wholehearted embrace of technological progress, the verbal interpretation accompanying it is not univocal in this respect. The narrative voice celebrating progress is repeatedly interrupted by a nostalgic undervoice filled with longing for a past shaped by heroic values and deeds, an ethos of production glorifying manual labor and a close contact with the land as spiritual fulfillment, not mere utilitarian necessity. This undervoice breaks through at particular narrative junctures, as in the story about the pioneer Yankelevich, a typical pioneer and an extraordinary person who Binyamin claimed he had known personally and admired a lot (interview, 8.23.91). In tours guided by Binyamin, the figure of Yankelevich often served as a narrative thread along the tour route (and it was sometimes borrowed by other guides, too). Yankelevich, the spiritual pioneer, refused to succumb to the high-handedness of progress and to make his work easier by using a newly invented plow that was attached to a tractor and was endowed with a seat. Instead, he insisted on walking behind a simple plow drawn by a mule as he had always done. A typical version of the story ran as follows:

> He wasn't religious, but he knew the whole Bible by heart, he knew the history of Israel and he knew the history of the valley…he had simply dreamed he would be able to come to the land of Israel and plow the earth here, sow it and plant it…And he arrives and he fulfills his dream and he is the happiest person on earth. And then what happens? As long as he works with the simple tools, everything is all right. Suddenly some instructor comes and tells him, "You are harnessing the horses [to the plow]? Get onto the seat." So he tells him, "Why should I get onto the seat? What am I, a banker or a clerk?" And he refused to accept it. So he harnessed the horses to the machine and walked beside the seat. The Arabs consider the Jews to be clever, so he [the Arab] says, "What is this crazy Jew doing walking beside the seat?…" Now that Jew, that Yankelevich…wanted to feel the earth with his feet because on that earth had passed the prophet Elijah, and King Solomon and King David and all that history…But later he got a plow that he had to get onto the seat [to drive], and he liked it. They told him, "Yankelevich, get off," but he wouldn't. It was difficult to get him onto the seat, but it was even more difficult to get him off it. (Binyamin, Yifat, 6.22.89)

This narrative gives voice to the problematics that surrounded techno-logical progress in the ideological climate of pioneering days. This climate was shaped by the Zionist ethos of return to the land, which was interpreted both as a return to the land of Israel and as a return to an organic way of life and to a direct contact with nature. In this view, technological efficiency was set against a world of meaning and value; a world where work was a mere necessity was set against a world where work was to be ecstatically experienced as a source of personal redemption. The final twist given to the tale, Yankelevich's responsiveness to the voices of progress and the promise of technology, as evidenced by his newly acquired taste for the comforts of the tractor seat, exemplify the self-directed irony that is sometimes added to these stories by way of both denigrating the present and casting a shadow of self-questioning on the loftily declaimed ideological certainties of the past. The ironical edge is increased by the allegorical word play associated with the phrase, "holding on to your seat," which is used in contemporary parlance to refer to those who self-righteously cling to public office with undue fervor, an allegation that was often made against founders turned politicians.

Notably, the Arabs emerge from these agricultural tales doubly short-shrifted: They are as mystified by the ideological commitment of the Jewish pioneers as they are baffled by the technological wonders the latter have introduced. The clash between a romantic attachment to the land and a technologically driven, pragmatic attitude toward it is obviously foreign to the Arabs' cultural experience as viewed from the standpoint of the Jewish pioneers. It is the predicament only of those Jewish idealists for whom cultivation of the land is not a natural way of life but part of a newly embraced personal and collective identification. And the collective memory of this idealistic attitude comes to anchor a complex attitude toward past and present, an Israeli version of contemporary nostalgia, as the story proceeds to tell how Yankelevich, in a quasi-religious pioneering outpour, insists on walking along the fields and sowing the seeds by hand, because

> ... he knows that here, in this valley, who worked in this valley? The Prophet Elijah, in Megiddo were King David and King Solomon. He knows that this is a truly sacred place...[and when the green shoots appeared], he ran into the field shouting "New life! New life!" And he began to caress the shoots, to kiss them, that's how much he loved agriculture, such a special man, we don't come across them any more. Today they sow with large machines, with a radio and a television inside, and everyone has a clock and they work by the clock. Then there was no such thing. Then, everything had value, with a great love for the land, for sowing it, and for the wheat ...(Binyamin, Yifat, 6.22.89)

In this, as in other stories, working the land was presented as a form of worship that is incommensurate with the distant and pragmatic attitude associated with technological development. The ambivalence associated in pioneering days with the ethos of progress, concretized in the negotiations surrounding the introduction of technologically advanced agricultural machinery, is also invoked in the story that was told in this shed to a group of my graduate students by Avi, a second-generation guide. Like Binyamin's story about Yankelevich, this story concerns the shift away from the use of mules or horses for plowing the fields to the use of tractors:

> Imagine, when the first tractor comes in, there is an argument, Meir Zarchi, Shai's father, you may have met him, Shai's grandfather, from Genigar, says, "Over my dead body!" We came to be connected to this land. You bring in the tractor, it creates a distance from the soil, it goes against the principles we've all discussed. So the folk tell him, "Listen, this is progress," and so on, but he says, "I've heard all about progress, but I won't have any of it. I'll show you, I'll lock the gates." And when Meir Zarchi says he'll lock the gates and won't let it happen, everybody got scared because he was a very big guy, and a man of principle, too. It wasn't a simple situation, so what could they do? They challenged him with a contest, because he loved contests. They told him, "You know what? We'll get the tractor on loan. No, we'll buy it and you will work with the horse and the tractor will work with the plow and we'll see

who does better." The first day Meir worked with all his might, and the guys were novices on the tractor, and he won, he made it and was very happy. The second day it was much harder. The guys were beginning to develop their skills riding the tractor, they're doing better and he begins to worry. The third day the tractor wins, but Meir doesn't give in. He didn't give up his horse...(Avi, Yifat, 11.8.91)

The Community/Individual Dialectic

Many corners in the museum are devoted to representations of the pioneers' domestic life. In these sections, the distinctive communal ideology and way of life of the *kibbutz* are explicated and celebrated. Just as the agricultural implements depicted in the work sphere anchor narratives that invoke the larger cultural ideology of productive labor associated with the Jews' return to the land, so the objects assembled and displayed in the domestic life sections, especially in the inner yard, invoke the social dimensions of the cultural revolution of Zionism as articulated in the *kibbutz* search for new forms of communal life. The focus here shifts from the values of productive labor and land to the values of communal feeling, simplicity in ways of life, and personal sacrifices to communal needs. The pioneer is now represented as the antibourgeois who willingly exchanged the genteel porcelain, fine food, and elegant clothing of his or her parental home for the badly cooked basic diet of the communal dining room, and the communal sharing of clothes known as *shituf* (partnership), which served to maximize the use of clothing because everybody could use everybody's clothes, as well as to help reduce the pioneers' bourgeois attachment to the individual ownership of personal possessions.

The representational logic most often employed in the domestic sphere corners tends to be mimetic, that is, reconstructed scenes of typical pioneering settings, rather than classificatory, that is, spatially arranged taxonomies of particular categories of artifacts, which was the most typical arrangement found in the agricultural sections of the display. A reconstructed collective-clothing shed, where the pioneers could go for a change of clothes, provides an opportunity to discuss the relentless demands of communal life; the laundry corner next to it, dominated by an enlarged photograph of male pioneers engaged in a handwash of clothes, becomes an occasion to reinforce statements made earlier concerning gender equality in pioneering days. A cabin added to the display in recent years, depicting a typical family house in a noncommunal settlement (*moshav*), provides an occasion for contrastive comments that highlight the special characteristics of communal as compared to noncommunal farming life; the reconstructed clinic, with its olden days' medical implements and cures, provides an occasion for a discussion of the health hazards and personal sacrifices faced by the early pioneers, and the sparse medical support they could rely on. Reconstructions of a communal shower and an outdoor restroom follow, drawing out humorous tales about life's basic bodily needs, sometimes with erotic overtones. A small-size model of a schoolroom with an old, enlarged map of the land of Israel and an enlarged photograph depicting pupils on one of the famous school excursions (*tiyulim*) of early days ends this part of the display.

The most central displays relating to the pioneers' way of life, however, are the communal kitchen and dining room, the family tent or cabin, and the babies' nursery. These three sections of the museum provide occasions for telling stories that give voice to the social utopia of close-knit, solidary, and egalitarian relations that grounded the *kibbutz* experience on the one hand, and to the enormous difficulties and personal costs associated with the implementation of this social vision on the other hand.

The items in the communal domestic sphere sections of the display thus provide anchors for narrating the way of life aspect of the pioneering experience: the crowded living conditions in the tent with its bare furnishings, testimonies of shortages in food supplies, the crude tin dishes on the dining room table, the makeshift baby cot constructed out of an orange crate. Major themes heard in this part of the tour relate to the hardships experienced by the pioneers and the largely successful efforts they made to overcome them. Consider, for example, stories related to the scarcity of food and the crudity of kitchen utensils, like the story told by Binyamin to a group of young children:

> These were the cups they used to drink tea, tin cups, because they didn't have plates and cups made out of ceramics, these were extremely simple plates and cups, the most modern things they had at the time. These plates don't break, they can fall down and not break.... Now in the morning, you see what they'd eat? They ate bread dipped in olive oil and onions. At noon they ate bread dipped in olive oil and soup, in these plates they'd put the soup. And they didn't always like the food, because the young woman didn't know how to cook, and she'd burn the soup, so they would return it to the kitchen, and she was very sad and cried, "Oy vey, I work all morning and prepare the soup and they don't eat it." And it was very disheartening, the full plates coming back to the kitchen. (Binyamin, Yifat, 7.21.91)

The communal dining room was not only or primarily the place for physical nourishment, however. It was the social heart of the community, where group solidarity was most fully experienced and cultivated. Thus, the first black-and-white brochure of the museum (now replaced by the less wordy and more colorful one cited earlier) vividly describes the central role the dining room played in the life of the pioneering group, an account that was echoed orally in most of the tours I attended:

FIG. 3.2. The communal dining room display in the Yifat museum.

The dining room itself was the heart of "togetherness"...Here in the dining room discussions were conducted, at times even very arduous "soul talks." Here they arranged the work schedule for the next day. In the dining room they danced almost every night. Dancing gave the strength to start all over again the next day.

The place's communal orientation was expressed not only in activities such as dancing and group singing, but also in the fact that it housed the library and the musical instruments originally brought by individuals, as well as the one radio the group possessed, all of which are now on display in the reconstructed dining room cabin. It also finds expression in group pictures of pioneers and in icons of national membership—such as the legendary blue box designed for donations for Jewish Agency pioneering enterprises such as land purchase and tree planting—and pictures of prominent Zionist leaders.

The intensity of communal experience sought by the young pioneers is reflected in the story of the debate over whether individual chairs or benches should be used in the dining room. The decision to use benches is presented not as a technical matter but as a rejection of individually oriented bourgeois values because on a bench, you can always move and add another person, unlike chairs (or so the doctrine goes).

Whereas the benches symbolize the essential openness of the group to new members, the bell placed outside the dining room door symbolizes the community's responsiveness to the needs of individuals. In the groups' unwritten code, an individual who woke up in the middle of the night, agonizing over some personal problem such as homesickness or self-doubts, could summon his or her bleary-eyed friends by sounding the outdoor bell, expecting them to share in his or her moment of agony and provide much-needed social support.

These stories of personal agony provide a context for discussing the pioneers' youthfulness (they were all in their late teens and early 20s) and the theme of the psychological cost of their separation from family and childhood friends. Indeed, it is often stressed that the ideological embracing of a communal, self-effacing way of life did not obliterate the personal costs involved in the decision to mold a new society in the land of Israel. The dialectical tension between the individual and the community, the private and the public, is narratively dramatized in the vignettes told at many junctures along the tour route, but most significantly so in the Way of Life sections of the display. The dining room, the public heart and symbol of community, and the tent, the private seat of romantic and conjugal life, flank the inner yard on opposite sides, visually encapsulating the polarity and tension between the pioneers' private worlds and their communal participation. Thus, whereas the dining room is narrated as an all-inclusive hub of the community, the tent stands for the striving for exclusive social

FIG. 3.3. A pioneers' tent in the Yifat museum.

FIG. 3.4. Making pioneers' herbal tea on a *primus*, a three-legged stove.

relationships that pose a threat to the solidarity of the community at large. And just as the building of community was enhanced by the pioneers' poverty, so the greater material comfort gradually achieved through hard work and technological progress is held partly responsible for triggering the process of communal fragmentation. As Binyamin once put it:

> ... When electricity arrived and they turned on the first light, then the change began. Because there was light in the tents, too.... whoever wanted to come to the dining room came to the dining room, but people preferred to stay in the tents and began to withdraw more. (Binyamin, Yifat, 6.22.89)

Whereas in this comment, the tent as a private enclosure marks a hazard to communal living, in another narrative, the community's heavy-handed invasion of the private sphere is concretized through the living arrangements whereby a third person (nicknamed *primus* after the popular three-legged stove) was assigned as a tentmate to a conjugal couple. The stories of the negotiations, spoken and unspoken, that were needed to ensure a measure of privacy, although generally recounted with a smile, are sometimes also accompanied by a harsh reassessment of these past practices. Binyamin, interpreting the tent display to a group of high-school students whom he judged to be particularly interested in stories surrounding romantic relations and conjugal arrangements in pioneering days, again invoked the figure of Yankelevich, his favorite pioneer, as he stressed the ideological significance of this arrangement in terms of the tension between communal and personal needs:

> We asked the oldest among the old-timers: "How could you do such a thing, bring a third person into your intimate life?" And one of them said: "We needed to break up the family cell. That Yankelevich and his Zladka were always together, they stopped coming to the dining room, stopped attending the parties, and all that." But some of the others were not quite comfortable with this and said that there was a shortage of living space, and perhaps that was the reason. (Binyamin, Yifat, 8.1.89)

One of the second-generation guides echoed the bewilderment and the note of disapproval that now accompany many of the *primus* stories, over-

FIG. 3.5. The communal clothes' cabin; the clothes, shared through the arrangement known as *shituf* (partnership) are arranged according to size: big (*gadol*); medium (*beynoni*); small (*katan*); and depleted (*yarud*), a local term designating the physical state of persons who have been ill, especially with malaria.

shadowing some of the earlier admiration for them, when he told me in one of our conversations that the one display in the museum he finds difficult to interpret is the tent and the *primus* stories associated with it. There was much feeling in his voice when he said, "I don't understand how they could have done it."

The communal babies' nursery, which is often the next stop in the tour, provides an occasion for both recognition of past difficulties and reassessment of past practices. Sarah's narration proceeds from the point of view of the caretaker (*metapelet*) as she herself has had first-hand experience working in the communal nursery in her own day, and remained sensitive to the health issues they were facing at the time:

> When more children were born, we already built a cot, you see there's a cot here, and there's even a bath and there was even a caretaker who received special training. And what I want to tell you, you know, that once we didn't have antibiotics, right? So in order to see that children didn't get sick, we first of all wanted to cover them at night with this net, so that the flies and mosquitoes don't eat them up...And the mother would come in and wear this mask and put on a white apron, clean, very sterile, so as not to infect the child with her cold if she had one, or with her sore throat, we saw to it that she doesn't infect her baby. We took great care of the children, because if they fell ill we had not enough means to cure them and we didn't have the immunizations you are now getting, the injections, right? (Sarah, Yifat, 12.5.89)

Although this account justifies the caretaker's obsessive hygienic measures in view of the health hazards and shortage of medication during early pioneering days, many of the retrospective accounts relating to the communal nursery provide an embittered commentary on these same childrearing practices and controlling measures (Leshem, 1991). All in all, a more complex attitude toward communal childrearing practices has been inscribed in the collective memory of the *kibbutz* than Sarah's account would suggest. The most poignant stories in this section of the museum depict the (always female) caretaker as a daunting figure, both highly respected and at the same time greatly feared by the young parents. She embodied the public voice of the community, institutionalizing a series of standardized childrearing measures that involved the appropriation of broad aspects of children's lives from the private sphere of parental guardianship and care. Given the communal childrearing arrangements, parents both depended on the caretaker and resented her for this very dependency, and for the power she yielded over the construction and maintenance of the parent–child bonding experience. Mediating the spheres of the public and private, she made stringent demands for hygienic procedures and the regimentation of children's daily schedules, and thus controlled child–parent interactions in the name of her pedagogical expertise. In some of the retrospective accounts of this highly problematic juncture in early *kibbutz* ideology and practice, the *metapelet* is not represented as an effective community worker who took responsibility for the babies' welfare under very difficult circumstances, but is, rather, folklorized into demonic proportions as a communal tyrant. This is suggested in the following story:

> What was terrible in the *kibbutz*? In the *kibbutz* there was this Zladka that I told you about, she was a real witch. They made a *metapelet* of her. She was supposed to take care of the kids. Now, she takes her job seriously, she says, "Kids have to be protected. A father who comes from the field he brings all kinds of germs, and we don't have medications here, and we don't have doctors, we have nothing, it's not like it was overseas." So I had to look at my baby through the net, that was the only way I was allowed to see him, God forbid I should go in, she [the caretaker] made all the parents tremble at her sight. The mother, she could go in because she needed to breastfeed the baby. But when she [the caretaker] saw the mother feeding the baby with a bottle, she says, "You're feeding with a bottle! You have no milk! I, too, can feed with a bottle. Go to the field, what are you doing here?" It was such cruelty, it is even hard to talk about it, but that's the truth, even a mother who wanted to feed her child with a bottle was not allowed to come in...Today it's a real revolution, today all parents get to take their children home...(Binyamin, Yifat, 8.13.91)

Indeed, although the health hazards that gave rise to many of the cautionary measures insisted on by the caretaker are acknowledged, many of the anecdotes associated with childrearing practices bring out the caretaker's oppressive control of natural desires and her role-related intrusion into the private sphere. In particular, her obsessive insistence on the rules of hygiene and the control of physical contact between parent and child are presented as the fanatical expression of a code of professional rationality backed by collective consent. This depiction of the female caretaker as a proponent of a professionalized system of childrearing, which signals expert authority and pedagogical progress, epitomizes the communal control exerted over individual lives. Its gender dimensions stand out in particular when compared to the treatment of professionalism and progress in the male-dominated occupational sphere of agricultural labor and technological improvement. As we have seen, in this sphere, too, some ambivalence is expressed in anecdotes about old-time farmers for whom the switch from a horse-drawn wagon to an engine-propelled tractor marks an objectionable and unnecessary surrender to the forces of modernity. But in these latter anecdotes, it is the old-time farmer who is affectionately portrayed as a somewhat comical hero, and the modernizing, technological spirit of agricultural expertise is ultimately vindicated. None of the demonizing that attends the portrayal of the professional caretaker and her occupational practices is found in the agricultural tales.

Update: Some Recent Renovations

Although I completed my composite, written tour of Yifat before the most recent changes were introduced into the museum's display area, a few words about these renovations seem warranted. On my last visit to the museum (in April 1996), I noticed three kinds of changes in the organization and layout of the display that I find significant from the standpoint of my study. First of all, the different corners of the museum were somewhat rearranged, for example, the tent and communal washroom were moved from the inner circle of the courtyard to the outer one in a different part of the museum. Thus, the circles representing work life and communal life have become more integrated into a holistic tale of an all-encompassing way of life with less specific emphasis on the centrality of agricultural production. Second, to some of the key displays—for example, the tent, the communal wash-room, the dining room—were added large, lettered inscriptions in three languages (Hebrew, English, and Arabic!) that single out these corners, name, and interpret them for all visitors independent of the guide's accompanying discourse. The inscriptions echo in skeletal form the kind of anecdotal information presented by the guides when they choose to pause in that particular corner, but they clearly make a move toward standardizing what is thought to be the core knowledge imparted by the museum. For example, the inscription on the large plastic plaque placed in front of the washroom reads as follows:

The Communal Washroom

This is the real center of social life in the settlement. The place for expressing opinions, transferring information, disseminating knowledge. A platform for language, ideal for voice development and for gymnastics. The washroom inherited the primitive shower unit from the first Aliyah but was only recognized as a common social institution in the period between the third and fourth Aliyah. The settlement saw in the washroom an expression of the communal spirit.

Third, a couple of new corners were added that seem to me to make interesting statements concerning points of controversy previously raised in relation to the museum story. One of them is a corner that on the one hand adds a historical note about an important endeavor of the pioneers—the drying of the swamps—but it also indirectly addresses the argument over whether there had been swamps in the Jezreel Valley. This new museum corner does not in fact make any explicit allusion to this contentious issue (from the standpoint of settlement mythology), but neither its title (Draining the Swamps) nor its text leave much doubt as to the museum's position in this matter. The claim concerning the existence and magnitude of the swamps is authenticated by citing the eyewitness account of a well-known personality in pioneering days, the physician Dr. Hillel Jaffe, who wrote to the Workers' Union:

> The danger in the valley (Jezreel) is very great. Apart from small swamps there is a large swampy area between two springs which will be extremely difficult to contend with, and one of them is called Ein al-Bidha. It will take a long time to dry this swampland completely because a part of it is not under Jewish control...We must not settle in the valley except on the hills in the North East. Under no circumstances must we settle on the small hill adjacent to Ein al-Bidha.

The other new museum corner marked by a plaque, which was introduced recently, deals with the contentious issue of gender equality in pioneering days. In most of the guided tours I have observed and recorded in the past, the myth of gender equality was rather consistently reiterated. This was usually done when the tour paused in front of a blown-up photograph of women engaged (like men) in road construction. The inscription given on the plaque designed for the new corner entitled Pioneer Women presents a less straightforward picture, diffusely attributing the gap between the ideals of gender equality and women's actual experiences to society. It reads:

> Equality of the sexes as an integral part of a system of social justice was one of the foremost objectives during the time of the second and third *aliyahs*. Women struggled to play an equal part in the building of the infrastructure of the Homeland although the more traditional "role" of cooking, clothing the family, and looking after the children's education became the norm. The gap between women's expectations and the reality of the situation expanded more and more and was a constant source of frustration. Discussion groups on this topic were used as a substitute for the inability of society to fulfill the inherent desires of the womenfolk. More and more discussions ensued!

As I stood reading this plaque, I was reminded of a guided tour I had participated in about a year earlier during which the guide presented what now seemed to be the museum's older storyline, which spoke not of expectations concerning gender equality but of its actual attainment in pioneering days. His version was challenged by one of the visitors who happened to be a well-known feminist scholar who had written extensively about the position and role of women in prestate years. That discussion ended on a bit of an acrimonious note, but it may have opened the way to a more focused and more nuanced presentation of gender issues in the museum.

The museum director told me that these new corners were not yet completed—as background to them, they intended to place very large photographs that would illustrate and authenticate their contents, relating the pictographic material to elements of the object on display. The picture showing the pioneer women working in road construction was chosen for this corner.

I would argue, then, that the changes and additions introduced into the museum display, whereas they have certainly contributed much to the aesthetics of the museum as a whole, can also be made sense of in terms of the cultural negotiation of images in which the museum participates. By providing an arena for an imaginative, dialectical engagement with images of cultural others—the Diaspora Jew, the pioneer, the Arab, the woman—the settlement museum invites contemporary Israeli visitors—men and women—to participate in the construction of a culturally constituted self. Whether they wear pioneer clothing before entering the time tunnel that transforms them into early settlers, or whether they are walking in their own shoes, the inducement to participate in the museum's representation of the past actually invites visitors to refigure themselves. Thus, visitors play themselves against the various images presented in fragmentary fashion at different points along the tour route—the romanticized Arab at one point, the Diaspora Jew at another, the idealized pioneer at a third. I believe that it is the particular form of this semiludic process of self-invention that gives this museum experience its distinctive flavor both in Yifat and in The Old Courtyard in Ein Shemer, where our next tour will take us.

A WINDOW TO THE KIBBUTZ EXPERIENCE: THE OLD COURTYARD IN EIN SHEMER

The Museum and Its Story

The Old Courtyard in *kibbutz* Ein Shemer is a site museum constructed around the very place where the *kibbutz* originated in 1927, following several previous settlement attempts on the same site that began as early as 1920. It was in that earlier period of the third immigration wave (1919 to 1923) that the stone wall surrounding the courtyard and the impressive stone house built as a hostel for Jewish travelers were constructed, and they have served as cornerstones in the further development of the settlement. The museum brochure includes the following description about the history of the place:

FIG. 3.6. The entrance to The Old Courtyard in Ein Shemer.

The old courtyard in Ein Shemer is a precise and most beautiful reconstruction of the days of early settlement. It is the only place in the area—and in the country as a whole—where a fortified courtyard from the days of Hashomer and Gdud Ha'avoda [names of two pioneering organizations] was preserved and reconstructed. It is the only place where the seeds of a *kibbutz* were sown in a fortified courtyard—*kibbutz* Ein Shemer, one of the founding settlements of the *kibbutz* movement ...

The heart of the museum is what used to be the old dining room of the *kibbutz*, which was located inside the old courtyard. The original section has been reconstructed as a communal dining room and forms the central focus of the contemporary display, whereas the dining room's later extension houses the rest of the exhibits. The main part of the tour takes visitors through the museum complex that encompasses the courtyard and the various thematic corners found in it. It is all suffused by a sense of place and roots, concretized in the actual traces of the past that give shape and feeling to the whole tour: the original stone house, the authentic wall, and the huge, beautiful date trees that were planted by the early settlers some 70 years ago and now greet visitors into the courtyard's enclave. As we shall see, many of the tour guides' accounts incorporate references to the authenticity of the place through an idiom of historical preservation and architectural reconstruction. The story told in Ein Shemer, unlike the tale recounted in Yifat, relates more specifically to the history of that particular *kibbutz* as a specific expression of the larger idea of the communal experiment and as an emblem of Zionist settlement.

Some visitor groups visit only the museum itself although some groups opt for an additional tour (for an increased fee), which takes them around the present-day *kibbutz* (such an option exists in the Yifat museum but is much more rarely taken). The *kibbutz* tour is conducted on a tractor-led large carriage, which was especially converted for touristic purposes following the example, I was told, of similar transport found in national parks in the United States. The combined tour of the *kibbutz* adds an explicitly chronological and comparative flavor to the tour as a whole, serving to underline both continuities and discontinuities between past and present. Much like the description of the surrounding landscape of the valley that prefaces the tour at the observation post in front of the Yifat museum, the brief view given in Ein Shemer of the contemporary *kibbutz* scene carries a largely celebratory note. Whether it comes before or after the round of the museum itself, it frames (or reframes) the stories about the hardships and triumphs of the first years of settlement with the knowledge of things to come in a way that allows for reassessments of the *kibbutz* as a cultural project without undermining its essential value and its important role in the country's history.

FIG. 3.7. The stone building and stone wall around which the settlement was originally built. The second floor of the building now houses the weapons display.

FIG. 3.8. The Old Courtyard in Ein Shemer. The reconstructed bakery (left corner) gives out delicious smells of newly baked bread; the granary to its right houses an exhibit of farm implements.

Similar framing can be found in the lively and humorous slide presentation that either opens or closes the museum tour: It tells the story of Ein Shemer as it is personified in the life of a pioneer called Aryeh who was among the founders of the settlement. It is a story of hardships, trials, and errors but also of the great accomplishments of a satisfying life and the making of place. More than most accounts I have encountered in settlement museums, but like the retrospective assessment associated in Yifat with the *primus* arrangement or the childrearing practices of the communal caretaker, this narrative of Ein Shemer also acknowledges problematic aspects associated with *kibbutz* life: children's communal living arrangements that meant many nights filled with anxiety and loneliness without accessible adults who could help the children overcome their fears, the financial bankruptcy of many *kibbutzim*; the unwillingness of many *kibbutz*-raised children to stay in the *kibbutz*, and the fact that some of them even left the country to go and live in the United States or elsewhere. The problematic state of the *kibbutz*—often referred to as the *kibbutz* crisis—is a well-known fact in Israeli life. The *kibbutz* inability to transmit its communal and egalitarian ideology to the younger generations, its failure to combat the capitalistic spirit of the day and to sustain its social vision in an increasingly individualistic age, all these serve as a backdrop to the way the story told in the museum is heard. And even though the flourishing *kibbutz*—as the aforementioned slide show points out—is an unmistakable presence and undeniable proof of accomplishment, it falls short of a vision come true. And perhaps it is the very questionable nature of this accomplishment that makes the museum and

FIG. 3.9. Makeshift furniture in a pioneers' cabin in The Old Courtyard: an earthen jar for cold water, a wood crate for a table, and covered tin boxes for chairs. A copy of Marx's book *Das Kapital* signals the inhabitants' left-wing political leanings.

the story it tells so necessary and so tenuous. Somewhat paradoxically, the most poignantly expressed sense of accomplishment I heard related to the founding of the museum, not to the founding of the *kibbutz*. At one point, the museum founder proudly told me how the whole *kibbutz* had participated in the reconstruction project that turned the museum from a run-down relic into the thriving place it is today, saying, "You see this roof? Every *kibbutz* member has his own personal tile in this roof." Indeed, it is by participating in the museum-making project as a communal enterprise that *kibbutz* members can now partake in the dream that has held them together for so many years, and that has itself now become an object of nostalgia.[2]

---

[2] A similar feeling—that the museum was more viable than its surrounding *kibbutz* life—was expressed by the director of the Yifat museum in responding to the question of what he imagined the museum would be like in 30 years' time. He said, "In 30 years? In 30 years I am not sure the *kibbutz* will be around, but I'm certain the museum will."

Thus, in Ein Shemer the purpose of the tour in the museum itself tends to be defined both locally, with stress on the social history and everyday life of the young men and women who had arrived in the land of Israel in semiorganized youth groups after the first World War, and more generically as a tale of the *kibbutz* idea as it was developed in the most radical, left-wing socialist strand of the *kibbutz* movement to which Ein Shemer belonged.[3]

A typical opening to a tour of the *kibbutz* itself emphasizes the more general relevance it has in contemporary life:

> What is the idea of the *kibbutz*? Perhaps many of you have been to or seen a *kibbutz*, there are relatives or acquaintances, the idea is to try and understand what is the life force of a *kibbutz*, of an agricultural settlement that lives from farming and a little industry, like a *moshav* or *moshava* (noncommunal settlements) or any other village. What makes the *kibbutz* special is that it is organized like a large family. Think about a large *chamula* (extended family in Arabic) of many people. In our case we have about 800 people, some 200 families. And their basic principles are these: All property is shared, they have one bank account, everybody puts their salary into the same account. The children are all educated in the same school. That's it, these three principles, and that's what makes this place what it is. (Ronen, Ein Shemer, 10.22.91)

On Place and Roots

The museum part of the tour typically starts with an attempt to help visitors make an imaginative leap back to the early 1920s and 1930s through the use of old photographs of the courtyard and its surrounding area, and with the help of a model reconstruction of the way The Old Courtyard looked in the early days. The tour guides' sensitivity to the political question of the ownership of the land finds its expression in comments stating the fact that the *kibbutz* was situated on land legally purchased by Yehoshua Hankin (a well-known Zionist activist and "redeemer of the land") from Arab owners who were glad to be rid of the swampy terrain. The landscape is similarly interpreted with reference to the photographs on display:

> [Pointing to a photograph] This is the courtyard, where we stood earlier, the way it was in the 1920s, and [pointing to the model] this is how it was already in the 1930s: the stone house, the sheds, the granary, and we can observe the changes that take place from the 1920s to the 1930s. But the most interesting item for you to notice as visitors is this photograph of a landscape. The year is 1934, a moment before the establishment of the state—just 14 years—it's unbelievable that this is what the northern Sharon looked like. The beginning

---

[3]Yifat and Ein Shemer belong to two different strands in the *kibbutz* movement, differentiated in terms of political shades within the Socialist left. The more radical left-wing leanings of Ein Shemer may partly account for the stronger emphasis the guides put on *kibbutz*-related issues of communal life and radical secularism.

of settlement, 1920, and what you had then were just Petah Tikva, Hadera, Zichron, but we're already 14 years after the British took over the country, more than that even, and still the Sharon area is all empty spaces. (Ronen, Ein Shemer, 8. 2.91)

Having oriented visitors to the past and present landscapes in which The Old Courtyard has found its place, photographic allusions take them on a short detour that depicts part of the story of early settlement not emphasized in Yifat—a peek at the corner known as *beit aba* (the parental home), which shows typical pictures of the *shtetl* (traditional Eastern-European Jewish towns) with bearded, religious Jews. These pictures provide a context for discussing the pioneers' attitudes toward tradition and religion. This aspect of the pioneering tale is particularly stressed in Ein Shemer, a *kibbutz* whose orientation has been radically secular. Pointing at the pictures on the wall, the tour guide says to a group of children from another (secular) *kibbutz*:

> I want to move on to a short but somewhat heavier display, *Beit Aba* [the parental home]. As you see, the museum is built up of different sections, and this one is about the parental home, in the beginning, in the Diaspora. Let me take for example my great grandfather, who can be seen up there, a merchant from Warsaw, the picture was taken in 1920. Why is it important for me that you see it? This Rabbi Shmuel Levy, what was he then? [Child's voice: A rabbi] He was a very religious man, right? Or at least religious. Folks, you should remember that the newcomers who arrived here in those days all came from very religious homes. In your *kibbutzim*, in our *kibbutzim*, were the people religious?
> [Child's voice: No]
> So what happened to them here? Wait a minute, they were religious in the Diaspora, but when they came to the land of Israel they were not religious any more. Most of them were people who had left religion behind, at the same time that they left their homes, even a little earlier. Most of them left religion. Their parents were mostly very very religious, and they came here as secular people, and developed a secular culture here. Today, even the holidays you celebrate, *kibbutz* holidays like *Shavuot*, although it is a holiday that's written in the Bible, but you mainly deal with its agricultural aspects, right? The same in *Rosh Hashana* [New Year], the same in *Succoth*, it's not the specifically religious aspects of these holidays that we deal with. Therefore, the culture they developed here was a secular culture. I am not just telling you all of this; because most of the newcomers at the time arrived as secular people and wanted to develop a counter-culture to the culture of the *shtetl* [East European Jewish town] and you see this in your *kibbutzim* as well. (Gadi, Ein Shemer, 10.31.91)

This excerpt in fact encodes a complex attitude toward religion and tradition. Alongside the rhetoric of beginnings that traces the foundational moments of the *kibbutz* to The Old Courtyard and the pioneers who constructed it, the parental home section suggests the possibility of another, more elaborate story line, in which the *kibbutz* beginnings are traced to an earlier moment of cultural rejection. According to this tale, traditional Jewish beliefs and ways of life had to be actively left behind by the young pioneers with their departure from the parental home. This recognition of the cultural erasure associated with immigration generally and with the revolutionary spirit of the early pioneers more particularly, which was known as "the negation of the Diaspora," marks a recent reorientation to the story of modern Jewry in Israeli culture. During the nation-building era, this erasure tended to be either ignored or even celebrated. The acknowledgment of the parental home as part of the pioneers' story signals a certain acceptance of traditional Jewish Eastern European culture, to which more and more Israelis of Ashkenazi descent trace their personal and familial roots.

The Communal Dining Room

This gesture of acknowledgment notwithstanding, the focus of the museum nevertheless remains with the group of early pioneers who settled in the place. Thus, the next major display along the tour invites visitors to an encounter with some representatives of that group in the reconstructed dining room at the center of the museum, where several mannequins of

FIG. 3.10. The communal dining room in The Old Courtyard: A pioneer wearing a *rubashka*, a Russian peasant shirt (front left); a pioneer seated in front of newcomers dressed in European clothes (left back); visitors to the settlement—a British officer and an Arab Sheikh (right, with back to table); the *kibbutz's* first washing machine in the right-hand corner. Along the walls are thematically arranged pictures and visual displays of *kibbutz* life past and present.

pioneers are positioned in such a way as to allow the guides to introduce each figure and his or her story to the visitors who are crowded around the display area. In the following account the pioneers are introduced to a group of grade-school children:

> We are standing inside the old dining room shed that was built here 60 years ago, and I want to introduce you to the characters here. Now, 60 years ago they weren't dressed the way you are with a T-shirt, there were no T-shirts. You see how they were dressed? This guy has a special shirt that the newcomers brought from abroad. It is a Russian shirt and it is a fashion that was common then in Russia. Anybody know what it's called in Russian? *Rubashka*...Now let's get to know this group of pioneers. That's their dining hall, the utensils, the tables, the benches. They came from well-established families. They all belonged to what we now call *zfonim* [northerners—a class-colored slang term used to represent the inhabitants of the affluent northern neighborhoods of Tel Aviv]—a good home, property, University studies...They had everything but left their parents and came to the land of Israel...You see, the one who is standing here is called Levy, he was appointed *mukhtar* [leader, an Arabic word] because he knew Arabic and English. Here across, you see, are seated Sergeant Smith and Sheikh Ali, the Sheikh of all the Bedouins in the area, who is a friend of theirs [of the pioneers]. He teaches them how to go out herding, how to work in agriculture. And Sergeant Smith, he is a policeman from the neighboring British camp, he came to sniff around because he heard that the Jews were hiding weapons...And you see Chaim? Chaim arranges the work schedule. He tells everyone where they should work...[turning to some kids] If you were part of the group he'd tell you, "You're going to work in the orchard tomorrow, and you girls are going to work in construction, girls were doing the same work as boys in those days, and you're going to pick oranges, and that one is going to work in the field and that one in the cowshed." That was his job, to tell people where to work, and he also worked in the cowshed. And who is sitting across the table from him? Franz and Masha, a pioneering couple who came by ship yesterday. He tells them, "You have to go and work in the field." Franz answers, "Me? I have a tie and a jacket, I can't work in the field. I am a photographer...I'll take pictures in the courtyard, we'll send them abroad, all the Jews will see the photographs, and they will all come to the land of Israel. What do you think about it?" Chaim says to him, "It's a nice idea, but here you can't live on photography, you can't make money from it. In the morning you'll work in the cowshed, and in the afternoon, after you've done your day's work, you can make it your hobby, we don't mind ..." (Ronen, Ein Shemer, 10.22.91)

As we see, the interpretation in the dining room in the Ein Shemer museum, just as in Yifat, underlines the social dimensions of the pioneers' experience, but, on the whole, emphasis is placed here on the dining room as a place where the community engaged in open argument about principled matters rather than on the supportive dimension of group life that played itself out in the confessional soul talks that were frequently mentioned in the Yifat museum. This story concerning an argument over a work assignment is an example of the kind of discussion said to be held in the dining room, and so is the following story concerning an argument over private possession. Both of these stories involve newcomers to the group, whose status as novices to the pioneering experience provides a narrative anchor for explicating taken-for-granted group norms that were part of the pioneers' social life but were unfamiliar to the newcomers, as they probably are to contemporary audiences:

> Imagine, a newcomer boy or girl arrives, they came straight from home. New clothes, shoes. Beautiful clothes compared to the worn, torn and patched up clothes the group had. These were what we call now "grade A" clothes, Sabbath clothes. They were put aside, and anybody who went out to town would wear the beautiful clothes and the pretty shoes, that's what you'd wear to go to Tel Aviv. For example, you want to go to Tel Aviv so you go to the wardrobe, and you see—hey, someone has already gone to Tel Aviv. So never mind, you go to the railway station, there, near Gan Shmuel, you wait. And when she comes back from Tel Aviv, you both go behind the bushes, exchange clothes, you give her your work clothes, and put on the good clothes, and travel *farandji* [well-dressed, Arabic], as they say, in good clothes. But she, Sonya, refuses. What does Ya'acov say? "She refuses to give her shoes to the *shituf* [partnership]. She has the newest shoes. All the girls in the group will have to go to Tel Aviv and Haifa in their worn-out shoes, they'll have no shoes to wear. This is a matter of principle. If you don't give your things to the *shituf*, listen, if you don't play our game, then go to another place. It can't work this way, or the group will fall apart. The *shituf*, it starts with shoes, then it'll be the clothes, then they'll take a tea kettle to their rooms, then they'll start reading their newspapers in their rooms, and all the companionship and equality will fall apart." This is what Ya'acov explains, it all begins with one pair of shoes, but it is a matter of principle. (Ronen, Ein Shemer, 10.15.91)

The opening of this story, "imagine," underlines the overtly fictive quality of the tale and its protagonists. Whether they are spoken of generically as a boy or a girl or specifically named as Sonya or Ya'acov, the figures in these tales are generic representatives of pioneering types, and the stories told about them are heard as speculative rather than factual accounts. At points, they even sound as parables used to substantiate abstract issues—as when the sharing of one's clothes in the *shituf* stands for the principle of communality.

Like the agricultural tools and household implements in the Yifat museum, the human figures in the dining room offer occasions for fictionalized accounts of pioneering life. The stress here is not so much on the processes of agricultural production as on the human interest stories associated with communal life. The processes of agricultural production are discussed briefly later in the tour, as visitors are taken through the appropriate corner in the yard, the one concerned with field cultivation. It is quite clear, however, that the dining room and its adjacent displays form the heart and soul of the exhibit, whatever other stops are made along the tour route.

As we have seen, the stories woven around the different figures in the dining room give expression to dilemmas surrounding central values of pioneering life and provide occasions for acknowledging the hardships the pioneers faced and for celebrating their ways of dealing with them. A stylized model of a well and a picture of arid land that is contrasted with one of green and fertile fields provides a visual context for narrating the hardships associated in early years with the shortage of water, which had to be brought in by carriage, and the joy of the discovery of water sources by the quaint expert geologist who was brought in for that purpose. Next to it, the carriage that served the famous pioneer physician, Dr. Hillel Jaffe, and a display of medical instruments allow the guide to dwell on the health problems encountered by the early pioneers, and the limited forms of treatment available to them. Further exhibits along the wall that surrounds the central dining room area mainly involve photographic displays relating to children and family life, to cultural life, and to the newer, industrial endeavors currently found on the *kibbutz*.[4]

The Family Cabin

A narrative line similar to the one that dominates the dining room display, one that is also familiar from our tour in Yifat, can be traced in the cabin where the pioneers established their humble lodgings, the local equivalent of the tent in the Yifat museum. Here, too, the simple and modest quality of the furnishing is stressed in a seminostalgic vein, invoking a sense of pity as well as a touch of admiration for a time when people were not as driven by materialism as they are today:

> This is the first room they had. What is it made of? Wood, and it is hot in the summer and cold and wet in the winter, and it's very unpleasant. Today

---

[4]Two sections within the extended dining room area are part of the museum but not part of its pioneering tale. One is a rather impressive archaeological exhibition that is based on digs conducted in the area and is quite visibly and attractively laid out, but is rarely made part of the guided tour. It is interpreted only for groups who specifically request a focus on archaeological matters. The other section is a nature corner, which has a nice display of stuffed animals representing the fauna of the area. Although this section is not part of the story line of the pioneering tale, its attractiveness to children makes it a favorite, often-short stop along the tour route. It is sometimes incorporated into the nostalgic spirit of the tour guide's narrative through moralizing, ecologically oriented comments about the extinction of various animal species in the area as a result of the ills of modernity and the overall thoughtlessness of human intervention in the natural landscape.

we build with blocks. What does a home need?

[Child's voice: A fan!]

A ventilator, indeed, no ventilator around here. What else does a home need? A stove, two beds, living room furniture, a couch, a television, a bath, so let's see what we have here. Can you hand me that "armchair" [pointing to a rectangular tin box covered with jute cloth]? Today we spend a lot of money to buy an armchair, look, in early days they used to take such a tin box, put some jute cloth over it, and they would have a wonderful armchair. You can make anything you want. The mattress is made out of a sack filled with straw. (Tal, Ein Shemer, 7. 30.91)

And as was the case in the Yifat tour, stories about the *primus*, the third person assigned to a family cabin, abound with much emphasis placed on the humorous aspects of this unusual arrangement, as in the following, personalized account:

I want to ask you, have you heard the term *primus* that is used in *kibbutz* language?

[Child's voice: The third person]

The third person. In the *kibbutzim* they decided, when there was a large immigration in the 1930s, that any family that already had a tent or a room will take in another person to live with them. So imagine right here, this was a cabin in those days, it belonged to Ignaz and Idit...and here they add another bed, for either a guy or a girl, and he or she lives with the couple until they build new rooms or tents...We asked Ignaz before he passed away, 2 years ago, an old person walking with a stick, 87 years old, we asked him, "Ignaz, how could you make children with the *primus* right here at home?" And he said, "What's the problem? There was a knock on the door and the *kibbutz* secretary comes in, and a kind of transparent-looking guy follows him carrying a folding bed and a suitcase. He sits down, greets us, and says, 'They told me this is my room.' The first moment we were in shock, but then we figured, it's a decision of the *kibbutz*...We sat quietly and explained to him, 'Look, it's your room but it's also our room, and if we don't make children there will be no next generation of the *kibbutz*, and the idea of the *kibbutz* will be lost.'...So we told him, 'Every evening, when you come back from the dining room, we will leave you a sign outside the door, if you can disturb us or not.'" "What's the sign?" we asked Ignaz. He says, "We took the broom of the room, there, we took that broom and told the guy, 'Listen, when you come from the dining room you look and see, if the broom is upside down, with the hair up, it means we're making children. If the hair is down, we're finished.'" We asked, "And was there discipline?" "And how," [Ignaz replied], "this was the Fifth immigration wave, the *yekes* [German Jews known for their punctuality and love of order]...A *yeke* sees the broom with the hair up, children are being made, the *yeke* sits outside on the heap of straw and waits. Waits till 10:00, till 12:00...sometimes we would fall asleep but the *yeke* sat outside till morning, there's order. These were the *yekes*, and that's how the second generation came to be." (Ronen, Ein Shemer, 10.18.91)

The stories told in the reconstructed dining room and family cabin mainly revolve around a major problem of *kibbutz* life—the tension between the personal and the communal, the pull of individual needs and desires as against the unrelenting demands of group life. As we have seen, this theme is central to the interpretive agenda in the Yifat museum as well, where it is similarly encapsulated in strings of frequently entertaining anecdotes. The lighthearted tone of these narrative segments does not, however, conceal the weight of the message they cumulatively convey. Within the setting of a museum designed to celebrate the communal ethos of pioneering life, the balance tends to be pushed toward embracing group values, but personal experiences and individual voices are not completely muted. These voices are heard in accounts describing communal arguments and disagreements on the one hand, and in written testimonies found in personal diaries, letters to the editor, and other group outlets—which are preserved in the local archive attached to the museum—on the other. These expressive traces of personal perspectives and feelings are now mobilized in narrating the pioneering past in museums whose communal messages seek to capture the imaginations of contemporary audiences, children of our new, much more individualistic age. Indeed, it is the constant presence of the dialectical tension between the individual and the communal that gives the museum story its sense of poignancy, not the momentary resolutions it reaches at various points in its narrative. In the tour guides' performances, stories of individual persons and of group life are forever intertwined. The communal spirit is most prominently celebrated through the mention of the personal sacrifices its achievement entails, and the personal voice is allowed to come through most clearly as it struggles against the heavy-handedness of communal demands. Given the centrality of this theme, it is not surprising that those corners of the museum that address it are favorite stops along the tour route and give rise to the use of some of the most potent images repeatedly invoked by the guides.

Notably, whereas this central tension of pioneering life (as well as of contemporary *kibbutz* reality) is rendered prominent in the museum narrative through the telling of mutually reinforcing anecdotes, the fragmentary nature of the museum tour also allows for the presentation of noncohering attitudes, so that one anecdotal stop along the tour route may provide an occasion for articulating a particular position or perspective that may then be contradicted by the ones that follow. This structural possibility of providing narrative support for conflicting attitudes on an issue or theme, which are expressed at different, separate junctures of the tour, is as intrinsic to the museum's spatial and temporal organization as is the possibility of reinforcement through repetition. Thus, no particular effort is made to control contradictions and ambiguities in the museum story. The following three narrative segments, which take us through three typical stops along the tour route in Ein Shemer, exemplify the possibility of articulating a theme in ways that do not add up into a coherent attitude. They are all taken from the same guided tour by Dan, a seasoned and enthusiastic museum guide in his 30s, in a tour given to a group of grade-school children from another *kibbutz*. All these segments relate in one way or another to the theme of women and the attitudes expressed toward them.

Narrative Disjunctions: A Note on Woman's Place

An upstairs room in the old stone building, called the weapons room, houses an exhibit of many different guns from several countries that were at the disposal of the pioneers during prestate years. This section of the museum provides an opportunity to discuss security needs, the development of Jewish self-defense, Arab attacks, and the British regulations against the Jews' ownership of weapons. Part of the tour guides' interpretation involves the story of the hiding of weapons that were held against British regulations in hide outs popularly known as *sliks* (from the verb *lesalek*, to put away). One place where *sliks* were commonly located were holes dug (and covered over) under the beds in the pioneers' sleeping quarters. It was hoped that British searches would not include those private areas of the *kibbutz*. One story about a *slik*, which I have heard in the family cabin, too, is constructed around an excerpt of a woman's diary that was reproduced on the wall of the weapons' room. It tells how for several years the author of the diary noticed that while she was out at work, all kinds of repair work was taking place in her family cabin, and she wondered at the care and effort that the *kibbutz* handyman, who was not known for his diligence, was putting into the maintenance of her room. The mystery was solved when once she happened to return to her room at midday and found out that the floor under her bed was being used as a *slik*, without anybody—including her male partner—bothering to tell her anything about it. The story is told quite casually, without any trace of annoyance, and its discussion gave rise to the following exchange, after one of the boys was asked to read the excerpt on the wall:

Guide: What is it you are telling us about?
  Boy: They were hiding a *slik*.
Guide: Hiding a *slik*. For how long?
  Boy: Three years.
Guide: Three years, and 3 more years, and she didn't understand why, what was happening there. Did her husband know it?
  Boy: Yes.
Guide: Right, it says, "my partner knew of the secret." Now, much more important, who should have known?
[Unclear children's voices]
Guide: All those who lived in the room. Why didn't all those [pronominal reference to females] who lived in the room know?

> Boy: Because they wouldn't have agreed.
> Guide: Oh, they wouldn't have agreed. Any other idea?
> Boy: They were women.
> Guide: They were women, so? So what? I can show you a picture from 1926 of a woman training with weapons. All the same, perhaps, why? You're getting very close.
> [A girl says something unclear on tape; my notes indicate that she said it was dangerous to tell women because they would not keep a secret]
> Guide: It's one of the few times I've heard it from a girl. Wow, girls! [paraphrasing the girl's remark] That they should allow a girl to disclose where the *sliks* are? If she's caught [and is interrogated], three–four times, and she'll say where it is…She'll sing it outright, not just tell it. They just have to ask and she'll tell…Women should definitely not be allowed to know where the weapons are. And indeed they didn't tell them…(Dan, Ein Shemer, 10.31.91)

This exchange exemplifies the force of the secondary messages and incidental learnings that accompany the main storyline of the museum tour. Although the official focus of this exchange is the pioneers' handling of the British restrictions against their ownership of arms, the previous exchange becomes first and foremost an occasion in which messages about women and their social place are conveyed. The story taps into widely held stereotypes of women as weak and therefore untrustworthy in a way that legitimates the tactic of marginalizing them. In this case, crucial information was withheld from the woman who wrote the diary concerning her own personal space. Indeed, the diary excerpt on display and the interpretation it was given in the exchange between the guide and his young audience confirmed this derogatory view of women, and the guide reinforced it by acting surprised at the fact that it was articulated by a girl (whose voice was given the status of a generic admission). At the same time, he subtly distanced himself from the sexist attitude he had helped to reproduce by offering data that challenged it (the 1926 picture of a woman training with weapons).

That the *slik* story in the foregoing example becomes an occasion for a discussion of the untrustworthiness of women and the need to exclude them from a central aspect of pioneering life and mythology is quite telling. It is an example of the way incidental comments about women's ineptitude, marginal to the museum's main storyline, serve to create an image of marked gender differentiation coupled with a marginalizing attitude toward women. This is of particular interest given the prevailing myth of gender equality associated with the pioneering era (Bernstein, 1992; Fogiel-Bijaoni, 1992), which is largely upheld in explicit references to gender issues at many other points along the museum tours I have observed.

Interestingly, this particular guide (in the very same guided tour) provided the only refutation to the gender equality myth in all the data I gathered, presenting a feminist-type critique of representations of gender relations as these are normally encountered in accounts of pioneering life, both inside and outside the museum walls. The following statement was made in the agricultural corner, the main stop along the tour route where the details of the pioneers' work arrangements become the central topic of discussion, and where comments about women, when these are made, usually celebrate their full and equal participation in pioneering life:

> I'm sure that when you were younger, even now perhaps, you've been told that there was equality between men and women in the *kibbutz*. Did they tell you anything like that?
> [Child: Yes]
> Folks, they told me the same story, too. They said, "Once, before you were born, when we were all young and beautiful, there was equality between men and women. The women worked in the fields." And that's where their explanation ended. I've grown up a little bit since then, not much, and here's a very interesting thing: Women did indeed work in the fields, but mainly they worked at things that weren't so highly considered at the time: in the kitchen, in the dining room, in the laundry, in the clothes cabin, with children, not as teachers but as caretakers (*metaplot*). I haven't heard of any man who worked in those things in that period. We know in most *kibbutzim* today there are men working as cooks, in the laundry here are quite a number of men, in the dining room certainly there are quite a few, there are also many educators who are men. And it's quite accepted. In that period it was not accepted, so what kind of equality was that? And what's interesting is that women were assigned to all the female tasks, and when there was no need for them there, then they'd get sent to work in the field so that they didn't laze away. That was their equality. Perhaps I don't understand this concept...(Dan, Ein Shemer, 10.31.91)

This statement contradicts received wisdom concerning the status of women in pioneering days, but it also reverses the by-now-accustomed, nostalgic spirit of settlement museum representation with its elevation of the past and denigration of the present. The guide here positions himself at the receiving end of the chain of tradition, conveyed through stories of the past, and refuses to accept it at face value. In so doing, however, he nevertheless upholds the value of gender equality that finds its expression in the rejected myth. Just a few minutes earlier, in interpreting the weapons exhibition, the guide led his young audience in an exchange that denigrated women as not trustworthy enough to partake in the weighty affairs of weapon hiding. He only indirectly indicated a sense of discomfort with the implications of this story by mentioning evidence of women's participation in military training. Both these narratives actually convey the message that women were not in fact equal to men in pioneering days, but the value orientations attached to this factual depiction are very different. Women's inequality is justified in the *slik* story—as in its retellings—but is mildly objected to in the last account. It is unlikely that this kind of inconsistency could have passed unnoticed in a written text, or even in an oral presentation of a different kind, as it did on this occasion. It is precisely due to the fragmentary nature of the guided tour, with its distinctive spatial and topical organization, that each of these narrative segments can be experienced as cognitively distinct and self-contained. Sometimes these segments reinforce each other in both fact and orientation, as in the case of the individual–communal dialectic discussed earlier; sometimes they don't, presenting a loosely inconsistent orientation, as in the previous case, to which the next narrative segment adds another layer.

The following story was told by the same guide in the granary section, performing against a background of a stylized display of agricultural tools and incorporating an actual demonstration of how the tool worked:

> Not only the Jews have love stories related to the granary. The Arabs do, too. But their stories are very very different and have to do with this instrument [picks the sieve from the wall]…This sieve, who worked with it? Men or women?
>
> [Children's voices: Women]
>
> Mainly women. Are any of the girls prepared to show us how one works with it? No? So let's take one of the boys. Come, what's your name? Itay, come give us an illustration…[the child stands beside the guide, vigorously moving the sieve from side to side]
>
> We're talking about a married woman, with a veil over her face, only the eyes can be seen, sleeves pulled down. By contrast the unmarried ones, their faces and eyes can be uncovered…The men would bring the wheat, would thresh it and the women would separate out the grains. You know, the wheat was their money, all the food they had for the next year…[urging the boy who is impersonating the woman with the sieve] Move on, move on, more energy, everything about her is moving, all kinds of things in front [children laughing], all kinds of things behind, oh, and suddenly there comes a young fellow, and she starts working harder, to make a good impression on him, to show that she's working properly, perhaps a good match can be made. These things work great. And later, when she begins to sweat—[pointing to the child with the sieve] see, I'm sweating just by talking, so with all this hard work he'll certainly start sweating soon, too—the dress sticks just in the right places, and it's wonderful, with this you can make love like you could never imagine [children laughing]…. (Dan, Ein Shemer, 10.31.91)

This is a localized version of the sieve story, which originally belonged to the personal repertoire of the old-timer guide, Binyamin from the Yifat museum, and some version of it has become part of the interpretive repertoire of most of the guides I have observed in both museums. In this version, there is a particularly striking chain of watching: The kids watch the boy who acts as a stand-in for the guide who tells about how the Arab men watched the woman the boy has been made to impersonate. Like the *primus* stories, this story makes quite explicit allusions to sexual matters, which apparently adds to its entertainment value. Although the sexual overtones are somewhat neutralized by the playful choice of a boy to play the part of the Arab woman, this rather blatant depiction of Arab women as objects of the male gaze is unmistakably sexist and a far cry from the message of gender equality the museum ordinarily associates with pioneering days. It seems to me that the crudeness of this tale is allowed to pass because the objectification of women is displaced onto Arab women, not Jewish ones. The tale comes under the rubric of the museum's interest in the Arab as cultural other, whose image is contrasted with that of the Jew. One implication in this case is that Jewish women fared better, whatever the complaints they might have had concerning gender equality in pioneering days. Thus, a third position on women's social place is narratively articulated on this stop along the tour. The theme of gender inequality is reiterated but this gross depiction of Arab women's unequal status and the objectifying practices they had to face is met with a striking degree of amused acceptance. Spoken in a self-assured, unself-conscious, patriarchal voice, this attitude is projected on the girls and women in both the tale and—at least in one telling of it—among the audience as well.

On this, as on many other occasions, the museum's rhetoric of identification was allowed to hold sway. Visitors' overt responses indicated various degrees of appreciation—as was reflected in their attentive demeanors, their maintenance of eye contact with the guide, and the questions and comments they addressed to him, as well as the entries they later put into the Visitor Book.[5] Museum encounters may also involve various degrees of indifference as expressed in listlessness, lack of attention, and a noninquisitive attitude, as well as an oppositional stance toward aspects of the museum story that may be expressed through direct challenges, ironic comments, and signs of displeasure. The next chapters thus consider further aspects of the interactional work involved in settlement-museum interpre-

---

[5]Visitor Books give audience responses in the highly constraining frame of a tradition of self-selected, appreciative responses given out from guests to their hosts thereby affirming that the museum has accomplished its rhetorical mission. In writing their words of thanks in the book, visitors can be said to inscribe themselves into the museum text as an audience-contributed gesture of closure, not really to provide well-balanced feedback on their museum experience. Indeed, most of the thousands of entries I have read in the visitor books in both museums (and others) during the time of the research include highly appreciative notes by both adults and children, who express their gratitude to the museum makers or to individual guides for a moving and edifying experience in semiritualized terms. Very few comments I have seen were critical or indifferent in their response, and the few that were pointed out the need to improve one aspect of the display or another but never questioned the value or relevance of the enterprise as a whole.

tation, particularly as it relates to the different positionings of both tour guides and audience groups vis-à-vis each other and vis-à-vis the museum story. As we shall see, the touristic project of sight sacralization that is grounded in a vision of an undifferentiated imagined community to be ritually generated through museum patronage (among other social practices), is more complicated than my preceding account has suggested. A more differentiated view of both tour guides and their audiences is required, one that will lead us to a more dialogic conception of museum discourse (Bakhtin, 1981). This more nuanced view conceives of museum presentations not as reports or assertions but as responses whose multivocality can be brought forth through a closer look at the participants in museum encounters.

Chapter 4

Generational Styles
in Settlement Museum
Interpretation

ɮ ∎ ʗ

THE NARRATIVE POSITIONING
OF SETTLEMENT MUSEUM GUIDES

This chapter is devoted to a further exploration of the discursive dimensions of museum interpretation, focusing on the crucial role played by the tour guides in shaping the form and texture of settlement museum discourse. Every guided tour, like any other oral performance, constitutes a unique encounter unto itself, and involves some degree of audience accommodation based on the guide's assumptions about the particular group he or she is addressing and his or her response to the visitors' perceived degree of attentiveness and interest. Most guides, however, develop and cherish their individual styles, which tend to constitute inflections on a basically stable interpretive stance and expressive repertoire. Beyond these individual variations, one can discern differences in the guides' presentational styles that relate to their shared generational affiliation. Old-timers and younger guides relate to the museum story and the *kibbutz* foundation mythology in quite different ways, and this substantive difference is reflected in their modes of presentation. These generational differences are informed by the larger context of intergenerational relations in *kibbutz* society.

Indeed, the problematics of intergenerational relations is a much discussed issue in *kibbutz* life because it bears on the very possibility of cultural continuity between the founders' generation and the ones that followed it. In an early study of *kibbutz* society, Talmon-Garber (1970) already discussed the ideological implications of the generational affiliation of *kibbutz* members, and in a recent anthropological study of *kibbutz* life (Evens, 1995), the cultural import of the intergenerational conflict model for the under-

standing of the *kibbutz* is again highlighted. My own observations of settlement museum discourse, too, have convinced me that generational affiliation should provide the most central differentiating parameter for
considering the performative dimensions of the guides' presentational styles.
As Evens pointed out in discussing social succession in *kibbutz* life, the
principle of voluntarism, which implies ethical commitment, is the central
idiom of *kibbutz* pioneering ideology, and accounts for what he considered
the exceptional sociological significance of the essentially paradoxical nature of the generational relationship on the *kibbutz*, which he explained as:

> instead of being compelled to perpetuate the institutional world of their
> fathers, the sons should be given the option. But the choice confronting the
> sons is internally inconsistent. If the sons were to choose (as urged) always to
> comply and never to deviate, the inference would then be warranted that
> they really do not have a choice but are instead behaving mechanically.... In
> effect, the sons are caught in a radial bind, a lived paradox. They are urged
> to *choose* to perpetuate the institutional world their fathers built. But insofar
> as they do so unfailingly, they cannot but fail to demonstrate that they have
> so chosen.... That is to say, in order to comply they must somehow falter in
> their charge. That is to say, by the logic of their moral order, the sons are *bound*
> at once to comply and not to comply. (pp. 81–82)

As we shall see, the reiteration of the pioneering foundation mythology in
settlement museums by representatives of the generations of founders and sons
is complexly structured in terms of this essential paradox of social succession
in the particular context of *kibbutz* life. The museum thus becomes an enclave
where intergenerational tensions can be simultaneously articulated and
smoothed over in performative acts of narration. In what follows, I pursue this
line of thought by comparing the interpretive agendas and verbal performances
of old-timer guides as compared to those of the younger guides. Specifically, my
analysis will contrast the interpretive styles of first-generation guides (in their
70s and 80s) for whom telling the museum story involves a strong autobiographical component, with the interpretive styles of second and third generation guides (in their 20s to 50s), whose personal relationship to the museum
story has been mediated in a variety of ways. Thus, as I hope to show, the guides'
generationally based narrative positions vis-à-vis the contents of the museum
messages shape the kinds of claims for narrative authority and relevance they
can make as narrators of the museum tale, and the metacommunicative devices
they employ in so doing.

I then take up one particular guided tour of The Old Courtyard in Ein
Shemer in which the issue of generational affiliation became topicalized in
a unique way. This tour involved a second-generation guide from Ein
Shemer as narrator and members of the old-timers' club in *kibbutz* Yifat—including two of the three old-timer guides from the Yifat museum—as

audience. In this rather unusual intergenerational encounter, it became the daunting task of the younger guide to relate to the old-timers a museumified version of what he assumed represented their own life histories. How does one tell an audience the story of their own life without appearing either utterly presumptuous or utterly trivial, or both? The discussion of the narrative strategies the young guide employed in dealing with this museum-specific situation of performative role reversal will help us illuminate further such issues as the handing down of the museum narrator role as part of an inevitable intergenerational process. Having become sensitized to the way guides and their audiences negotiate their generational and cultural positionings vis-à-vis each other, I was challenged to consider my own positioning in relation to the settlement museum narratives I was studying, which inevitably colored my reading of the museum encounters of which I was a part. I undertake this problematic but, I believe, essential introspective move in the next chapter.

Clearly, settlement museums, like other institutionalized contexts for the preservation and representation of the past, are given cultural recognition and entitlement to tell a particular story by virtue of their official role as culturally named and framed contexts for the production of discourses about the past. This institutionally supported cultural warrant gives tour guides authority as cultural brokers. In other words, it endows them with what Shuman (1986) termed *storytelling rights*. These rights involve two major claims: First, the claim to narrative fidelity and authenticity; namely, the claim that true stories are narrated in conjunction with authentic objects. The assumption of narrative authority and the stress on the authentication of tales and objects are common features of touristic quests. The concern with authenticity is an especially prominent part of the living history enterprise, as pointed out by Handler and Saxton (1988), "Authenticity is a dominant value of living history, and we speak of the *quest* for authenticity to suggest the fervor with which it is pursued" (p. 242). And second, the claim to relevance. The relevance the story of the past is said to hold for the present and future justifies the very establishment of institutionalized contexts specifically devoted to the material preservation and narrative reconstruction of a particular version of the past. The museumification of the Zionist past in settlement museums thus compels the refiguring of a line of connection between past times and present concerns and sensibilities as part of the museum's interpretive project.

As we shall see, the rhetorical projects of tour guides of the first and following generations are essentially different with regard to their claims to authenticity and relevance, and this difference affects their performances in interesting ways. Thus, old-timer guides draw their narrative authority from their active participation in the events narrated in the museum's object stories. This is reflected in their unmediated familiarity with the objects on display and their fund of personal stories about the past. In both cases, we get an "I was there" claim. In terms of the categorization of narrator roles proposed by Booth (1961, pp. 149–165), we can say that old-timer guides often assume the role of *participant–narrators*. They participate in the tale as either *narrator–protagonists* who partake in the narrative action or as *narrator–witnesses* who bear witness to it. Visitors often respond to this construction of the narrator role on the old-timers' part by considering them "almost part of the museum itself," as I have heard it expressed again and again. Although the old-timers were generally more successful than the younger guides at authenticating the museum tale and thus establishing their narrative authority, they found it more difficult to convey to younger audiences a persuasive message of relevance regarding the values, events, and accomplishments of the past. As I observed them in action, or heard them recount experiences of guided tours I had not attended—reports freely volunteered, and often prefaced by the heart-pinching, "It's a pity you weren't here..."—I realized that to the old-timer guides, every successful tour was much more than a job well done. It was a reaffirmation of the relevance of the past, and at least to some extent a vindication of their personal histories and life trajectories.

Younger guides, of course, cannot employ the testimonial rhetoric that is so effectively used by the old-timers even though they often personalize their accounts in a variety of ways. Their main problem as inheritors rather than makers of the history represented in the museum lies in their need to find alternative ways of constructing their narrative authority. At the same time, in their very willingness to participate in the myth-making enterprise that is at the heart of museum storytelling, and by employing a marked idiom of identification, the younger guides actually embody and symbolize the museum's claim for the continued relevance its story holds for present and future generations.

HAVING STORIES TO TELL:
OLD-TIMERS' TESTIMONIAL RHETORIC

For old-timer guides, museum interpretation is not primarily a matter of professional engagement, and it is more than a matter of an ideological–pedagogical mission. Most fundamentally, they speak from the standpoint of people who have a story to tell, a cultural position that in this case goes even beyond old folks' familiar desire to share their life story with members of following generations.[1] As it became clear to me during my fieldwork, the position of having stories to tell carries distinctive localized meanings in the sociocultural world in which I had situated my inquiry. The

---

[1]The significance storytelling holds in the life of the elderly has been pointed out, and beautifully demonstrated, in Myerhoff's seminal work (1979, 1992).

significance of being identified—by oneself and others—as someone with a lot of stories to tell was brought home to me as I accompanied Binyamin, the old-timer guide from Yifat, to the Friday afternoon gatherings held in the *kibbutz*, which are known as the Parliament of Yifat. These club-like weekly gatherings bring together men from the whole region who loosely share a background in agricultural life.

These are semiritualized occasions of heightened sociability and are held in a specially designated part of the local stable, with participants seated on benches at the rough wooden tables for several hours each week. The age range in these gatherings is impressive—from old-timers in their 80s to young folk in their 20s. They come together for sessions of storytelling, gossiping, and political debating on a voluntary and regular basis, enjoying a make-shift meal of homemade produce, barbecue, and drinks. The food is served in simple kitchenware, the menu is basic and unchanging—and features delicious homemade pickled cabbages and *labane* (a dairy product adopted from Arab cuisine) that are eaten by hand with pita bread. One person is responsible for the barbecued chicken parts that are made on the spot, picnic style, and passed around the table whenever they are ready. They are usually eaten without the use of cutlery, and eating with fingers—in a style of antigentility—seems to have become part of the ritualized texture of the occasion, one that helps to set it apart as a unique context of male sociability.

The 20 to 30 men who are usually present—coming and going at will—are sometimes joined by a couple of women, but women are generally felt to be out of place there, as I was specifically told by an old-timer who at the same time embraced me with good cheer and profusely played the role of host, stuffing my plate to overflowing. During the 3 months or so of participant observation in these gatherings (in the spring of 1990), which seemed to me as a kind of backdrop scene for my museum work, my presence as someone interested in the folklore of the valley was amiably but rather indifferently received. It was generally accepted as sensible that I would attach myself to Binyamin, who had prodded me to come along with him, promising I would get a chance to see moustaches of a magnitude I'd never seen before—a promise well kept. Binyamin was often spoken of by other parliament participants as someone who has lots of stories to tell, an image that earned him much affection and respect, and went along with him to the museum as well. In the course of my visits, however, I was also often advised to talk to this person or that who had great stories to tell about the first days of the village of Nahalal, or the skirmishes with the Arabs in prestate years or the War of Independence, as the case might be. The statement that a person has lots of stories to tell was often accompanied by an appreciative statement concerning that person's participation in all manner of important enterprises in the past, often memorable agricultural feats or issues related to security matters.

It became quite clear to me that in this sociocultural context, the position of having stories to tell amounts to a claim of involvement in communally significant deeds and events of the past, a statement of social worth. It is also a testimony to a person's qualities as a storyteller, whose privileged narrative positioning bridges over undeniable individual variations and personal agendas in narrative deployment. Both the parliament encounters on Friday afternoons and the settlement-museum daily narrations provide contexts for folk–historical inscription. In both these contexts, the people who have stories to tell are presented as the true makers of history, and their present repertoire of tales is a measure of and a testimony to their past exploits. Old-timer guides thus position themselves as people who have stories to tell, as doers become speakers. They are narrators whose contribution goes far beyond a sympathetic sponsorship of the museum's tale, and for whom the museum encounter becomes another arena in which the significance and value of their life and life's work can be repeatedly reaffirmed through their shaping of the museum's oral text.

The performances of old-timer guides are thus replete with self-references. The use of first-person narration, or testimonial rhetoric, is grounded in the narrator's personal history. The use of the first person plural often signals their self-inclusion in a wider, more encompassing group of like-minded people. Thus, to heighten the dramatic effect of their story, they may purposefully blur the protagonist and witness roles in constructing their roles as narrator–participants, leaving it unclear whether the story relates to their personal past or is about someone they knew, or some generic member of a pioneering group. The figure of Yankelevich, the fervor-filled pioneer frequently invoked in Binyamin's stories, is a case in point. Although Binyamin often claimed that Yankelevich had been a real person from another *kibbutz*, and the stories about him were things that really happened, at other times he would present him as a fictionalized figure (e.g., "There was a pioneer, let's say his name was Yankelevich…"), and in an interview with me he conceded that he felt a profound sense of identification with the pioneering image of Yankelevich that he painted in his narratives, and did not object when I suggested that this may be an indirect way for him to tell about himself. Such presentational strategies may open up old-timer guides to accusations of fabrication (often referred to as *folklorizing*), that is, narrative practices that go against the museum's claim to fact-oriented representation. Usually, however, these practices are condoned as a matter of a special narrative license enjoyed by the old-timer guides. As one of them said in an interview:

> Older people certainly recount their own experiences, what they lived through, and even if it was not their personal story, they insert themselves into it, out of a sense of truth, definitely a sense of truth—if it didn't happen to them it happened

to a friend of theirs. They were simply part of all these experiences, even if it didn't happen to them specifically…(Yehudit,10.16.91)

And much as the older folks relished in and encouraged younger people's willingness to become part of the museum enterprise, they did not hesitate to point out what to them was the special narrative seduction of old timers' voices, which were a projection of lived experience, not of merely handed-down stories or even book knowledge. In an interview, Binyamin said that the main criterion for selecting a new, younger guide should be the extent to which he is felt to be able to tell the museum story with inner conviction, identifying with its emotional tone and spirit. He pointed out that some of the young guides were doing quite well, each telling the museum story in his or her own way. But then, unable to uphold this note of acceptance for long, he added:

> People who lived through the period have a special quality to them because they experienced all of this on their own flesh, and someone who hasn't experienced this in agriculture, in a first settlement, going out to the shower, to the restrooms, the laundry and making do—if you just read about these things, only from reading, I don't know, I don't think that a person who reads and studies and then passes it on like a parrot, I don't like it, what can I do? I don't have a good feeling when I guide, let's say, at some Crusader castle…I didn't live in those times, just heard about it from someone who knows the material, but I just recite it, and I don't feel good about it, what can I do? (Binyamin, Yifat, 10.11.91)

In considering the kinds of autobiographical insertions, or at least first-person narrative segments, typically introduced into the guides' renditions of the museum story, I pay special attention to the pronominal usage they contain. The analytic value of such a move has been pointed out by Babcock (1977), following Jakobson (1960), when she said that pronominal usage can be quite revealing for an understanding of the working of language in its interactional context because, as she put it, "pronouns are 'purely relational units' that encode the relationship obtaining between sender and receiver and as such may be used … to shift one's attention from the narrated event to the speech event and vice-versa" (p. 67). The following four segments thus exemplify ways in which the museum tale becomes explicitly anchored in personal experience through the reiteration of the first-person singular and the verbal construction of a narrator–participant role. In the first two segments, the narrator assumes the protagonist role, the central figure in his or her story; in the second two segments, the narrator assumes the witness role, a secondary figure in the story he or she is narrating. Both positions serve to reinforce the guides' narrative authority as authentic speakers, anchoring the act of narration in a personally experienced reality.

As the following two exceprts from a tour addressing a group of elderly visitors indicate, for Sarah, an old-timer guide whose first steps in cooking were taken in the kitchen of a pioneering group, the story of the pioneers' nutritional efforts is a personal testimony, a tale of woe retrospectively sprinkled with humor, and so is the memory of the already discussed *primus* arrangement, of which she has also had firsthand experience:

> Now suppose we want to cook a meal…I asked the *ekonom*, you know what an *ekonom* is? The one who is responsible for the food supplies, I asked, "Srulik, what is there to cook?" And he would say to *me*, "You've got a sack of lentils and a sack of beans, perhaps there's some rice here in some tin box, you've got to manage with that." I said, "That's okay for today, but I've got to prepare something to eat tomorrow as well." So he said, "Today make some soup with the beans and porridge with the lentils, and tomorrow the other way round." And that's what happened…I knew the food I cooked was quite tasteless…. because I couldn't cook…So when they just made a train on the table, one plate behind the other, and at the head of the train they put the kettle, making a "too-too-too" noise like a train that's about to depart, and the train begins to come back to the kitchen with all the dishes and all the food…I would go and cry and friends would come and comfort *me*…I was supposed to take it as some kind of a joke, but in fact all they had to eat was a cup of tea and some bread…. (Sarah, Yifat, 11.5.91)
>
> And I remember that in *my* tent there lived a guy from Germany…He was called Shmuel A. and *my* husband was called Shmuel B…. Now this guy, the German, he had a girlfriend from Syria. He couldn't speak one word that was not German, and she doesn't know a word of German or Hebrew. I speak some Yiddish so I say to him, "How do you manage with her?" And he says, 'With the hands, we speak with our hands." [Laughter] (Sarah, Yifat, 11.5.91)

Many of Sarah's autobiographical insertions are tales of affirmation—in one way or another, they tell of the good spirit in which she and others handled what could have been experienced as difficult situations, turning hardships and bitterness into moments of triumph, both at the time and in retrospect. After she shared with me her pain of bereavement over her fallen son, who was killed in the 1973 war, I began to hear what at first sounded to me like an old-timer's ideological urge to reaffirm the Zionist vision (and her own part in upholding it) in more poignantly personal terms. It all had to be worth a great deal to be worth such a loss.

For the old-timer guide, Binyamin, some of the happiest memories of his past relate to the times he worked as a shepherd. The shepherds' corner, as he told me, was his favorite stop on the tour route. Here he liked to insert an autobiographical segment about his special relationship with the goat named *Chumtche* (translatable as *Brownie*), giving expression to his views concerning the need for farmers to cultivate a strong attachment to the domestic animals they worked with. Like the stories about the pioneer called Yankelevich, this story highlights the emotional, noninstrumental dimension of the pioneers' endeavors, but it is also a clear example of an autobiographically anchored tale. I have heard Binyamin tell it on several occasions, at various levels of elaboration. During a guided tour he gave to a group of university students whom I had brought to the museum, he launched into an extended version of the *Chumtche* tale, some parts of which are recaptured in what follows:

> [pointing to a picture on the wall] Here am *I*, and here there's another person, and here's a goat with whom *I* had friendly relations. *I* gave her a name. She was like *my* friend. *I* called her *Chumtche*. Why? Because she was a bit blonde, a bit of a brownie. She was very clever, she was an extraordinary goat, and she always walked first, she wouldn't let anyone walk ahead of her…*I* fell in love with this *Chumtche*, she was *my* friend, and *I* would call her, and *we* would eat together, from this bag [pointing to a bag on display]…And one day the herd had spread all over and *I* wanted to bring them together. *I* put the bag on the ground, took up my *nabut* [herdsmen's stick] and went off to gather the sheep. And when *I* put the bag on the ground, *Chumtche* came over and had a *kumzitz* [campfire party], opened the bag and ate up all the food. And you know, herdsmen go out for the whole day, from morning till night, and *I* was young then and liked to eat a lot, and after *I* came back *I* wanted to eat and saw that my food was scattered all over. And then, of course, a hungry person is irritable, so *I* got angry, took hold of the *nabut* and wanted to catch her and give it to her. But she was cleverer than *me*. What did she do? When she saw *me* holding the *nabut* she ran to the back of the herd and mingled with the goats and *I* was unable to catch her. [the story goes on to tell at considerable length how *Chumtche* disappeared and was found by Binyamin after much searching only after dark with a leg injury]. So *I* called the doctor, he came and bandaged her leg, and *I* came home and got reprimanded by the wife because it was late. Go tell her that *I* have another love. It's quite a story, so *I* didn't say anything. *I* said, "Work, what can *I* do?" [laughter]…The next day when *I* took her out *I* made another attempt, to see if she'd learned any lesson. *I* took the bag, walked around, and then *I* put it down. She was sitting next to the bag and didn't touch it. No way. She waited for *me* to come, and when *I* came, *I* opened the bag and *we* had lunch together, and she constantly wagged her tail in agreement. She's all right. So what *I* want to tell you with all of this is that a person who is an agriculturist, he should love the animal he is working with…. (Binyamin, Yifat, 11.8.91)

Although this was clearly presented as a personal experience story, it also had the shape of a parable, ending in a pedagogical note, a general statement about the appropriate relationship between a farmer and his animals. This very personal story is thus enlarged and depersonalized. Watching Binyamin time and again, I realized that for him museum narrating was not only a public site where he could insert personal stories and give voice to his lived experience, but also a public arena, some of whose features he could personalize by appropriating stories that did not seem to be part of his personal history. For example, one time as he was addressing a group of young children in the reconstructed dining room, he wanted to impress them with the sacrifices made by the pioneers who had given up their affluent lives in Europe for the frugal existence of the new settlements in the land of Israel. To heighten the effect of his story, he launched it with the words, "When I was 17 and came to the land of Israel as a young pioneer...." Having spent many hours with him taping his life history, I realized he was using a fake first-person form for dramatic effect, appropriating a museum tale for dramatic purposes in a way that accentuated his museum-related role as a human embodiment of times past. At times it was not quite clear to me whether I was hearing a personal recollection or a stylized use of the first-person singular, as in the case of the following version of the widely circulating sieve story (for other versions of this story, see earlier excerpts). I knew he was considered to be the source of this story but have also heard him tell it to some groups with no mention of the autobiographical component that appears in this version:

> In one house, in the yard of one house, *I* went in and saw something that at first appeared strange. *I* saw two girls sitting outside working with the sieve, and two girls sitting in the house doing the same work. *I* tell them in Arabic, greet them and so on, and ask, "Why are the two girls sitting outside?" [the story continues to point out the matchmaking function of this seating arrangement] (Binyamin, Yifat, 11.8.91)

When I asked Binyamin whether such a visit had really taken place, he emphatically assured me of the truthfulness of the story, as he put it, but a smile spread over his face and I noticed a twinkle in his eyes, which is probably why I was not completely relieved of my doubts and remain uncertain as to whether this was or was not another example of a fake first-person tale.

Whereas the first-person singular brings out the testimonial flavor of the narrator's tale (whether he or she assumes the role of protagonist or witness), the first-person plural functions as a special kind of pronoun or shifter (Silverstein, 1976), providing a pronominal bridge between the story and the audience through the persona of the narrator. Thus, in the following two segments, the first-person plural—the generic *we*—used by the old-timer guide manifests this shifting pronominal quality as it slips between reference to the legendary pioneers who founded the early settlements, the contemporary *kibbutz* community whose enterprising spirit is evidenced by its continued desire for self-improvement, and the narratively engaged participants in the museum encounter itself:

We want to make progress all the time. I told you, the farmer had to cover a lot of ground, he has lots of land, it's all a matter of scale…*We* need to improve *our* tools, *we* can't plough as *we* used to any more, *we're* already working with completely different tools, not a sickle any more, not a scythe any more—here are the sickles, you see?—*We're* already using a reaping machine. *We* will talk about this threshing machine that's used for threshing the corn…(Sarah, Yifat, 12.5.89)

The first *we* ("*We* want to make progress all the time") in this example is part of a general ideological assertion that represents the enterprising spirit of the community of Jewish settlers (past and present), who constantly developed and promoted new agricultural methods and tools in their pursuit of efficiency and progress. The speaker then switches to the historical present, which is often used in museum discourse, and here the *we* clearly refers to the early pioneers only ("*We* need to improve *our* tools, *we* can't plough as *we* used to anymore, *we're* already working with different tools," etc.). The last *we* in this excerpt shifts attention to the situational level of the encounter itself, referring to the guide and the particular audience present ("*We* will talk about the threshing machine…"). A similar pattern of pronominal usage can be observed in the following excerpt:

The great and rare collection of tools you'll see inside is a collection of tools that are not in use anymore. For over 40 years, because *we've* made so much progress that these tools seem to us outdated. They are not in use. You'll see how *we* make progress, that's why *we* have brought you here to show you and all the people of Israel who visit *us* in great numbers, including adults and old-timers, all of them come here to see how *we* started to build *our* beautiful land of Israel. How *we* began to settle this land, how *we* dried the swamps. All this you can see by looking at *our* slides… (Sarah, Yifat, 10.9.91)

In this example, the narrator exploits the metacommunicative role of pronominal usage, moving with her listeners between the narrated events ("*we* dried the swamps" in reference to the pioneers; "*we* collected the tools" in reference to the museum makers) and the storytelling situation (audience–inclusive use of "these tools seem to *us* outdated"; "*our* land of Israel"). This referential shift is accomplished through the special elasticity of the first-person plural, which in this case is anchored in the narrator's role as a participant in or witness to past events. Pronominal usage in this case serves a subtle but important metanarrative function. Utilizing the referential versatility of *we* in this particular performative situation, the narrator encompasses within a shared discursive space the early pioneers who made history through their settlement efforts, their contemporary offspring who, in their turn, made history by establishing the museum, and the museum visitors—in the previous cases, grade school children and non-*kibbutz* adults—who are invited to participate vicariously in this double-layered, history-making endeavor.

Explicit autobiographical insertions serve to further authenticate old-timers' tales, providing a testimonial backdrop to the public story's unfolding. However, the old-timers are sometimes perceived by younger guides to be overly zealous in their storytelling urge, too overtly ideological and pathos-filled in their narrative styles, too prone to folklorizing. When taken too far, as it is sometimes claimed to be, the old-timers' presentational style runs the risk of losing touch with young audiences. Moreover, their understandable tendency to narrate in a nostalgic vein, mythologizing the pioneering past and denigrating the present, is argued by some of the younger guides to create an additional barrier for the identification of contemporary audiences with the museum tale. So the old-timers' authentic presentational style, which they use to perform and celebrate themselves in and out of the museum context, is both admired and shunned by the younger guides. The younger folks borrow the old-timers' stories and generally valorize their meanings, yet they tell them in their own way, discursively negotiating their distance from the museum story in constructing their position as narrators much as the old-timers underscore their proximity to it.

AMBIVALENCE AND RESISTANCE: YOUNGER GUIDES' PERFORMATIVE STYLES

On Passing on the Torch

It is well understood by one and all that in order for the museum story to continue to be told, its interpretive project must sooner or later be passed onto the shoulders of the younger guides. At the time I was conducting fieldwork for this study, only three old-timer guides were working in the Yifat museum on a regular basis. All the other guides in both museums were younger guides working in the museum either full time, part time, or on an occasional basis. As mentioned already, at the time of this writing, Binyamin has retired and Yehudit is mainly working in the archive and helps out in times of pressure as an occasional guide; Sarah is the only one of the three for whom the museum is an occupational engagement, and she works there whenever her health permits. When we discussed the process of passing on the torch to members of the younger generations of the *kibbutz* in an interview setting, the old-timer guide Yehudit remarked:

> We already want to pass on the task of guiding tours [*hadracha*] to the younger people. And some of the [young] guides I've seen here—although I haven't been able to follow a guided tour in its entirety—I definitely see a breath of fresh air—they bring many examples I don't bring; for example, they make

comparisons very nicely, comparing work as it is today or life as it is today, to how it was in the past. They do it very nicely. (Yehudit, Yifat, 10.16.91)

This comment highlights the special texture and value of the museum interpretations conducted by younger guides in terms of their ability to relate to young audiences and to make the story of the past—albeit one they did not experience themselves—relevant to contemporary life. It reveals a growing awareness of the difficulty inherent in the museum's rhetorical mission of communicating the past to younger audiences—who make up the bulk of their patronage—not in the sense of establishing the authenticity of the displays, or the truthfulness of the stories, but in the sense of persuading them of their relevance. It is the younger guides' special gift to reinsert the museum story into the contemporary scene, to reinfuse it with life and meaning in a way that can speak to present-day visitors. Yet even while recounting the museum tale, they constantly negotiate their distance from it, simultaneously highlighting continuities and differences between past and present, us and them. Continuities are often framed in terms of precedence—for example, the intense contemporary debate about the ways and the degree to which the *kibbutz* should and can change was addressed by a young guide throughout a tour in which he stressed the processes of change that have marked *kibbutz* life throughout its history, making the present crisis appear like another link in this ongoing process. Differences are marked by a stress on technological progress but often also by humorously underlining the quaintness and naivite of past ways. In this case, visitors are invited not only to identify with the museum story, but also to join the younger guides' metacommunicative dance along the continuum marked by a position of complete identification at its one end, and a position of ironic detachment at its other.

Thus, even though the narrative performances of the old-timers form one of the bases for the interpretive styles developed by the younger guides, the latter make no attempt to emulate the old folks' styles in giving shape to their own performances. Rather, as they narrate the museum story, they continuously negotiate their story-telling rights, and their claims to relevance, through the use of a variety of discursive strategies, some of which are discussed later.

As many of the younger guides testified, their very choice to work in the museum had to do with their sense of identification with its story and with its pedagogical agenda. Indeed, a person's willingness to identify with the museum story was cited by museum personnel as the prime criterion for the selection of new museum guides. However, identifying with a story and the values it articulates is very different from personifying it. Indeed, whereas the old-timer guides stood in for themselves, serving as a metonymic extension of the museum story, the younger guides devised the use of the playfully authenticating practice of period attire. Many of them dress in the

Russian shirt, the *rubashka*, which is a widely recognized pioneering icon. It was introduced by the guides in Ein Shemer (and has been partially adopted by younger guides in Yifat), and it serves to dramatize the semiplayful gestures of identification that mark the younger guides' performances of the pioneering past. In Ein Shemer, they appear before their audiences as make-believe participants in the past they fictionalize, supposedly joined by the similarly clad museum mannequins that they introduce by name as part of their interpretation. In Yifat, similarly clad images of pioneers are pointed out in the pictures on the wall. Alternatively, children are invited to enter an imaginary time machine and don pioneering attire in the communal clothes cabin. These performances bring the museum story to life, adding a dramatic component along the lines discussed by Snow (1993) in relation to the Plymouth Plantation. The guides' oft-repeated statement that the museum is as much about the tools as it is about the people behind the tools is given embodiment through the actual enactment of pioneering types. The purpose is, of course, to facilitate audience identification with the museum story through a fictionalized presentation of self, which playfully frames the museum's claim to authenticity. The realness of the objects as relics of the past is thus counteracted by the sense of fabrication suggested in the guides' dramatizations and the young visitors' experimental dressing-up sessions. At the same time, their interest value and identification potential are clearly enhanced.

Identification-Within-Distance

The younger guides' ambivalence toward the museum story generates a sense of identification-within-distance, which has a double-edged quality to it, and serves to shape their presentational style in a number of ways. Thus, their very participation in the museum enterprise, and their occasional use of autobiographical insertions, which are modeled on the old timers' style, are clearly designed to invite identification, yet their performances often seem to convey their sense of distance from the stories they tell. In resisting the official museum story, the younger guides employ a variety of narrative and metanarrative devices. The rhetorical devices that have emerged as most relevant to the identification-within-distance dialectic concern the distinctive ways in which they use autobiographical insertions and shared texts in mediating and authenticating their narratives.

Some of the younger guides' autobiographical insertions are actual personal experience stories associated with their childhood on the *kibbutz*. Many of them are not first-person testimonials, but rather overtly mediated versions of the old-timers' tales. One form they may take is that of second-order reminiscences such as reports based on stories the narrator had heard from a family member who belonged to the pioneering generation. In recounting these storytelling occasions, they retell stories rather than recounting events, assuming the role of narrator–witnesses, never that of narrator–protagonists. However, their positioning as narrator-witnesses is not that of secondary participants in the events narrated, but of privileged audiences of the old timers' tales. The following two stories exemplify this kind of mediating strategy. The first tells about the aforementioned *primus*—that is, the third person who was allocated to the tent of a conjugal couple, and the arrangements made by the cohabiting pioneers to alleviate the awkwardness of the situation. It is a personalized version of the story given in chapter 3, and is given as a citation of an old-timer's report:

> My *grandfather* tells a lot of stories…*My grandfather* tells the story that one day he came back from work…Without going into details, after a while he fell asleep, probably he was tired from all the work and things like that. He fell asleep, finally at 3 a.m. he wakes up in panic, looks at the watch, 3 a.m., of course it's the middle of the night. He looks at the broom—the *primus!* He gets up in all speed, turns the broom upside down, and begins to run, looking for the *primus*. He comes up to the *primus*—the *primus* is sitting in the kitchen, the only place he could still sit, where it was still a bit warm. He can't sit outside all night, can he?…He didn't talk to *my grandfather* some 10 or 12 years after that. So what must we always remember to do? Turn the broom upside down. (Rami, Ein Shemer, 10.31.91)

The grandfather figure here serves as a narrative anchor for a story, many other versions of which I have heard on other occasions. This personalizing strategy clearly enhances the speaker's narrative authority by highlighting his—albeit mediated—proximity to the museum tale through the original figure of his grandfather, the story's protagonist. Notably, this personalizing strategy counter-balances the overall distancing effect of this genre of tales, which focus on the quaintness of the ways of the past as seen from a contemporary perspective. The closing of the story, which gives it the enlarging impact of a parable, humorously asserts its pedagogical value through a claim of mock relevance, and demonstrates the mobilization of a playful attitude in enacting the complex dialectic of identification and detachment that characterizes the younger guides' performative styles.

Another example of such vicarious reminiscing, which makes use of the narrator–witness role, is the following:

> There's a mosquito called Anopheles, and when that mosquito stings, the person becomes very ill with a disease called malaria. My *father* was ill with malaria. He had very high fever. He had such high fever there was no place on the thermometer for it. His head was aching, he was sweating, and after that he was very cold and he suffered a lot. And anybody who sees a person suffer like that, they'd understand why they were using these nets. You see these nets? They would put such a net and protect themselves from the mosquitoes, so the mosquitoes couldn't come in…That's how it was in the

past, not how it is now. Here, you see, they were so poor, these were all the clothes they had. And in the summer, when it was very very hot, and it was impossible to live inside the cabin, and it was so hot they would throw water on the floor, and lay down like this on the floor with only their underwear on, and that was their cooling system. Imagine! (Rami, Ein Shemer, 10. 21.91)

In this example, again, although the personalizing strategy enhances identification, distance is created through the explicit assertion of contrast between past and present, through a call to try and imagine a situation that is by now barely imaginable. The narrator mobilizes the founding generation's narrative authority, but rather than assuming the standpoint of the pioneers, he assumes the stance of the audience who is finding it difficult to imagine the past. Positioning himself at the receiving end of his father's story, and acknowledging the audience's positioning at the receiving end of his own tale, he actually models the role of receptive audience member for his listeners. His tale is simultaneously a story and a metastory—what he says and the saying of it are both foregrounded and intertwined in such a way as to make up his personalized version of the museum tale.

These mediated personal stories are typical in their use of the first-person singular, which is also found in old-timers' narrations, although more prominently so. Old-timers' uses of the first-person plural, the idiom of *we* that is discussed in the previous subsection, is, however, absent from the younger guides' discourse. The younger guides use the first person pronoun (*my*) in order to establish their personal credibility as narrators, not in order to weave a narrative web of identification around themselves and their audiences. The link they establish with their audience flows from a dramatized sense of a shared present, which involves negotiating the distance of both narrators and audience members from the past they attempt to bring to life in the museum encounter. Indeed, the use of the third person, which casts the pioneers as *they* set against *us*, the speaker and his or her contemporaries, is the most typical pronominal form in the younger guides' performances. This distancing usage extends the linguistic game of pronominal reference employed in museum discourse beyond the identificatory *I* and *we* to the potentially alienated and critical *they*.

This form of discourse is further reinforced by a strategy of citation I refer to as *textual mediation*. In its minimal form, textual mediation finds its expression in evidentiary statements indicating sources such as, "It says in the book of Ein Shemer..." or, "A woman writes in the *kibbutz* journal..." A more elaborated form of textual mediation involves a strategy of direct citation. On several occasions, I observed guides dramatically pull out fragments of paper with excerpts from old timers' diaries or communal journals, which they had found in the *kibbutz* archive. Their narration thus gained a double-layered quality, and was structured as a narrative within a narrative, with the narrator–guide citing a *narrative narrator* (the author of the diary or journal excerpt) whose story conveyed the message associated with that particular juncture along the museum route (cf. Chatman, 1978, for a discussion of narrator roles). These dramatized accounts of past events thus served to bring the museum story closer to the audience and to authenticate it through the use of an original text. At the same time, by focusing on factual items that sound outlandish in contemporary terms, and/or by maintaining linguistic fidelity to the idiom of the past in the language of the narrative narrator that is cited as part of the performance, this reading aloud also accentuated the distance between past and present, between the voice of the narrator–guide and the voice of the story's protagonist. Take the following example of such a reading, which relates to the pioneers' practice of naming a newborn child by communal consensus rather than by parental choice:

> A woman, in the year 1929, writes in her diary—I am reading an excerpt from a diary that I photocopied in the archive; I photocopy a lot of excerpts, cross out the name so as not to invade people's privacy—note, I am standing in front of the children's corner. The topic is children—to understand how they thought in the past. I need to understand, "When I was about to give birth to Yael [her daughter], it was clear to me as it was to everybody else that I am not allowed to give her whatever name I like. The child belonged to the *kibbutz*, and the *kibbutz* has to determine the name, that was the custom. They brought me two alternatives to the hospital from the *kibbutz*, Yael or Tamar. They did not force a decision on me [*lo kafu alay har kegigit*], God forbid, but rather, as you see, they let me make my own choice, which shows that we enjoy a spirit of liberalism in everything we do…" (Ronen, Ein Shemer, 8.2.91)

In this example, as in the next, a long-abandoned, common practice of pioneering days is brought to the visitors' attention in the form of little stories that concretize the past. Here the description of a past practice is recounted in an attitude of humorous detachment. The narrator–guide uses the narrative narrator's voice to position himself outside the story frame, as someone trying to understand the strange ways of his predecessors. In the following example, the by now familiar *primus* story is narrated with a similar use of the strategy of textual mediation. Highlighting the personal cost that attended this arrangement, the person cited here, the narrative narrator, prefigures the disapproval contemporary audiences (and guides) are assumed to feel vis-à-vis this practice, creating a sense of shared attitudinal ground with his audience while at the same time generating a sense of distance from past practices:

> I want to read to you an excerpt from the journal *mibefnim* [from inside], "We began to build the tents. It was decided that every tent will house three persons. Apart from us, there were a few more couples in the camp, and every couple had to receive a single person to their tent…B. and I received two

primusim, Y. and P...Even at a later period, when there were additional newcomers and we could give up on one *primus*, three of us continued to live together and we were called the big family. We lived like this for 2 years." And the last excerpt I'll read to you, it belongs here, and it is a cry of protest by the same girl who wrote the excerpt we just read: "What did they do to me?.... The sacred duty to absorb new immigrants, the most sacred duty in the land of Israel, is accompanied with the desecration of my love. Yes, there is no other word—*chilul* (desecration). Is this great sacrifice really demanded of me?" (Dan, Ein Shemer, 10.31.91)

This strategy of textual mediation, of narrative within narrative, is another way in which younger guides negotiate their own and their audience's distance from the museum story: On the one hand, the past is exoticized and distanced in terms of the particular social practices singled out for narrative elaboration as well as through the sense of authenticity invoked by the use of an archaic linguistic variety anchored in traditional texts; on the other hand, the attitudes expressed by either the narrator–guide or the narrative narrators that are cited on these occasions are intelligible to contemporary museum-goers, and are made into a matter of focused interest and discussion, even though they are obviously not fully shared by either the guides or their audiences.

In this respect, the textual mediation strategy is very different from yet another narrative strategy employed by younger guides, which involves the invocation of autobiographical fragments, mainly involuntary childhood memories triggered by the museum's material display—its pictorially depicted scenes, its objects, sounds, and smells—all of which are used to articulate personal scenes and powerful feelings of rootedness on the part of the narrators, and possibly invoke similar feelings and yearnings in the hearts of their listeners. This narrative strategy is particularly effective in the case of adults for whom the museum visit is a nostalgic journey into long-forgotten regions of their past, an opportunity to re-affirm an experientially and sensually based sense of home.

The autobiographical insertions used by the younger guides, however, are quite different from those used by the old-timers: they occur in the flow of the guides' interpretive talk as casually flowing reminiscences of a very personal childhood world rather than as pathos-filled, semistylized anecdotes of personal participation in communal life. These autobiographical segments rarely make use of the verbal signs and visual emblems that make up the core of pioneering tales, but rather register a more privatized response to the scenes and meanings of the pioneer world, a skirting at the edges of the collective tale.

Thus, often citing a well-known line by one of Israel's foremost national poets, Shaul Tshernichovsky, which says that a person is formed as "a pattern of his homeland's landscape" [*ha'adam hu tavnit nof moladeto*], the younger guides frequently applied it to themselves as they subtly reinscribed the museum's story in a language of place and roots, but without partaking of the ideological fervor and pathos of the founders.[2] Countering charges of ideological indifference leveled against the offspring of the pioneers, they in fact suggested through their autobiographical insertions an alternative form of participation in the communal story. They clearly did not personify the image of the early Zionist pioneers, but they could personify the human product of the Zionist dream of creating a new Jewish person as rooted in place and as harmoniously linked to his or her natural surroundings. Their position vis-à-vis the Zionist ethos is one of lived, taken-for-granted experience, not one of ideological assertion. Although often left implicit, this position was sometimes explicitly stated in autobiographical segments inserted into the museum story:

> A homeland is first of all the physical environment on which the emotional experience and the historical experience are built, and so on. Cultural heritage, homeland. But first of all, if we speak of physical environment, we're talking about the land, the landscape you know, which everybody is attached to...I want to tell you about two experiences related to this...After the war [referring to the Six Day War] we went from Jenin to Kabatieh [in the West Bank], and after Jenin I suddenly had this strange feeling, I was suddenly moving back in time through a time tunnel—buch, buch, buch, buch—the sound of the water pumps in the orange grove....A day after the Six Day War was over, we went up to the Golan Heights and I spent the night in the [Syrian] town of Kuneitra. It was very cold and suddenly we heard the voices of the jackals. I had almost forgotten about them, but in my childhood I used to go to sleep with those sounds every night...And suddenly there was this strange feeling of going back to your childhood, a kind of trembling, this issue of the sounds. What is a homeland? It's the smells and the sounds...(Raviv, Yifat, 12.6.89)

Notably, the attachment to home and place, and the invocation of the intimacy of childhood scenes, is spoken here in a gendered idiom of war and is framed within an encounter with the enemy. The narrator then contrasts this profound (if paradoxical) sense of belonging, of being part of the landscape, with his own father's immigration experience, citing what to him was presumably a family story he had heard at home:

> One of the most difficult problems a person can have is the sense of alienation. People came to the land and on the one hand they felt that this is our country. My father told me that when he came to Jerusalem for the first time he felt as if he'd been here already. Jerusalem was real to him...but there was another

---

[2]See Gurevitch and Aran (1991) for a fascinating discussion of the implications for an Israeli sense of place of different conceptions of the land of Israel—as an idea or as a concretely experienced reality.

part of it he couldn't connect with—the touch, the smell, the contact with the land, this needed to be reconstructed anew. Toynbee, the Canadian [*sic* British] historian (who didn't like us) once said that the cunning Jews, who were expelled from their land, packed it up in a little book and took it with them. But you can't pack up smells, and the Bible indeed brought Jews back to the land and gave them a sense of home, but somewhere there remained a feeling of alienation. (Raviv, Yifat, 12.6.89)

Interestingly, the problematic of negotiating narrative distance from the museum tale that I have identified as central to the younger guides' rhetorical task becomes, in this excerpt, part of the actual story of the past. In a way reminiscent of, yet quite different from, the narrative positioning of old-timer guides, the narrator here, too, reflects on his act of telling and injects into his interpretive account his reflective comments about what it means for him to be telling the story of the land of Israel. In this case, however, the cultural warrant he derives from his firsthand knowledge of the land does not become an authenticating gesture; rather, it is a radically reflexive move, which forces into view the negotiated, constructed nature of both the story-telling occasion and the historical tale at its center. By casting himself as the native Israeli, the one mythic role his pioneering father could never assume, the narrator renegotiates his positioning vis-à-vis the museum story.

For younger guides and younger audiences, participating in this story is made more complex than the simple formula of participation–via–identification would suggest. It is no longer simply a matter of bridging generational distances through gestures of identification with the old-timers' myths of "making place" and "making history" (Katriel & Shenhar, 1990). In a very real sense, the younger guides are inscribing and reclaiming their own distinctive part in the Zionist tale both as agents, that is, the soldiers–heroes who reclaim the land by fighting Israel's wars, and as part of the scene (Burke, 1969), as products and beneficiaries of the pioneering era. This is a different claim of belonging, one that is all-too-often overshadowed by the ideological pathos that dominates the museum discourse. It speaks to a sense of affiliation that is grounded in the life world of the native, not in that of the newcomer to the land, and it therefore spells a promise for the continued relevance of the museum message.

Participating in the retelling of the museum story, embodying the very possibility of its continuing relevance, the younger guides' presentations can nevertheless interrogate this story in far-reaching ways, bringing up pointed questions only their generation has begun to ask: What does it mean to be part of this land and its stories? Ploughing its fields? Singing its praises? Dreaming its smells? Longing for its lost sounds and voices? And by introducing the possibility of this interrogative mood, they reflexively invite the basic question: What does it mean to be telling these particular museum stories at this time, at this place?

These implicit self-doubts and self-questionings, which accompany the museum enterprise as it makes its uncertain way across generational lines, cannot be easily dispelled even though the dynamics of this process can be probed. Framed within the museum walls as the discourse of yesteryear, settlement museum interpretation is shaped by the situation of its enclosure within these walls. Settlement museum guides' ideological assertions thus tend to remain largely self-contained, myth-making gestures harking back to glorified days of beginning. In their standard form, they are discursively constructed in such a way as to ignore, as much as possible, contemporary concerns and encompassing realities of political strife and widespread disillusionment with the present outcomes of the communal, socialist, and egalitarian spirit of pioneering days. They often resolve their narrative difficulties by injecting humor, irony, and hyperbole into their storytelling, as the extended example given in the next section demonstrates.

Thus, although old-timers' testimonial rhetoric clearly reproduces the official, canonical version of the museum story, the younger guides' experientially based identification with its objects, sounds and smells may make its retelling appear quite superfluous. Paradoxically, the young guides' discomfort with the canonical version of settlement museum narration does not stem from a critique of Zionist ideology and practice, but from its wholehearted embrace. Indeed, in pointing out the fundamental success of the Zionist enterprise in the lived experience of the younger generations (as did the last guide cited), the revival of the old-timers' Zionist ideological fervor is put into question even though it is the very focus of the museum enterprise. Why preach Zionism to the new generations of Sabras, the fruit of this earth? The answer I was repeatedly given when I asked this provocative question came in the form of references to the threat of social demise symbolized by the emigration of native Israelis from Israel (a phenomenon natively known as *yeridah* or "descendance," the opposite of *aliyah* or "ascendance" to the land of Israel).

Time and time again I have heard guides say during tours, as well as in interviews and informal conversations, that the museum experience is expected to enhance young visitors' sense of roots and commitment to their native land. It is hoped to help combat young Israelis' readiness to emigrate, deserting their people and land for the lure of a more affluent life abroad. Basically identifying with this pedagogical mission, the younger guides willingly partake in the narrative reproduction of the museum story, even while they constantly signal their ambivalence toward its message, strategically crafting a presentational style they can comfortably employ, appropriating the museum to make it their own, in their own ways.

Jostling for Narrative Position: A Young Guide
With Old-Timers

Clearly, my own participation in settlement museum encounters represents
one particular version of the routine intergenerational encounters that
museum visits may occasion. A rather unique opportunity to observe the
dynamics of a different kind of intergenerational encounter in a settlement
museum setting presented itself in the fall of 1991. On one of my visits to
Yifat, the old-timer guide, Binyamin, who knew I was collecting data in Ein
Shemer as well, told me that a group of old-timers, including two of the
guides from Yifat, were going on a trip to the Ein Shemer museum the
following week. At that time, I was already beginning to ponder issues
related to the relative positioning of narrators and their audiences vis-à-vis
the museum story and in relation to each other. This seemed a wonderful
opportunity to observe what was bound to be an interesting intergenerational encounter between a younger guide and old-timers who were not only
kibbutz members but also representatives of the first pioneering settlement
museum that served as a model for museum making in Ein Shemer as well
as elsewhere. In what follows, I examine some of the communicative features
associated with the unfolding of this unique encounter, which took place
on October 21, 1991.

The overall jocular tone of the encounter was set right at the start by the
guide named Rami, a *kibbutz* member in his mid-30s. As the Yifat elders
were thronging into the screening room, where they were about to be shown
the slide show that tells the story of Ein Shemer, he smilingly used the
familiar address term *chevre* (buddies) in ushering them in. His opening
remarks testified to the extraordinariness of the situation:

> I have been a guide here for 3 years and I guess that an experience like this
> has never come my way before. There's a limit to the tricks that can be played
> [*jesh gvul lekol ta'alul*, an idiomatic expression which utilizes a rhyming effect].
> But to bring here the old-timers from Yifat? This…You know, I get here
> old-timers from [*kibbutz*] Sha'ar Ha'amakim. They say [impersonating an older
> person's speech], "Just a minute, just a minute, a courtyard like this, it's
> strange—sure, we've already seen it in Yifat, well, you've copied from Yifat,
> good bye!" and they don't want to see it…. But I really have to tell you that
> when we established the museum, we didn't know what to put into our guiding
> here, so we dressed up, all very hushed, and went to Yifat. Everyday we would
> go back there again to listen to Binyamin, to learn all his jokes, only after that
> we dared to come back here and learn how to do the guiding. I'm not joking,
> I was in Yifat perhaps a whole year, we kept stealing [stories] from them. So
> I want to tell—the fact that our museum is better, that's a sure thing…
>
> [Binyamin: "Now you blew it [*fishalta*], no such thing, never say such a
> thing."]

The better parts, the better parts we learned from you, a great deal, I say this with all due respect. First of all, see who's sitting here, people who have plowed the land of Israel with their own hands. You want *me* to tell *you* [about it]? [gesturing toward the seats in the screening room] It's a shame, one of you should be getting up here and I should sit down. [Shift to a more conversational tone] There's one question I really want to ask you. Is there anybody here who was somebody else's *primus*?

[Many voices throw out positive responses, but nobody is asked to elaborate. The guide continues, hushing them down]

Why am I asking? I'll tell you why I'm asking. You see? Why am I asking? [more voices]

Just a moment, just a moment, comrades [*chaverim*, a common form of address in *kibbutz* parlance], one at a time,

[more voices]

because I tell, I'll tell you what I tell, we just had a visit here of a class of 11th graders from Haifa. I just told them about the *primus*. We have this cabin with three beds, and Ignaz, an Ein Shemer [elderly] member told us stories, and believe me, every time I tell those stories and every time I don't believe what I'm saying...How could three people live in this two by three meter space? This is obviously a lie, bluffing, you're just fabricating this, it's impossible. And the kids say, "For 2 years they lived in a threesome?" And I tell them, "You know what, today we have a large immigration from Russia, let's see you bring a [Russian] family to live together with you." They burst out laughing, "What? Are you nuts? We have a separate room for each one of us." And the families there, from the villas in Denya [an affluent neighborhood in Haifa], you should have seen them. So I want to tell you that I really, I take off my hat to your generation.... (Rami, Ein Shemer, 10.21.91)

These rather lengthy introductory comments encapsulate many of the themes and foreshadow many of the rhetorical strategies that are later utilized and further elaborated in this guided tour. Pointing out the sense of absurdity associated with the task of telling old-timers about their own life and history, the guide sets aside the question of narrative authority while at the same time defending his right to the floor throughout the tour. As on so many other occasions in settlement museum encounters, the question about the *primus* was more a rhetorical ploy than a genuine query, as the guide's struggle to protect his speaking rights attest. In fact, openly and playfully admitting that there is nothing new he can tell them about pioneering days, the guide re-establishes his leading-narrator role by shifting attention from the historical era that is the object of the museum display to the museum-making enterprise itself. He casts his audience in the position of representatives of the Yifat museum (an attribution that was directly relevant to just two members of the group) and only later acknowledges their generational position as old-timers. This is an equalizing gesture, using shop talk to put museum makers of all generations and in all places on at least a shared footing, playfully displacing intergenerational tensions and the profound social and personal implications they may have with a rather flippant image of rivalry between similar museums in the touristic market-place.

Having shifted the focus of attention from the museum story to museum making and museum storytelling, the guide can now engage in a metadiscourse—a discourse about museum discourse—that allows him to tell his special audience things they do not know. These include local frame narratives about the preservation of the site, the collection of museum items and the organization of the display, including the playful account about stealing their stories—as represented by Binyamin's museum narratives—for narrating the past in Ein Shemer. Frame narratives are sometimes couched in terms of a comparison or even competition with the Yifat museum. This playful move is possible because of the strong perception of an ideological and preservationist agenda shared by the founders and staff of these two museums and because of the memories of various moments and forms of cooperation between them. Thus, following the viewing of the introductory video, Rami led the old-timers into the dining room area, and offered the following introductory remarks to the museum as a whole, underwriting its authenticity as a site museum, which the museum in Yifat is not:

> Ein Shemer, this courtyard, and this may indeed be the difference between you Yifat and us: Here the courtyard—they didn't take a large tractor shed or cowshed and filled it up with display items. This courtyard is the real courtyard of Ein Shemer. From here you can see the stone house, you see it in this model, too, and indeed, the stone house is here...Fortunately for us, this stone house has remained intact since 1921, when they started building it, and it attracted the guys who came here. Already 40 years ago they wanted to build a house here in the middle of the yard that you'll see in a moment, a children's house, and Ignaz, one of our members, said, "No. Perhaps in so and so many years we'll do something here." He didn't dare to utter the word *museum* then, but it's lucky that they didn't build anything, and it's lucky that the wall remained, and a bit of the water tower and the bakery and the granary, a bit remained of everything, and the stories remained, and from the stories and the bit that remained we built and reconstructed the whole courtyard as it had really been. (Rami, Ein Shemer, 10.21.91)

In this account, as in others, the museum-making enterprise is presented as a collaborative intergenerational project: The old-timer, Ignaz, was the one who had the vision to see what the old courtyard could become at a time when the thought of preservation was very distant from most people's minds. On other occasions I have heard him spoken of with respect and gratitude in this visionary role, whereas a younger generation member, Ran, was spoken of as the "nut" or enthusiast (*meshuga ladavar*) who was the great pusher (or "bulldozer," as he was also referred to) who made it all possible

by orchestrating a wide range of collection, reconstruction, and maintenance activities. As mentioned earlier, the same wording was employed by
my informants in Yifat to talk about Oded Artzi, the founder of their
museum. The preface to the museum in this case also becomes a testimony
to the possibility and value of intergenerational collaboration, an underlying
theme that re-emerges a few minutes later in the story of how the display
of the dining hall was organized:

> Let me tell you a story, it's one that's just right for you. When we brought in
> the tables, there was this little shed here, which was the original dining room
> of Ein Shemer, then it was enlarged to this hall [as it stands now]. When we
> brought in the tables, me and Ran, Ran will soon show you a tractor, he's the
> big "nut" who built the museum, we didn't know how to arrange the tables.
> We didn't know how to arrange the dining room at all. At 6:00 in the evening,
> we suddenly had an idea: We called in the elderly people of Ein Shemer, and
> told them, "Come, arrange the dining room." They came in here, what shall
> I tell you, there was such excitement, their legs were trembling. After 50 years
> they are told to arrange the dining room as it used to be 50 years ago. They
> started arguing if the kitchen was here or there. H. says to S., "Are you crazy?
> How come the kitchen is here? The kitchen was there…" It was something,
> we were standing here, laughing our heads off. Okay, they agreed about where
> the kitchen had been, now where had the tea kettle been? Then they began
> telling where they had sat and how many people on each bench. Two nights
> we sat here with 20 old-timers from Ein Shemer and learned all the stories.
> (Ronen, Ein Shemer, 10.21.91)

This account of how the dining room display was arranged is a hallmark
of vernacular museum design. According to this story, no professionals were
consulted in erecting this house of memories. The museum display is
presented here as a mimetic reconstruction grounded in old-timers' testimonial role. Old-timers' testimonies and collectively constructed memories
were sought out and relied on. Even though the fragility of the elders'
recollections was recognized, the guide further played out the self-effacing
presentational strategy he adopted from the very beginning of the tour. That
way, he highlighted the lack of historical knowledge and precarious narrative authority of second-generation members, who had to put all their faith
in the testimonies their elders could provide. The public recognition given
to this role in shaping the museum display seems to be asserted with special
force for this particular audience of old-timers, whose special status as
first-hand witnesses is thereby acknowledged. At the same time, the description of the process of attempting to arrange the dining room highlights the
problem of personal memory and presents the arguments between the
old-timers as a source of entertainment for the younger people in less than
reverential tones. This depiction sounds a familiar note that runs through
this guide's interpretive account as he mingles appreciation and respect with

a sense of amusement and disbelief. The same ambivalent effect could be heard in the self-mocking statement at the introduction about the elders' personal sacrifice in relation to the *primus* stories. This arrangement is presented as so fantastic—both in the sense of wonderful and in the sense of unreal—that younger people, including the guide, found it hard to believe. In one interpretation, the issue is what young audiences hear as the hyperbolic nature of the old-timers' stories, whereas in the other, it is the issue of the validity of their powers of recollection. In both interpretations, however, the old-timers' narrative authority is simultaneously asserted and humorously subverted as the guide both acknowledges their participation in the museum-making enterprise and at the same time projects an ambivalent reading on this very gesture of recognition.

A somewhat similar, paradoxical effect can be discerned as the guide claims that the mannequins placed in the reconstructed dining room represent authentic figures of old-timers from Ein Shemer (both alive and dead), and are actually named after them in the interpretive oral commentary that accompanies the display. Although given a place of honor in this pantheon of settlement history, these old-timers are museumified beyond remorse. Although the old-timers from Ein Shemer apparently accepted this practice, the old-timer guides from Yifat told me on different occasions that they objected to the use of mannequins and avoided introducing them in their own museum, as they thought they detract from the authenticity of the museum display. The intensity of feeling associated with this objection suggested to me that the idea of encountering a museumified version of their contemporaries, or generic representations of themselves, as part of the museum display was distasteful to them as the museological gesture of veneration can come so dangerously close to a gesture of removal or even dismissal. No wonder that the old-timer guides did not want to face the possibility of such an implication in their day-to-day environment.

Another important strand in the guide's discourse on this occasion involved stories about the responses of young audiences to the museum display, which gave the old-timers a glimpse of how the generic story of their life resonates (or fails to do so) in the contemporary sociocultural scene. The guide thus positions himself in a familiar role as mediator, but in this case he mediates the present to those who know much about the past, rather than the past to those contemporary audiences who know little about it. Stories about audience responses to the museum tale are a type of frame narratives. As such, they are more about the project of museum making than they are about the pioneering ethos itself. Unlike the frame narratives considered earlier, however, they are not about the museum-making activities of preservation, collecting and restoration but rather about the process of museum interpretation and its effects. The focus in these narrative segments is thus more on the receivers of the museum message than on its producers.

Rami referred to audience responses at a number of junctures along this tour, saying such things as, "The children go wild when I tell them about the *slik* [weapons hideaway], they want to go and find it." A more extended example appears in the following segment, which deals with the traditional healing practice of administering an enema in cases of indigestion. The guide here begins with a comment that acknowledges the superiority of Binyamin's narrative repertoire as a token of old timers' privileged knowledge. But he then inserts a new element into his narrative act by drawing attention to the way in which visitors respond to museum narration. By shifting the focus from the tale to the storytelling situation, the guide underscores his own position as regular participant in museum encounters, which gives him access to audience responses to the museum story. He thereby marks a domain of experience in which a claim for a privileged position as narrator is warranted:

> Let's look at a couple more pictures. By the way, don't miss the *choken* [enema] here, but I'm sure the stories I know about the *choken* are nothing compared to those Binyamin can tell. Nevertheless, last year a child who was here says to me, looks at this thing here and says to me, "This is not a *choken*, this is an Arab *nargileh* [smoking implement]." So the teacher says to him, "You know, kid, the only difference between them is where you put the mouthpiece. That's the only difference." [laughter] It's the teacher who said that, not me. Binyamin, write it down [for future incorporation in guided tours]. You're not writing.
> [Binyamin], "I'm not writing, you've learned all these stories from me."
> (Rami, Ein Shemer, 10.21.91)

Although many of Rami's stories, as he admitted earlier, were indeed taken from Binyamin's repertoire, audience response stories of this kind were not a product of old times or old-timers' tales but of the museum context itself, a context shared by older and younger guides alike. By asking Binyamin to write down his audience tale, the guide here playfully pushed toward a role reversal of his actual position as Binyamin's self-appointed disciple. He had earlier told the audience that he had spent a whole year listening to Binyamin's stories before he dared to tell them in Ein Shemer, wildly exaggerating the scope of a real exchange that had lasted one day (as Binyamin later told me). Now he jokingly suggested that Binyamin take down his stories as a resource for his own museum interpretation, assigning a more open-ended texture to the museum narrative and more equal narrator roles than Binyamin was willing to concede.

Indeed, citations or descriptions of audience responses were occasionally injected into interpretations of other guides, too. Most often, naturally, what gets cited is audience approval, as in general comments like, "the children love this, they say…" or in more specific ones like, "the other day a man came and he recognized his grandfather in this picture," which contribute both to the immediacy and to the authenticity of the museum display. At times, the frame narrative may come in the form of a self-citation, as the guide reports on his or her own interpretive performance in front of another audience. This usually occurs in addressing adult audiences, and the self-citation alludes to a previous guided tour given to children, allowing the guide to inject a higher level of dramatization into his or her presentation than a normal group of adults would probably stomach, and thus to model a more enthusiastic and immediate response than could probably be elicited from his or her actual audience. Examples of this strategy in the particular guided tour we are examining abound:

> There are *sliks* here, if anybody has a mind to look for weapons, he shouldn't bother, you won't find them. The British didn't find them so you won't either. I say this with a smile because the kids keep looking for the *slik* and it drives them bananas, and I tell them, "What do you think, the British were experts at this, so you will find them?" But then I fill up some *sliks* for them...(Rami, Ein Shemer, 10.21.91)

> Let's have a quick look at the dining-room. Look at this, it's even strange to ask you, but look [picking up a special tea-making spoon], you know how much fun I have with this? The kids go nuts, "Is it a *falafel* [popular Mid-Eastern dish] spoon? Is it for making yogurt?" (Rami, Ein Shemer, 10.21.91)

> Here you see Shoshana the cook. She started working at 4 a.m., and the night watchman, the moment he heard the dishes, came running to get a cup of tea. But the night watchman in Ein Shemer, unlike the one in Yifat, he didn't come just for the tea, he had a book of poems by Pushkin [Russian poet], love poems, and he would sit down here at 4 a.m., put up his leg and read her a love poem. At your place, did they read out love poems at 4 a.m.? [laughter] Nothing, don't you tell me, this happened only in Ein Shemer...Well, you see, that's what I tell the children, "Kids," I tell them, the older ones, "*chevre* [you guys], you're always stuck with that television and video, why don't you read the girls some love poem?" I tell them, and I read them some love poem here, and they look at me as if I came from some other planet, "What is it, reading love poems? We come to the girls, we want to get on with it without love poems, what's the story?" [laughter] (Rami, Ein Shemer, 10.21.91)

> Now I want to tell you another thing. I stand here, and in front of me stand all the children of Israel...but when they see this Arab [mannequin] and I tell them about it there's always some kid on the margin there who utters a curse word about the Arabs. And first of all I look at the teacher, she looks like she'd like the earth to swallow her up, what's this? She's ashamed. And I tell them, "Kids, you know, my best friends—I'm telling this to you, too, but to you it was clear—you know Baq'a el Garbiya [an Arab village], instead of

going to buy nails in Hadera [a nearby Jewish town] I'll go to Baq'a, I have a
family there [that I befriended] but also regular neighborly relations, we have
lived with them for 70 years now," so I tell them about the Arabs in the area.
(Rami, Ein Shemer, 10.21.91)

In all of these examples, the guide underscores the extraordinariness of
this particular interpretive situation, which hinges on the special identity of
his audience, yet he normalizes his account through the use of self-citation
strategies relating to other tours he had led in the past, especially tours
addressing kids. Framing his story as a telling about a telling, he gets to tell
old-timers a story that he would otherwise hesitate to address to them. This
way, the present tour becomes laminated with recollections of previous tours
that address children who constitute the museum's more accustomed patrons. At the same time, the guide repeatedly indicates his attentiveness to
what he considers to be his audience's special interests—by citing incidents
involving old-timers, by highlighting their contributions to the making of
the museum, by acknowledging their narrative authority and playfully
effacing his own, or by injecting well-known anecdotes of pioneering life
(like the one about the reading of Pushkin's love poems) and humorously
claiming them as local fare by such prefaces as, "This happened here in Ein
Shemer," or, "It is written in the book of Ein Shemer," and so on. Yet the
self-citations are also constant reminders that old-timers do not constitute
the natural audience for the museum story as it is told by the young guide.

Toward the end of the tour, as he tells them about the first washing
machine brought to Ein Shemer, which had been operated by the pioneers
in the dining room and was therefore put on display as part of the exhibit
there, the guide explicitly shifts to a metadiscussion of the museum interpretive agenda itself, finally coming full circle to a point where his initial
self-effacement is all gone and he can urge the old-timers from Yifat to do
more with their museum, to support it more enthusiastically as a *kibbutz*
venture. The makers of history in the pioneering sense thus become subsumed into the heroics of history-making in the contemporary scene, that
is, the remaking of history in the museum context:

An old-timer from Ein Shemer tells us one day, "The washer that was in the
dining room, do you know where it is?" Ran [the museum founder] heard this
and almost fainted. What washer in the dining room? We started looking for
pictures, and he couldn't explain to us what it was. What shall I tell you, we
turned every stone in the land of Israel to find this washer. Where did we find
it? I won't go into it, some village, in the north of the country at the house of
some *yekes* [German Jews], the real washer, with this soap, you see, you close
it with the clothes inside, it's working, wow, and how it's working! [operates
it, it makes quite a noise]...Now, another thing, suppose I show this washer,
finishing the tour right here. A hundred meters from here we have Ein
Shemer's contemporary laundrette with the computer cards and all, and I

take the kids there…and they see how the laundry is done today on the *kibbutz*…And this is the idea behind the guided tour, Ein Shemer of bygone days and Ein Shemer of today out there. Without this [comparison] the point of it is lost. And I want to tell you, really, you have such a diamond of a place, and you don't utilize it as much as you could. Really, your museum with your *kibbutz*, it's the diamond of the valley, you should take note of this…(Rami, Ein Shemer, 10.21.91)

Throughout this tour, as we have seen, the young guide constantly negotiated his narrative positioning vis-à-vis his audience of old-timers—deferring to them, ironizing their stories, defining their stance in relation to contemporary audiences, elevating and all but denigrating them in the same breath. The tour is completely anchored in the present moment of encounter and it has much more to say—whether explicitly or implicitly—about narrative positioning and intergenerational relations than about the ins and outs of pioneering days.

In this respect, and as I have tried to show throughout this chapter, settlement museum encounters are not standardized, reiterative, storytelling occasions, but rather dynamic and diversified communicative events that are shaped and reshaped in and through participants' construction of their narrative roles. Their positioning vis-à-vis the museum tale as well as their positioning vis-à-vis each other as narrators and audience members are important dimensions in this situated process of meaning construction.

In all the cases discussed, however, the basic assumption of all the parties involved was that the guides and their audiences either naturally belonged to, or would like to be part of the imagined community (Anderson, 1991) of mainstream Israeli culture (and its anchoring in pioneering mythology). It is within this shared assumptive framework that all the various negotiations described in this chapter took place. In the next chapter, I discuss the case of guided tours for which this assumption has to be modified in various ways. By attending to the particular inflections of settlement museum interpretations that address some problematic audiences, as locally constructed, I hope that some of the more subtle aspects of the interpretive agenda of settlement museums can be fruitfully probed. A consideration of these tours will bring us as close to an appreciation of both the cultural limits and the hegemonic power of the settlement museum narrative as we come to in the present study.

Chapter 5

Museum Encounters
as Potentially Contested Sites

ഔ∎ॐ

Settlement museum discourse, as we have seen, is infused with a rhetoric of identification. It is by dramatizing their sense of identification with the museum story and its ideological stance that the guides claim narrative authority, and it is through their working assumption that the audiences they address both can and should be coaxed into becoming more involved with the museum's version of the past that they seek to win adherence to it. That the history of pioneering and the values associated with it constitute a foundation mythology to be collectively cherished by all members of the Israeli public is thus the taken-for-granted of settlement museum encounters. Visitors are assumed to have at least a basic knowledge of pioneering history to which the guides can add some bits of information, but their main task is to reconfirm and enliven this knowledge through emotional appeal. And even though most museum visitors can hardly be said to trace their personal histories to the story of pioneering, and therefore cannot take the guides' self-identification with it as a model for their own involvement in it in any straightforward manner, it is only on rare occasions that these underlying assumptions are questioned.

Such questioning may occur when museum encounters involve visitor groups whose identification with the Socialist Zionist foundation mythology can neither be assumed nor easily induced, given the recognition of cultural distance, an underlying ideological gap, or even political struggle between the visitors' positions and those that underwrite the museum tale. Whereas all museum encounters, as we have seen in the previous chapter, inevitably involve some form of audience accommodation, those museum encounters that are fraught with ideological tensions invite the telling of more conspicuously inflected versions of the museum narrative. In the context of Israeli settlement museums, the main junctures of ideological struggle that seem to be foregrounded can be mapped onto the larger societal rifts in Israel: the ethnic rift between Ashkenazi (European) Jews and Mizrahi Jews from Middle Eastern and North African lands, the rift between secular and religious Jews, and the rift between Arabs and Jews.

I was particularly intrigued by the discursive accommodations involving these issues in settlement museum tours, and have observed and recorded guided tours addressing elderly Mizrahi women and Arab visitors in Yifat as well as religious Jewish visitors to The Old Courtyard in Ein Shemer. These observations enabled me to explore some of the dynamics of settlement museum encounters whose rhetoric of identification becomes subsumed by participants' actual experience of the museum setting, and the ideologies to which they give voice, as precarious arenas of potential contestation. In this chapter I thus trace the contours of such tours in which not only cultural but also ideological boundaries were crossed, and in which the potential for oppositional voices had to be inevitably taken into account by the guides as they rhetorically constructed the museum tale.

PIONEERS, IMMIGRANTS, AND THE ETHNIC DIVIDE

Generational Proximity, Ethnic Cleavage

As we saw in the previous chapter, the question of generational affiliation is crucial to the shaping of the guides' performative role. It is no less significant in relation to the visitors. Museum tours that are led by old-timer guides who address elderly audiences are of particular interest, as they represent the clearest case in which a shared footing between the guide and his or her audience can be assumed. Although younger guides often expressed concern about addressing elderly audiences who may be critical of their performances, the old-timer guides did not share these misgivings. Sarah, in particular, who guided the two tours I discuss in this section, both of which addressed elderly Mizrahi women from the greater Haifa area, relished the opportunity to participate in what she hoped would become an occasion for shared reminiscing. These tours took place on consecutive days in the fall of 1991, and they provide an example of how the guide's assumptions concerning shared generational and gender affiliation are played up against the recognition of a considerable cultural gap between her and her ethnically different audience. Throughout the tours, she never made any reference to ethnic matters, which reflected the suppression of ethnicity in settlement museum discourse more generally.

This is quite notable, given the fact that the rift between secular and religious Jews, and the one between Jews and Arabs, were acknowledged and addressed on various occasions in both settlement museums. Indeed, visiting groups from the ethnic enclaves of development towns in peripheral zones (Kellerman, 1993) were willingly received, but were not explicitly differentiated as to their backgrounds, and their potential sense of exclusion from the heroic tale of pioneering was never addressed. It was both repeatedly stated, and even more powerfully implied, that the story of the museum belonged to the nation as a whole in an undifferentiated way (basically excluding Arab citizens of the state). Indeed, it seems that it is partly through their participation in settlement museum encounters (and similarly oriented cultural mediations), that Mizrahi Jews, as well as other Israeli Jews of nonpioneering stock, can be hoped to identify with the Israeli pioneering saga. To this effect, the patently equal and equalizing position of museum visitors requires that their particular personal histories and ethnic heritage should become at least momentarily suspended. This is not always easily accomplished, as Sarah found out during the tours under discussion.

In constructing her presentation to her particular audience of elderly Mizrahi women, she foregrounded issues of age and shared generational affiliation. As will become apparent, however, the meta-narrative of shared experiential ground she was trying to weave collapsed time and again in the face of the cultural gap between her and her audience. This happened, for example, when she pointed to the pioneers' tent and one of the visitors spontaneously uttered *ma'abara*, a term referring to the tent encampments created in the late 1940s and early 1950s for the housing of Jewish refugees from Europe and newcomers from Middle Eastern and North African countries. The arrival of these various groups of immigrant–refugees more than doubled the Jewish population of Israel in the late 1940s and the tent encampments (*ma'abarot*) in which they were housed became a symbol of the hardships they faced in adapting to the new land. They later became a symbol of social deprivation because all those who could leave them did so as soon as possible. And because many of those who stayed behind for several years were newcomers from Middle Eastern and North African extraction, these tent towns also became marked for ethnicity. The negative connotations associated with the tent encampments in Israeli collective memory explain Sarah's rather startled response to the invocation of the *ma'abara* image at the sight of the tent (although it was not the first time I had heard it made by visitors I had observed). She replied:

> No, that's not a *ma'abara* [tent encampment], no, no, no. Excuse me, don't mix up everything. That was settlement. We started with tents, then we moved on to cabins until we moved into the houses. It took time. It took a lot of time. First we lived only in tents, and the tents usually stood in an open field, very close to the granary.
> [A few voices can be heard, people are trying to say something, but the guide presses on.] Please, my name is Sarah, anybody who wants to ask, please

ask questions in the end. I'll explain everything as we go along, but in the meantime I'm only asking you to listen.... (Sarah, Yifat, 11.5.91)

In fact, the account given of the difference between the pioneers' tents and a newcomers' *ma'abara* is not quite clear or particularly persuasive: Both early pioneers and later newcomers faced many hardships when they first came to the land and both moved similarly from tents to other makeshift arrangements before they came to live in regular houses. The adamant demand to draw a sharp line between the two visually similar images has little to do with the actual living conditions depicted in the museum display. Indeed, it is grounded in the mythological position of the pioneers as heroic founding figures, whose tents became symbols of voluntary sacrifice and an ideologically driven ascetic attitude to be sharply distinguished from tents that were the mere outcomes of dire circumstances. Thus, comparisons between *halutzim* (pioneers) and *olim* (immigrants), as this guide's reaction suggests, are not ones the guides normally encourage as these tend to go against the cultural project of enshrining the pioneering past by invoking uninvited ostensible commonalties of experience. The surplus, ideological meaning attending the pioneers' as compared to the newcomers' tents makes it harder for the guides to dwell on the distinctive hardships of pioneering days, which is one of the themes that runs through settlement museum interpretation. Indeed, the day before this very tour, while addressing a group of elderly women who had originally arrived in Israel from Iraq and had apparently been inhabitants of one of the aforementioned tent encampments, Sarah made the following fleeting reference to the tent, saying:

...And a tent. I lived in a tent, you know [assenting voices and nods of recognition]. Yes, many of you I think lived in a tent [mumbled voices]. You lived in a tent that was much better than this one...(Sarah, Yifat, 11.4.91)

Here, too, the guide attempted to valorize the pioneering enterprise through references to the sacrifices it demanded, pointing out the frugality of the pioneers' tent and recounting the pioneers' good will and self-sacrifice in absorbing new immigrants through the *primus* arrangement that housed a third person in the tent of a conjugal couple. Through the suggested comparison with her audience's past, she claimed the greatest (and most ennobling) hardships belonged to the pioneers, whose tents, she claimed, were simpler than those of the later newcomers.

In underlining the distinctiveness of the early pioneering experience as compared to all later arrivals in the land of Israel, the guide served the interest of distinction and enshrinement, but this worked against the museum's other goal, which is to enhance visitors' personal identification with the pioneering ethos and creating shared ground between them and the guide. This was accomplished to some extent in other parts of the tours when the guide invoked generational proximity in attempting to invite her audience's identification with the museum's preservationist agenda and the claims it makes about the importance of the past and its continued relevance in contemporary life. Thus, in addressing her elderly audiences, the theme of historical continuity and the need to valorize the ways of the past through the preservation and display of the artifacts that have come to represent it became a major strand in the guide's presentation.

Perhaps the clearest indication of what it meant for these elderly people to valorize old things was brought out in Sarah's opening remarks to the group of elderly Iraqi women. She prefaced the tour with her customary frame narrative about the making of the museum and this time the usual collecting story turned into a tale of the material salvage of old things and an assertion of the metaphorical salvage of old people:

> We found these things thrown away in some field, or in some tool shed, we gathered them here so we could show you, your children and your grandchildren how our land of Israel started, from the beginning, very simple, we thought it would be a great thing to preserve these tools. Although it's an old thing it's not to be thrown away, right? You don't throw away an old thing. Also an old person you don't throw away, right? You have to collect it, fix it, develop it. [responding to an unclear comment] No, an Old People's home doesn't mean you throw them away, it's great…(Sarah, Yifat, 11.4.91)

Thus, the museum-making enterprise is framed here as an affirmation of old things and old people, and the guided tour in this case becomes a gesture of self-approval, with the elderly people honoring themselves through the honor they give to the items on display in the very place where the people and things of the past, they are reassuringly told, are routinely honored by young people as well.

That this sense of self-approval is not easily attained in the world outside the museum walls was immediately brought forth in the visitors' spontaneous response to Sarah's foregoing introduction, "But our children said to throw away, throw away, it's no good, it's not beautiful." The guide's message about valorizing the past clearly contradicted the vision of cultural change and adaptation that motivated these old ladies' socially mobile offspring. The fact that throwing away old things and creating a new world of their own making was exactly what the young pioneers whose story is enshrined in the museum had done was not mentioned. The comment went unattended, and the basic paradox entailed by the museum project of preserving a moment of cultural change for audiences who are at best ambivalent toward its implications remained submerged here as elsewhere.

Indeed, the guides' ability to convey to their audiences messages that I would consider perplexing or even provocative without triggering any questioning, opposition, or open disaffection was really quite surprising. Sarah's commentary on issues of gender as related to the early pioneering groups during these tours is a case in point. Addressing these two groups of elderly, traditional women, she gave voice to a feminist, progressive perspective, which they listened to with an ear for comparisons between the pioneers' practices and contemporary ones:

> [pointing to a picture of a mixed-gender construction group] Note here, first of all, look, the girls are working together with the guys, and you'll see this all along, pay attention to this, because then the most fragile girl wanted to be strong, and wanted to be a pioneer, with all her might, "I came to the land [of Israel] to build it, I didn't come to be a housewife." She first and foremost wanted to build the land.
> [A woman's comment: "Not like nowadays."]
> Not like nowadays. Then she really wanted full equality. Without any conditions, no prior conditions. That's it, and she went to work with the guys. Note here, she's pushing the wheelbarrows together with the guys. (Sarah, Yifat,11.5.91)

A similar message was conveyed as the guide drew her audience's attention to a picture of men washing clothes by hand that hung in the laundry corner of the museum:

> We are standing here near the laundry corner, which was always behind the shared clothing cabin. And the women are standing, receiving the dirty clothes from the field, from the cowshed, from the stable. They have to wash them, and they developed a feeling of anti to this, "Did we come here just to do the washing? First of all we demand that the guys, too, will take part in the laundry duty. The guys, too, should do the laundry, we too want to go out to the granary, the cowshed, the field and the vegetable garden, we will not stay just here [in the yard], doing the laundry, cooking and taking care of the babies. No way." (Sarah, Yifat, 11.5.91)

Looking at these elderly Mizrahi women, I could not help thinking that for many of them, the traditional domestic chores so vehemently shunned by the young pioneer women must have been a lifelong project and a source of self-identification associated with the domain of family and homemaking. No comment came forth from the audience. A similarly nonchallenging attitude greeted the following, more extravagant statement in which not only homemaking but even mothering was presented as a potential obstacle in the way of women's participation in the pioneering enterprise:

> The girls wanted to work, yes, do the work of the guy. Even if she was thin and slim and weak she wanted to be strong and prove herself as a pioneer, she had come to build the land. Does she only want to be a homemaker? No.

She doesn't want to do the washing all day, to cook and take care of her child. She wants to do agricultural work, like the guys exactly. She's as strong as everybody else. Believe me, I was so thin I weighed 48 kg and I was very strong at work, yes. [in response to a question]

Pregnancy? When I was already pregnant, well, then I wasn't that happy anymore. That's all. Seriously I'm telling you, I didn't even have the time, I said, "It's a waste of time, I'm so busy, now I want to teach Hebrew, I have to teach [folk]dancing, I want to absorb the new immigrants, when do I have time to be pregnant? But what already happened—happened, you know, and the children came even when they weren't really waiting for them. And they came, so thank God there are the children—and let them all be healthy. (Sarah, Yifat, 11.4.91)

This view of mothering is certainly at odds with both past and present prevailing cultural attitudes about childbearing and mothering in main-stream Israeli culture, which is family-oriented and child-centered, or with the Middle Eastern tradition these women represented. A few minutes after the guide's foregoing personal account of the difficulties pioneering women faced in reconciling themselves to their mothering role, she launched into a detailed, very favorable account of the role of the caretaker (*metapelet*) who presided over the communal nursery where the babies of the *kibbutz* were raised:

The caretaker had to take care of the babies, and the mother could go to work. So if there was a mother who had milk she would still come by every few hours for breast feeding. But if she didn't have milk? Why should she come by? She would come in the evening. The caretaker was like a doctor, she changed the babies, she knew everything.

[Woman's voice]: Not like now, now it's the mother who comes first.

Right, exactly. She would bring the woman in labor to the hospital, she would get the instructions from the doctor, yes. (Sarah, Yifat, 11.4.91)

This account of the caretaker is unusual among other accounts of that role that I have heard in settlement museum interpretations, where it more usually appears in the context of bitter retrospective recriminations about the tyrannical figure of the caretaker who controlled parent–child contacts on the *kibbutz* (see earlier excerpts on pp. 50–51). This guide, who had herself worked as a caretaker, did not demonize that cultural figure either on this or on other occasions. Rather, she sounded an appreciative note to the caretaker's professionalism and dedication. Here she was apparently so intent on elevating the caretaker's role as a radical alternative to the traditional mothering role that she did not fully respond to a visitor's comparative comment about the primacy of the mother role today. This insertion, however, sought to redress the balance, gently reminding the guide and the other audience members that the gender and childrearing arrangements of the pioneers, however wonderfully exotic they may sound, did not take root either in *kibbutz* culture or in the wider society. Mothers come first, the traditionally oriented comment stated—whether they are elderly women from Iraq or young *kibbutz* women—and they are here to stay.

We see, then, that even though the old-timer guide tried to maximize the impact of the shared generational orientation she and her audience seemed to hold toward the past as a valuable resource, this museum encounter gave rise to conflicting attitudes. Indeed, the guide made many strategic attempts to highlight both her own and the visitors' old-timer status through references to the value of the past, the respect for old age and the authority of Jewish tradition as articulated in biblical texts and as expressed through biblical figures. In Brown and Levinson's terms (1987), one would speak of this as a massive employment of positive politeness strategies. The sense of solidarity the guide wished to cultivate was, however, undercut by the museum's project of enshrining the story of early settlement, which involved claims of uniqueness and separateness for the pioneering experience as compared to that of other newcomers to the land. It was also complicated by the fact that the valorization of settlement history implies the ideological rejection of another past, the Diaspora past, which weakens the guide's repeated claim for the essential need to value the past and its elderly bearers.

Through her use of personal anecdotes and her overall warmth and enthusiastic approach, the guide seemed to have aroused the women's interest and achieved a sense of bonding with her audience at different moments along the tour route. They often responded with smiles and encouraging nods. However, she did not really encourage these Mizrahi women to make their own contributions to the discursive construction of the tour, and they did not insist on giving voice to their own points of view. The cultural gap between the guide and her audience left little room for shared reminiscing, and the unexpected side comments sometimes initiated by the women only seemed to undercut the fragile, generationally based sense of affiliation she was able to generate. More often than not, these comments were either rejected or left unattended for fear of rocking the boat. The complexities associated with the Ashkenazi/Mizrahi societal rift, as locally encoded in the difference between pioneers and immigrants, were left unprobed. So were the social implications of making this privileged version of the pioneering story the foundation mythology of the nation as a whole.

Ethnic Convergence, Experiential Chasm

No such cultural gap between the guide and her audience was anticipated by either the guide or me as we discussed the imminent arrival of a group of elderly visitors from another *kibbutz*, who were coming to the museum as part of a day's trip to the north. These old-timers' prospective visit had jumped out at me from the museum work calendar, where I often looked in order to schedule my own field trips to the museum. They were coming from the *kibbutz* where I had gone to school during part of my childhood. Sarah told me happily that she was going to guide them, anticipating an occasion of reminiscing and bonding, which was the way she often said she experienced encounters with elderly *kibbutz* members, whose life–world she felt she could fully identify with. I made a point of being at the museum on the day of their tour, wondering if I would recognize any of the elderly people after all these years. As it turned out, only part of the guide's and my expectations were met, but for me the visit emerged as an important moment in my fieldwork. It made me recognize the power of social and autobiographical experience that takes us beyond the recognized categories of ethnicity dicussed in the previous section in a way that proved to be especially meaningful to my own experience of the museum story.

In constructing her commentary, Sarah assumed a great deal of solidarity and equal footing with her audience, whom she thought of as old-timer *kibbutz* members like herself. She even expressed a special sense of affiliation to this group because in her youth she had spent time in a *kibbutz* located not far from theirs. At times, she made explicit reference to this shared bond, as, for example, when she concluded her overview of the museum's internal yard, saying:

> For you it will be wonderful, to old-timers it will surely mean a great deal. I know that I sometimes guide old-timers around here and I won't tell you what they do when they see all this. It is simply world embracing. You can say that every one is suddenly part of this history...Because I feel it too, I want you to know that I came from [another *kibbutz*], so I am your neighbor, so that I, too, was a part of this history. And for you surely none of it will be new, but perhaps a little moving. (Sarah, Yifat, 12. 24.89)

Unlike the guided tours described in the previous section, in this case there seemed to be enough common ground in terms of their shared experience as *kibbutz* old-timers and founders so that the more general issues of respect for age and veneration of the past did not come up. The tour was to be a personalized, emotion-filled journey into precious memories of a shared past and was not expected to convey new information to the visitors. The old-timer guide constructed an interpretive account that blended factual details concerning the agricultural work of the pioneers, frame narratives relating to the making of the museum, and personal stories of her own life as a young pioneer. Her discourse was at the same time punctuated by a persistent effort to invoke her audience's memories, "You will see a tent, of course you all lived in a tent..." "I lived with a *primus*, you, too, probably had *primusim* [plural] in your tents..." "We have this big water pump, you'll hear it working as you used to hear it in your orange groves..." "Let's ask the old-timers, did you have a chance to work with these tools?" "Who doesn't remember that the kids were sleeping on [mattresses filled with] corn husks?" "You remember, they would make the hay into stacks…" "I do not have to tell you what this tin box is…" "The soup was, do you remember the soups? Just a minute, who remembers the soup: lentil soup or bean soup?" Here and there, a brief response was given and briefly acknowledged, but no extended dialogue developed at any point in the tour. Mostly, visitors either provided a line of information the guide elicited or confirmed the memories she attributed to them, as in, "I remember very well," or, "Even this tool I remember working with," and so on.

Much to my surprise, this turned out to be one of the least effective tours I had observed Sarah guiding along the museum route. As we were walking along the display, the group began to dwindle in size and many people opted out. Both before and after this tour, I saw Sarah charm many diverse visiting groups with her warm, lively, and interesting renderings of the museum story. She was even able to capture the attention of groups of restless teenagers from urban areas or newly arrived immigrants who had very little knowledge of what she was talking about.

It therefore seemed curious that despite her obvious delight in taking on this group, the audience's obvious familiarity with the pioneering world depicted in the display, her highly personalized style, and her expressed feelings of solidarity with her audience, a good many of the visitors left the guided tour in the middle and began to roam around the museum and in its garden on their own. Even the few who stayed throughout the tour did not seem to resonate with the story to the extent that both the guide and I had expected. It was clear that she was more invested in telling the story than they were interested in hearing it out. They had to be coaxed into attending to the guide's account with repeated requests for silence or attention:

Just a minute, just a minute, just a minute, I will allow you to walk around, later you'll be able to walk around, but here it's really important that you hear this. I know, old-timers know this, it's not that…

Please, I'm asking you, I was also curious to see all of this, but in order to see you have to know what you are looking at. Please, all the older people, I'm asking you [to come] here to this corner, for a few minutes. We will not stay here long, yes, please.

Please let me have quiet. We will walk around later, we will let you have the free walk for as long a you like. But let us at least make sure we're going in a particular direction, please I'm asking you to concentrate, because here it all begins…(Sarah, Yifat, 12.24.89)

Noting the elderly visitors drop out one after another, I followed the shrunken group to the end of the tour route, inwardly cringing at the guide's unaccustomed entreaties for silence and attention and wondering what had gone wrong. Some time later, I had the occasion to discuss this (to me) memorable museum visit with one of my former grade-school teachers who was one of the elderly *kibbutz* visitors to the museum that day. Obviously untouched by the display, he had retired very early in the tour and spent most of the time walking outside on the museum lawn. In this later conversation, he confirmed my feeling that he did not identify with the museum's pathos of heroic pioneering. I sensed a trace of annoyance in his tone. Clearly, he did not resonate with the museum's project of "turning an ankle-high site into castles floating in the air." Knowing him to be a highly respected biblical scholar, I wondered whether it was the recency of the past depicted in settlement museums that led to his disinterest. He agreed that he found archaeological sites much more interesting so I tried to get at the source of his anger by directly addressing the recency factor and asked, "What about the Holocaust museums that are being established now in so many places?" He gave me an incredulous look and said, "How can you compare?" And at that moment, it dawned on me why that particular guided tour, although it provided some occasion for shared reminiscing, had not generated the kind of human contact that both the guide and I had vaguely expected it to do.

Like my former teacher, many of the old-timers from that particular *kibbutz* were Holocaust survivors. While they were obviously familiar with the material world put on display in the museum setting, and from time to time found one object or another evocative of past days, they did not seem to be willing partners to the enshrinement process that the museum represented and enhanced. Reflecting on that tour, I realized that the pathos-filled discourse of the guide, which most visitors either resonate with or take in their stride, did not go down well with that group. For them, it seems to me, the drama of Jewish pioneering—which is the drama of the New Jew as an active, future-oriented maker of history—with its themes of personal sacrifice, collective struggle, and national revival, was eclipsed by the story of the destruction of Jewish life in Europe and the indelible personal and collective loss it entailed for them personally. From their point of view, apparently the celebration of the active and idealistic orientation to the renewal of Jewish life in the land of Israel by the few who were committed, far-sighted, or lucky enough to leave Europe behind them in the early part of the century is a reminder of what has been traditionally presented in Zionist historiography as the disastrous passivity, lack of foresight, or sheer bad fortune of the many who remained. They could not wholeheartedly or even indifferently participate in this celebration of the pioneering spirit without hearing in it the echoes of the cultural vindication, and even disapprobation, that greeted many Holocaust survivors who arrived in Israel as refugees in the late 1940s and early 1950s. The image of the Holocaust survivor, who was cast as the opposite pole of the Zionist pioneer, represented everything the pioneers wanted to distance themselves from. The survivors were the Jews who had not heard the call of history and had stayed in Europe rather than join the Zionist effort in the land of Israel; they were presented as passive victims of Nazi hostilities (with the exception of the few Ghetto fighters and Jewish partisans) rather than fighters and makers of history; they were eventually driven to Israel as refugees, rather than arriving out of choice and ideological commitment (Diner, 1995; Segev, 1986, 1991).

Given the particular background and apparently discordant set of expectations of these visitors, and the fact that the guided tour was actually tailored to what to the guide was an audience of presumably like-minded old-timers, the guide's style on this occasion was a performative misfire, so to speak. The unspoken gap between the guide's and the audience's positions vis-à-vis the museum story prevented them from effectively attaining or even seeking the moment of communion that can give museum encounters their distinctive ritual flavor. Unable or unwilling to articulate the source of their disaffection, the visitors opted out: Some of them began to drift around the museum, others went outside, and the few who stayed with the guide were only half-heartedly listening to what she had to say.

I was deeply troubled by this particular fieldwork experience, tried to talk to the guide about it and sensed her own discomfort and puzzlement. Then, having traced the problem to the visitors' background as Holocaust survivors, I came to realize that for this particular audience of elderly *kibbutz* members, the pathos of settlement museums was probably greatly overdone; it was tolerable at best. Even though they shared many aspects of the pioneering past depicted in the museum display, they could not significantly identify with the particular preservationist agenda associated with the settlement museum enterprise. Ethnic proximity was no help in this case. The gap was experiential, not cultural, and it suggested to me that a more nuanced account of the social positioning of visitors vis-à-vis the museum tale may sometimes be called for.

The Ethnographer's Positioning:
An Autobiographical Insertion

Following this incident, and my inexplicably strong reaction to it, I recalled a challenging question made by one of the readers of an early paper I had written about settlement museums. He required that I explicate my own positioning vis-à-vis the museum story. I realized that this was more than asking me to introduce a moment of reflexivity into fieldwork (a worthy goal in itself). It would be consistent with my overall contextualizing approach, and particularly my insistence on the importance of charting the positioning of different visitor groups toward the museum tale. How could I exempt myself from this requirement?

In fact, I had not considered the issue problematic until the incident just described. In this, as in my former ethnographic projects in Israel (Katriel, 1986, 1991), I had basically constructed myself as an ethnographer studying her own culture. It was only after considering this particular museum encounter, however, that I came to realize how ambivalent my own response to the settlement museum story actually was. Up to that point in the field research, I seemed to have experienced only the insider dimensions of my participation in mainstream Israeli culture whose master-narrative these museums reproduced. My marginal, first-hand experience of *kibbutz* life as a child was a help, but mainly, I think, it was the irresistible, unreflectively experienced magic of an overall promise of belongingness that the museum offered me. Even if, like most visitors to settlement museums, I did not in fact trace my personal roots to the pioneering past, we were all at least invited to share in a culturally constructed longing for it. It was to a powerful community of feeling that these museums invited their patrons, and most of those who came indeed responded to this seductive invitation with a basic sense of appreciation and identification. But at the same time, I remained an outsider, my family past in Nazi-ravaged Europe making me sensitive to the limits of the museum master-narrative, to its hegemonic nature and exclusionary potential.

Much as I wanted to fully identify with the museum story, that moment of self-recognition when my former teacher's astounded, softly spoken, "How can you compare?" taught me otherwise. It thundered in my ears—this unthinking comparison was mine, not his. I imagined that it would have sounded as irrelevant to my friends in settlement museums as it was unacceptable to him. What did the commemoration of Holocaust memory have to do with celebrating the master-narrative of Zionist pioneering of the 1920s and 1930? Indeed, it was just through this act of narrative separation, made explicit in this refusal of comparison, that I came to realize that my own positioning vis-à-vis the museum story had everything to do with the juxtaposition of these two themes.

So where was I in all of this? I was caught between two powerful master-narratives of modern Jewish existence, the story of victimization and loss and the story of a world redeemed by human creation. It seems, in fact, that in much of the contemporary Israeli official rhetoric the Holocaust Story has become foundational, displacing the centrality of the pioneering ethos by posing a storyline that traces a movement from catastrophe to redemption (Handelman, 1990), from the destruction of European Jewry to the establishment of a Jewish Homeland. To me, the pioneering and Holocaust narratives have always felt more like alternative constructions, encoding quite incompatible messages about the role of memory and of human agency in our lives.[1] Visiting settlement museums demanded that I negotiate my position vis-à-vis both these stories. Part of me resonated with the Holocaust narratives, which made the museums' stories of pioneering hardships and triumphs sound like pathos-filled overstatements, but I also realized that part of the fascination these pioneering tales held for me had to do with their unbridled affirmation of life, with the promise of self-making in a world where dreams are a powerful reality. Shaped by the surfeit of memory that filled my personal background, I found heart in the rhetoric of new beginnings that infused the cultural world I was studying. At the same time, I realized that my own research agenda, which has involved the tracing of processes of cultural production in contemporary Israeli culture—in museums and elsewhere—was an inevitably tenuous project, that tracing the construction of Israeli culture is as much an act of recognition as it is one of deconstruction.

I realized, too, that I had myself been lured by the museum's rhetoric of identification into denying the very distance that made my ethnography possible in the first place. Like all other participants in museum encounters—visitors as well as guides—I had to negotiate my positioning vis-à-vis the museum tale, discovering the ways in which it could become my own and the ways in which it could not. And to this day, as I turn to the road that takes me up the hill to the Yifat museum, or glimpse the top of the two old trees that pridefully announce one's approach to The Old Courtyard in Ein Shemer, my heart fills with a surge of unspeakable longing, a longing I have come to recognize in the voices of other visitors as they sight long-forgotten objects in a museum corner, for a moment transfixed in time and place. Yet I have known all along that the only way I can truly listen to the museum narrative is by lending it a dubious ear, by interrogating the representational practices it employs, by attending to the silences around its edges, for example, by producing a critical ethnography, an auto-ethnography that builds as much on my rootedness as on my inevitable estrangement from my field of study.

NEGOTIATING THE SECULAR/RELIGIOUS RIFT

A more openly spoken social cleavage than the ones discussed in the previous sections relates to the cultural and ideological gaps between secular and religious Jews. In what follows, I explore how this rift became articulated and negotiated in settlement museum presentations by discussing one

---

[1] In a recent article concerned with memorialism of national death in Israel, Handelman (1997) discusses changing trends in understandings of the relation between Zionism and the Holocaust, and suggested that if these trends develop further, the Holocaust may yet become a radical critique of the Zionist state.

particular tour of The Old Courtyard in Ein Shemer, which was led by
Ronen, the second-generation guide introduced in chapter 1. Ronen's
untrimmed beard with patches of gray made him look more like the bearded
rabbi whose picture hung high on the museum wall as an emblem of the
pioneers' East-European origins, than the pioneering type he was imperson-
ating by wearing the Russian *rubashka* shirt. I had observed him guide a
number of groups before, offering vivid and well-received performances of
the museum story, and we had talked at length on previous occasions. This
time, I interviewed him before the tour, specifically focusing on his thoughts
about how to handle the religious visitors he was expecting. I sensed that it
filled him with more than the usual degree of anticipation that seems to
color all tour guide performances, however routinized they may become. In
talking about how he intended to construct the tour, Ronen clearly indicated that he perceived it as a potentially conflictual encounter. He saw the
visitors primarily as religious Jews, who would not take kindly to that part
of the museum story that narrated the pioneers' rebellion against Jewish
tradition, which was part of their secular version of the Zionist revolution.
He was therefore determined to win them over, stating from the outset:

> I have prepared myself for this, to guide older, religious people. Moreover, the
> moment you speak in their language, you immediately become one of them,
> then it's easier. So because I know their language, it is very easy for me. I've
> stopped speaking in my own language, yes, and they immediately begin to
> communicate with me, because I am using their codes, their proverbs, their
> figures of speech…(Ronen, Ein Shemer, 8.2.91)

The fact that these religious visitors were also agriculturists and were
associated with the national–religious sector of the Zionist movement, did
not seem to affect his attitude to them. Although they were obviously
younger than the old-timers whose memories helped to construct the Ein
Shemer display, they could be assumed to have participated in the early days
of their own settlements as youngsters or children, or at least to have had
firsthand experience of agricultural life. He did not say a word that would
indicate recognition of the many everyday experiences and values these
religious farmers apparently shared with secular pioneers even though they
were central to the museum message. In fact, as it transpired early in the
tour, the visitors' identity as agriculturists had not registered with him in any
significant way. He had originally mistaken them for urbanites from a town
near their *kibbutz* that carried the same name. And although their correction
of his assumption about them did lead to a few references to their shared
agricultural experience, he continued to relate to them in terms of the one
social category that seemed most relevant to him—religious affiliation. Most
of the visitors, men and women alike, appeared to be in their middle years,
somewhere between their 40s and 60s.

Indeed, during the tour, he tried to speak what he considered to be their language, their version of Hebrew, and his presentational style on this occasion was different from that of the other occasions on which I had recorded him, and it was obviously shaped in such a way as to accommodate his particular audience. He sprinkled his talk with numerous expressions associated with traditional texts, Biblical and Talmudic allusions—textual resources that speakers of modern Hebrew immediately associate with the social dialect of religious groups. He made many references to Jewish life in the Diaspora that are only rarely heard in that museum context, and maintained a thematic focus on the spiritual dimensions of the pioneers' endeavors through repeated comparisons between the pioneering ethos and traditional Jewish life. But even as he made such a self-conscious effort to speak their language, his way of telling the pioneers' story seemed to underscore the very points of tension he was avowedly out to overcome. As we see next, the exhibits he chose to highlight as well as the interpretations he offered for them, however linguistically sweetened, conveyed a mounting sense of provocation until at a certain point, when he began to talk about the changes the pioneers had introduced into the traditional text of the Passover *Haggadah*, a visitor interrupted a comment he had begun to make, saying, "Please, do not be provocative." He himself was aware of the tightrope he had been walking, and twice along the tour said, "I hope I have not hurt anybody's feelings." This curious blend of provocative storytelling and audience-oriented discursive accommodation seems to me to have underscored the depth of the religious/secular ideological rift even while entertaining the possibility of mending it. I illustrate this with a few examples taken from the transcript of this tour, employing some of the original Hebrew terms in order to substantiate my point concerning the guide's double-edged rhetoric of religiosity.

The tour started out by placing the museum enterprise within a larger preservationist project. Citing a saying attributed to the late Labor leader Yig'al Alon, that "A people that does not preserve its past will have an uncertain future," which I have heard quoted many times as part of settlement museum discourse, the guide then stated that the museum was not about Ein Shemer in particular but about preservation efforts and the value they have in a larger educational agenda:

> Our problem as parents, as grandparents, as educators, as inhabitants of various places in this country, is to convey to the next generations the story of the place so they could look to the future. I will not deal with this issue any more but it's important to me that you take a good look at this place and when you go back to your place, get your council together...and decide when and how you can preserve the beginnings of your town....(Ronen, Ein Shemer, 8.2.91)

This emphatic assertion of the value of the past, and the guide's exhortation to his audience to become active participants in the efforts to preserve it so that their children and grandchildren will see where the story began, is an appeal well-directed to this particular audience of tradition-oriented, religious Jews. It is followed, however, by a series of interpretive comments that accentuate the centrality but also the problematics of the rejection of tradition by the early pioneers. Thus, standing in the small museum corner that depicts the pioneers' parental home through the use of enlarged photographic portraits of old-world, religious Jews, the guide began his narrative of the pioneers' collective biography:

> Where did these people come from? Mainly from Eastern Europe, Izmir, and Turkey. They came from religious-traditional families, all of them came from traditional-religious families, all of them had studied in the *cheder*, in *talmud Torah*, [traditional Jewish schools], in a religious high school, and so on, and so on. They went through a certain transformation in their lives as a result of which they *hitpakru* [became secular] and said, "Let's go to the land of Israel as a group." The skullcap they left at home, the ritual fringes [worn under the shirt by adult Jewish males] they left at home, the bag of the *sidur* [prayer book] they used to take to the synagogue on Saturday they left with their Mom, and made *aliyah* [emigrated; literally ascended] to the land of Israel, saying, "The *mitzvah* [duty] to settle the land of Israel and the duty to cultivate the holy soil in the land of Israel balances out all the other [religious] duties—and *dayenu* [we stand satisfied]. And they came here. (Ronen, Ein Shemer, 8.2.91)

This account launches a theme that is further elaborated along the tour route: The pioneers are presented as modern interpreters and adapters of Jewish tradition rather than as rebels against it. Their refusal of the many commandments of Jewish religious life is grounded in a reinterpretation of a Jew's religious duties, so that becoming agriculturists in the land of Israel is presented as a fulfillment and not as a rejection of religious commandments. Furthermore, the pioneers are credited with a lingering attachment to their traditional, Biblical text, as is dramatized in the following anecdote told about Ya'akov, one of the mannequin figures representing the pioneering group in Ein Shemer's restored dining room:

> A much more interesting figure is that of Ya'akov. Ya'akov is the group's secretary. Why was he elected to be the secretary? Because he is a thoughtful person. He had been a student in a rabbinical school and was captivated by the ideas of the socialists in 1917. He *zanach et torato* [left his study of Torah behind] and switched to another torah [used in a secular sense for "body of knowledge"], that of Marx. The story about him is that he used to walk in the *kibbutz* yard all day, deeply immersed in thought, and swaying. Why is he swaying?

[Visitor: He learned to sway in the *cheder* [traditional Jewish school, referring to the back and forth swaying movement of the body that tradition-ally accompanies Jewish men's study]

[Guide]: No. In the *cheder* he learned to sway this way [demonstrating a traditional back and forth swaying movement], here he walks and sways that way [demonstrating a sideways swaying movement]. He changed the direc-tion of his swaying [laughter]. Why? It's not accidental, it's a highly principled swaying. No, under one arm he holds a Bible, because he is a deep thinker, and under the second arm, *rachmana leitzlan* [God forbid]—Marx, Das Kapital. Can you imagine the struggle that goes on in his mind, not to speak of [the turmoil] in his heart and soul? (Ronen, Ein Shemer, 8.2.91)

This excerpt, like the previous one, is formulated from a decidedly secular point of view. No orthodox religious person could accept the liberty the early pioneers took to reinterpret the religious commandments in the way the guide described them, or the suggestion of an equivalency of status between the Bible and the writings of Marx made in his depiction of the deep-think-ing Ya'akov. The guide must have known all that, given his academic background in Jewish philosophy, yet he continued to confront his audience with the story of the pioneers' antireligious attitudes, both pushing at the limits of his audience's tolerance and subtly exploring what to him was an idiom of religiosity as a possible path to reconciliation. Thus, discussing male–female relations among the young pioneers, he recounted the stories about their sexual puritanism, attributing it to their religious backgrounds, and highlighting the many cultural uncertainties they had to face in their efforts to create the legendary new Jewish society and new Jewish person:

They really did nothing. Why? Think about it. A boy and a girl are sitting in the granary, alone, they came from traditional homes with deep Jewish roots. They *zanchu et toratam* [left their Torah behind]…they left the *Halachah* [Jewish code of conduct], anything that could be left behind, and came here. And they had to decide for themselves what to do, not just what to do in the daytime, but what does one do *bekumcha ubeshochvecha* [as one rises and as one lays down to sleep, a formulation that harks back to the central prayer in Jewish liturgy called *Shema*], how one eats, how one dresses, what is allowed and what is forbidden, what is a Sabbath and what is a regular day, and what is a holiday. What and how? Certainly [they deliberated] with regards to what a girl and a boy can do. Can they sit together in the granary? It's almost like having *hityachadut* [conjugal relations] before the wedding, and what kind of marriage will they have? Although externally they had made a very nice decision, "Listen, we'll start here from scratch." Pioneering; but deep inside something was ingrained, that Jewish something, the sense of order. They had to sit down and clarify for themselves what was allowed and what was not, so they had a discussion…And they really clarified things and constructed a new framework for their personal lives…(Ronen, Ein Shemer, 8.2.91)

Again, this recognition of the Jewish roots that fueled the pioneers' endeavors, both as personal traces of a cultural heritage and as the keenly felt absence of a socially binding behavioral code, is likely a double-handed gesture as far as the audience is concerned. The very cultural project of self-invention undertaken by the pioneers is highly unacceptable from a traditional Jewish point of view. For members of this particular audience, starting it all from scratch is a ludicrous and hazardous presumption. The guide's and the audience's divergent perspectives finally came into collision as they were pausing at the museum corner devoted to the theme of holidays [chag umoed]. The guide used the pioneers' efforts to adapt the celebration of the Jewish holiday of Passover to their own needs as an example of what he called their recipe for a tradition-oriented cultural inventiveness:

> They came to the land of Israel without the Gmara [the Aramaic portion of the Talmud, central text of traditional Jewish learning]. They came with only the Bible [Old Testament], and tarmil vetziklon [a light, poor person's bag] because they said, "This is the basis, the pshat [literal text], we'll take it, and it's the right and duty of every Jew lidrosh [to offer interpretations]. Kach garsu [that was their position]. Lo echlok itchem [let me not argue with you]. I'm just presenting it leshitatam [according to their system]. Now, this is easy to say but very complicated to do... Kashya [problem], what does one do? They started writing out the whole thing for themselves. So first of all what do I want to say? They made decisions in personal matters, the moment someone was born, or, chas vechalila [God forbid] the moment someone died, and when there's a wedding and when there's a Brith [circumcision] and when there's engagement, and so on. The bell starts ringing [summoning pioneer group members for discussion]. "What shall we do?" "What kind of ritual?" "What does one read, a text?" "Something needs to be done"...And what about the holidays celebrated by all Jews in the land of Israel and in the Diaspora? What do we do for Shavu'ot [the feast of Weeks]? And Rosh Hashanah [Jewish New Year]?... We want something new. Come, let's start afresh, let's open the book and write it all over again. And it's a problem. A part of it they managed to do and a part they didn't. Part of it they wrote and part of it they didn't write and f ir part of it there are still discussions going on, what to do next. There is ovdan derech [loss of the way], it's not by chance [that the issues have not been set], the way hasn't been all paved yet.
>
> [Visitor: Ovdan derech ve-ovdan dor [loss of the way and loss of a generation]]
>
> The People of Israel has been inscribing its heritage for 4,000 years? Zionism has been inscribing itself for 100 years? Have patience. It is written: Divrei chachamim benachat nishma'im [the words of the sages are listened to patiently]. We will all listen to them patiently, we are not rushing anywhere. What I want to show you is an experiment. [pointing] This is a Passover Haggadah [the traditional text read before the Passover meal, here a kibbutz version].

[Visitor: The Lord's name cannot be found in there.]
Just a minute.
[Another visitor: All the traditional *psukim* [citations] were taken out.]
    First of all, the Passover *Haggadah* is a concept all in itself, it's not a *midrash* [homiletic commentary]. You just take the book of *Shmot* [Exodus], read the story of the Exodus from Egypt, with the book of Exodus, you put some additional historical layers from here and from there, *tfilot upiyutim* [prayers and religious poetry] of one kind or another, and this is our *Haggadah*... (Ronen, Ein Shemer, 8.2.91)

Having laid out the view that religious texts are cultural constructions, the guide continues to detail some textual and ritual changes introduced by the pioneers in such a way as to stress the centrality of the land of Israel in the Passover ritual. This territorial refocusing of Jewish tradition elicited a cynical response on the part of one of the participants, who quipped, "But it did not help to prevent the sons [of the *kibbutz*] from emigrating." This comment by the visitor, in which he used the derogatory term for emigration, *yeridah* [descendance, as contrasted with the positive-sounding ascendance, *aliyah*], probably alluded to the slide presentation the visitors were shown at the beginning of the tour, which concluded with an open acknowledgment of the phenomenon of emigration [*yeridah*] among second and third generation *kibbutz* members. The rejection of *kibbutz* life, but more poignantly the rejection of the basic Zionist tenet of making a life for oneself in the land of Israel, is a sore point that has triggered a great deal of soul searching within the *kibbutz* movement. A number of guides in Ein Shemer told me they were proud that this point was not swept under the carpet in their slide show, and admitted that it had engendered a great deal of pained argument among the *kibbutz* members when it was first introduced. Thus, Ronen was not taken aback by the visitor's comment and offered an alternative interpretation of the emigration of young *kibbutz* members, relocating it in relation to traditional Jewish images rather than viewing it as an ideological failure specific to the pioneering project:

Believe me, to my heart's regret, not only does most of the Jewish people live outside [the land of Israel] but a good portion today [aborted sentence, probably alluding to the high incidence of assimilation]. There are those who say, pardon me, that our people is a people with wandering genes. So thousands of years ago it wandered from Egypt to Israel, a few thousand years later it wandered to Babylon, then it wandered to the *pzura* [Diaspora], and 100 years ago it wandered here, and then it wanders to Silicon Valley, and in 100 year's time it will wander back. So what's the panic? Some say we shouldn't panic, it's simply a wandering people. The problem is the *ziklon* [baggage]. What does it take in its baggage? ...One great and wise Jew had an answer to that. He said, "All the Torah on one foot: *Veahavta lere'acha kamocha* [love thy neighbor as thyself]..." (Ronen, Ein Shemer, 8.2.91)

The final challenge, however, came in the form of a question by a woman visitor who turned the guide's game of speaking their language back on him. Objecting to the pioneers' practice of inscribing the Zionist spirit into traditional texts in the form of textual alterations, elaborations, and omissions, she shifted the argumentative ground and claimed that she was not speaking from a religious standpoint but from an aesthetically grounded respect for the integrity of artistic and cultural works. She pressed her point by asking the guide:

> Visitor: If you dared to change the scriptures here, I'm asking, would you have made changes in a [literary] work? Not from respect for the Torah, but a respect for the text, would you make changes in Bialik [national poet]? Why did you change here? There's the matter of respect for the text. I'm not speaking out of Judaism.
> Guide: I'll think about it, Okay? (Ronen, Ein Shemer, 8.2.91)

The question, of course, remained dangling, and although there was clearly no meeting of minds, the tour calmly proceeded to the agricultural display area outside, moving, as the guide noted in terms familiar to religious Jews, from dealing with the spiritual realm (ru'ach) to the pragmatic realm of subsistence (tachles). The guide reminded the visitors, as he did on launching the tour, that they could walk around the museum on their own if they so chose, which in this case was also a reminder that they had elected to listen to what to them was a provocative and markedly secular version of recent Jewish history. Even after having made the choice of visiting the museum, they could still have avoided the tensions between secular and religious interpretations of the Zionist enterprise that the guided tour brought to the fore. This recognition of the gap between him and his audience resurfaced again in one of the guide's parting comments, when he noted that time was running short and it was already noon on Friday, Sabbath's eve. Assuming that they were in a bit of a hurry to get back home before the Sabbath, he sent them away, saying with a tinge of self-irony directed no less at them as at himself, "I can go on and on telling stories, but you are in a hurry, and soon the Sabbath will come in, and you'll say, 'It's because of that goy [non-Jew] from Ein Shemer that we had to break the Sabbath laws [of nontravel].'"

Because parts of this encounter were included in the instructional movie we produced on the basis of the videotaped material (as described in the introduction), I had numerous occasions to discuss Ronen's presentational style in these excerpts with people who had watched the film—museum personnel, students, scholars, and others. Notably, in the instructional video, this segment was juxtaposed to segments taken from another guided tour Ronen had given around that time to a group of very young religious children. It was clear that on this latter occasion, his main framing category for his audience related to their young age, and their religious affiliation remained completely submerged, which highlighted the discursive accommodations both these presentations entailed, each in its own way. Viewers' responses to this segment varied in what became a predictable range. Some thought the guide was unnecessarily provocative in telling the museum story to the group of adult religious visitors, and felt that his use of their language was a patronizing rather than a friendly gesture; some thought he had really reached out to them in trying to adapt his style and frame of reference to theirs; others thought he should not have made that effort—it was they who chose to come to a settlement museum located in a secular, left-wing *kibbutz*, and it was up to them to try and listen to the museum story without any religious coloring, as one person put it.

At times, the argument became quite heated and I realized that the discussion of performative style had stirred deeper waters. The very assumption I was making, in line with the contextualist, rhetorical framework of analysis I had adopted, was that the matter of audience accommodation had to be taken for granted as an aspect of all language use. In this conceptual framework, it is an inevitable, ideologically neutral feature of verbal performances whether meta-communicatively foregrounded or not. I spent a great deal of effort analyzing the varied and complex possibilities of this process as I was able to document it throughout my fieldwork. But, as it turned out, for many of the viewers of the video, this conception of performative accommodation did not provide a viable interpretive framework for understanding museum encounters that involved an ideological struggle and an agonistic potential, as in the earlier case. The question for them was not how to specify and interpret the details of the audience accommodation process, but how to view and assess narrators' willingness to embark on such a process in the first place. Those who objected to the guide's appropriation of the visitors' language in this context saw it as a self-effacing move, a lack of heart that prevented the guide from standing on his own and speaking in his own voice. To them, it was not a generous gesture of invitation. They saw the museum as a place of collective self-making and self-assertion and considered the discursive style supporting this process as intrinsic to it. It could not be compromised or even negotiated without seriously affecting participants' identity claims. According to this interpretation, it appears that it was the guide's very attempt to create a common discursive ground with his religious audience that turned the encounter into such a conflict-ridden, tenuous affair, one that sounded ingratiating to some and paternalistic to others.

A similar argument concerning the very viability of performative accommodation arose, following viewings of video segments of the last guided tour I shall consider, which involved Arab visitors to the Yifat museum. These segments, too, were included in the aforementioned video, but contrary to the case of the guided tour of Ein Shemer discussed in this section, the guide in this second case made very little effort to accommodate the tale to his Arab audience in a way that might address his visitors' potentially contentious views of Jewish settlement history. Again, some viewers of the video commended the guide for his lack of accommodation, interpreted as uprightness, or, as one viewer put it, his "unwillingness to bend his story" so as to please his audience. Other viewers were taken aback by what they considered to be a lack of sensitivity to the particular position of Arab visitors who could not be expected to identify with the Zionist settlement triumphs recounted by the guide with considerable enthusiasm. To them, Zionist settlement was associated with painful personal and collective losses and dislocations whose consequences were keenly felt and continuously deplored. Whatever the video viewers' positions concerning the guide's style were, it was obviously perceived and discussed in ideological terms as a refusal of performative accommodation that was applauded by some and frowned on by others. Again, I was alerted to the impossibility of viewing the discursive choices made by the tour guide as ideologically neutral. Indeed, when the settlement museums I was studying became most palpably sites of half-spoken contestation, the ideological underpinnings of their narrative practices jumped into view. But no less significantly for my analysis, so did the ideological implications of the rhetorical model that has grounded my reading of these discourses. This is an important theoretical reminder—the contextualization of context is itself an interpretive and an ideological act.

ARABS AND JEWS IN SETTLEMENT MUSEUM ENCOUNTERS

The most contentious juncture in settlement museum interpretation concerns the way in which the Arab–Jewish struggle over the land of Israel/Palestine has figured in this discourse. As was shown in the previous chapters, both Arab tales and tales about Arabs became incorporated into the museum narrative repertoire (especially in Yifat). I now wish to develop my account further and discuss the cultural politics associated with the representation of Arabs, and their tools and stories in settlement museums encounters. These representational practices become, of course, especially poignant and problematic when Arab visitors are guided along the museum display. I have therefore chosen to focus on one such tour in Yifat as a way of addressing the issues such an encounter raises.

Representational Practices

Through the narratives woven around them, the manual agricultural tools displayed in the Traditional Agriculture Corner are associated not only with the traditionality of the Arab villages in which they were actually found, but also with the antiquity of Jewish agricultural life. This link is accomplished through repeated allusions to the Biblical names of the tools and implements on display and the Biblical stories in which they are embedded. Take, for example, a story told by Binyamin to a group of grade-school children as they stood facing the implement used until some time ago as a measure for dry substances in traditional Arab households:

> I'll tell you a story, do you remember the story about the Patriarch Abraham? Oh, he was quite a man! Phee [Wow], he had lots of cows and sheep and lots of people working for him, and he used to wander from place to place, and he lived in the desert. He was the first Bedouin, the Bedouins weren't there yet, but he was there already. He was sitting in a tent, what was his wife's name? Sarah, Sarah sat with him in the tent, and three angels are coming, they are going around in the desert, and they see some old man sitting with a young and beautiful woman, so they say, "Let's go visit them," so they come, so Abraham says to them, "*Tefadalu* [Arabic], please, come in and be our guests," so he says, what does he say to Sarah? He whispers loudly in her ear, "Go get three measures of flour [*seot kemah*]." Here are the measures [pointing to the wall], *from the Bible straight here on this wall* [italics added]. You see, this is what they used to measure in, imagine, the Patriarch Abraham in his time. How many years already? Oh, it's impossible, I wasn't there, you weren't there, your parents weren't there, and he was already using this to measure with. (Binyamin, Yifat, 1.8.89)

In this story, a claim of priority is made for the Jews via the figure of the Patriarch Abraham who is at the same time presented as "the first Bedouin." Collapsing the image of Abraham onto the image of the Bedouin supports the logic of claiming a biblical provenance for the objects on display. Here the Bedouins are not cultural Others but, rather, stand-ins for the Jews, allowing for a direct, uninterrupted line to be drawn from the time of the Patriarchs to present days. The tools and implements on the wall are therefore attended to and valued not only for the aura of authenticity they carry as testimonials to a recent past when real, productive work was performed by human hands in a way that promotes attachment to soil and place. They also become textually sacralized through biblical allusions that reconfirm the link of contemporary (mainly Jewish) visitors to the ancient Israeli past—through a Bedouin detour—in the meantime appropriating the sense of rootedness projected on them by their actual Arab provenance. To Jewish audiences, the kind of story Binyamin told sounds like a playful elaboration of a well-known biblical tale, retold here as elsewhere by way of reiterating a largely accepted ideological claim concerning the historical depths of the Jews' roots in the land of Israel (despite the 2000 years of life in the Diaspora). Renaming Abraham as the first Bedouin, or recent Arab tools as biblical items, cannot be subsumed under the museum's commitment to factuality, which includes an accurate specification of the objects' provenance, but is intelligible in terms of its larger mission of refiguring Jewish–Israeli collective memory.

This story signals a deep identification with the image of the Arab, who is valued for his antiquity as well as for his role as custodian of the land during the years of Jewish exile. But it is also, of course, a gesture of appropriation toward the Arab past, actual and symbolic, that is a rarely spoken-of potential source of tension in the museum context. Although the sense of identification was an explicit element of many of Binyamin's stories, it was only in an interview I conducted with him well into the research (on August 23, 1991) that he elaborated on the tension he experienced in relation to the position of Arabs vis-à-vis the Jewish settlement story. He told me about an exchange he had had with a group of Arab teachers whom he had recently guided through the museum display. He had been obviously aggravated by the fact that they had openly raised the issue of the pre-state history of Yifat, which was roughly the location of the now-destroyed Arab village of Mdjedel, whose inhabitants fled with the outbreak of the 1948 war. Binyamin said he had had many friendly contacts with the Arabs of Mdjedel and the nearby village of Ma'alul during the British Mandate, because he had lived in the nearby *kibbutz* of Gvat from which Yifat later split off. Although he was quite firm in his belief in the rightfulness of the Zionist enterprise of creating a homeland in Israel for Jewish refugees from Europe and the Middle East, Binyamin, whose childhood was spent among Arabs in prestate Jaffa, strongly empathized with the plight of the Arab refugees as well, speaking of them as victims of the 1948 war rather than its aggressors. In line with the ideological position that equates the cultivation of the land with a sentimental attachment, and a moral even if not a legal right to it, he even refused to let their flight be interpreted as lack of attachment to the land and place, and insisted that they were driven away against their will by the Iraqi soldiers who were part of the invading Arab armies stationed in the area. By the time the war confusion was over and they may have been ready to return, he said, the place was already occupied by Jewish refugees from Germany, Iraq, and other countries who had nowhere else to go. But all this only emerged as a response to the visitors' comments, which he clearly perceived as a deliberate provocation. Ordinarily, even Binyamin did not allow any of this tension to insert itself into his interpretation of the Traditional Agriculture Corner, which was one of his favorite stops along the tour route.

The display in this corner collapses the pre-Zionist past—alternatively inhabited by timeless Arabs and textualized Jews—into a moment of stasis filled with authentic, picturesque and now obsolete tools and implements indexing a time-before-time. The Arabs are presented as unchanging, romantic figures whose lives follow the rhythms of natural and agricultural cycles; the tools and implements found in their villages are the same as those used in antiquity by the Jews, and they are simultaneously appreciated for their rootedness in the land and despised for their primitive ways and their inability to benefit from technological progress, unlike the Jews who developed new and more efficient forms of land cultivation, increasing productivity and minimizing physical labor. Notably, a similar set of representational strategies was found in depictions of Arabs in Israeli postcards (Cohen, 1995b).

The extent to which I had come to expect this kind of idyllic yet ambivalent representation of the relations between Arabs and Jews during prestate years as part of the museum's discourse was brought home to me forcefully one day when I visited it with an American friend who is pro-Palestinian in her politics. We were strolling along the Traditional Agriculture Corner of the museum when she suddenly stopped in front of one of the enlarged photographs and drew my attention to it with something of an exasperated tone of voice. The picture showed two men working along two adjacent fields—one was an Arab plowing his land with a horse and a wooden plow, and quite close to him was a Jew plowing his land while seated on a tractor. She interpreted it as a picture designed to point out the modernity gap between Arabs and Jews through blunt visual comparison. I had not thought of it that way but this interpretation seemed plausible given the ethos of technological progress that permeated the agricultural display. It wasn't a picture that was frequently narrated and I did not remember having heard it explicated by the guides. So the next time I came to the museum, this time with a group of students, I deliberately asked Binyamin, who was our guide on that day, to say something about the picture. He saw it quite differently. To him, it was a picture that demonstrated the possibility of mutual respect and harmony between Arabs and Jews. Each of the two farmers depicted in the picture, he said, had his own way of cultivating the land, each went about his own business, and each knew his place in a way that indicated that they lived in a world that could accommodate both. He made no reference to the technological superiority often symbolized by the tractor in other narrative segments routinely included in the museum tour. Where my friend saw conflict and one-upmanship, he saw the possibility for a separate, mutually respectful coexistence. The picture in itself, I realized, could support either reading.

Visions of Cooperation:
The Story of the Hybrid Plow

Various anecdotes pointing to pleasant neighborly Arab–Jewish relations were inserted into the guides' accounts, including stories about how the Jewish pioneers, who had no experience with agricultural work, were taught by the Arabs how to till the land (a situation that was sometimes half-jokingly referred to as Arab Zionism), as well as stories about how the Jews, in turn, taught the Arabs how to mobilize technological progress to improve their agricultural production. Another story, which is frequently retold in Yifat, seems to me to epitomize the museum's main narrative with regards to the representation of the early Arab–Jewish encounter in Palestine. It is the story of the hybrid plow, whose telling became an occasion for a fantasy-filled gloss on the relations between Arabs and Jews.

The ploughs used by biblical Jews in ancient times and by Arabs through the first part of the century were made of wood and could be adapted to fit the conditions of the soil in different places and seasons of the year. They were dependable and local in the most positive sense of the term, in that they reflected a responsiveness to the particularities of the place: They were built of local material and shaped by generations of human touch. Initially, the pioneers were incompetent farmers—having had none or very little agricultural background—and were unaccustomed to local conditions. They were taught how to work the land by the local Arabs who imparted to them the age-old agricultural tradition they practiced. The wooden plows they first adopted from the Arabs kept breaking down in their unaccustomed hands, whereas the iron plows sent to them from Europe by their benefactor, Baron Rothschild (the so-called "charity plows"), were unsuited to the hard, dry soil of Palestine. The solution, attributed to the blacksmith Lev Toporovsky from Rishon Le-Zion (see Avitsur, 1986), is recounted in the museum as a combination of the best of both worlds. In the tour guide's words:

> ...he turned the wooden plow into an iron plow. It is similar but is made entirely of iron, it doesn't break, it is completely stable and its capacity is much greater so that it is superior to the wooden plow. Now the Arabs called it a Jewish plow, and the Jews called it an Arab plow. Why? The Arabs know that it was produced by the Jews, but the Jews know it is an Arab product. (Binyamin, Yifat, 6.22. 89)

This hybrid plow, with its Middle Eastern shape and European substance, responded both to the demands of an efficiency-driven agriculture and to the particularity of local soil conditions. The repeated stories of its making encode the possibility of fruitful, creative developments out of the comingling of Arabs and (European) Jews in the land of Israel. Nostalgically set in the distant past and in what appears to be the politically neutral domain of agricultural method, the story of the hybrid plow points to a fantasy of mutual enrichment that was entertained even at a time when Arab–Jewish relations were reaching a peak of hostility. This was the second year of the Intifada, the Palestinian uprising in the Israeli-held territories of the West Bank and Gaza, and the conflict over contemporary Jewish settlement ideology as implemented in those areas remained a politically explosive issue.

The narrative omissions and tales of cooperation went unchallenged in addressing Jewish visitors, but the tension engendered by the political and ideological rift between Arabs and Jews over questions of land and settlement hovered at the edges of every museum encounter involving Arab visitors. The guides were keenly aware of it. Some of them told me quite openly and unapologetically that they found it uncomfortable to interpret the museum display for Arab visitors and preferred to leave this job to someone else, usually Binyamin who looked forward to these intercultural encounters. They said they were quite aware that it was the Jewish version of the Zionist settlement narrative that the museum was telling, and, fair-minded as they wanted to be, they did not think it was the role of Jewish settlement museums to tell the Arab version of this conflict-laden tale. Let them tell their own story, they said. Only on rare occasions was the potential for political tension overtly acknowledged and directly addressed, as it was in the case of the museum encounter I consider next.

Arab Visitors in a Settlement Museum Tour

The guide in the case of the tour I want to focus on was Raviv, who had experience as a teacher-guide with the Society for the Protection of Nature and was not a regular member of the museum staff. He was energetic and eloquent. Born to a non-*kibbutz* farming family in the area, he had a native familiarity with it, and a great deal of knowledge about its history and natural landscapes, as well as a love for transmitting it. He had personally known the founder of the Yifat museum, Oded Artzi, had followed the museum's development from its very beginning, and was highly appreciative of its accomplishments. I have three recordings of guided tours he led through the Yifat museum, one of which was addressed to the museum staff itself during the early part of my fieldwork. Out of respect for his knowledge and experience, they had invited him to help them restructure their guiding activities and teach them things they might not know about the artifacts on display or the history of the area.

The fact that Raviv was permitted to guide the group of visitors he had brought with him, rather than have a local guide do so, was a vote of confidence on the part of the staff. The group in question consisted of Arab teachers who were undergoing an in-service training program sponsored by the Society for the Protection of Nature, and the museum tour was one of their stops in their outing for that day. I was particularly keen to get a recording of this tour, as the ideological issues surrounding the representation of Arabs in museum discourse in general, and particularly when handled in actual encounters with Arab visitors, had begun to loom large in my thinking. It was clearly the most contentious representational problem settlement museums had to face, given the history of Arab–Jewish political and military strife that the Zionist settlement had brought in its wake.

Against the overall background of self-questioning and unease among museum guides that appeared to color many guides' thinking about how (or even whether) the story of Arab–Jewish relations could fit into settlement museum narration, Raviv's interpretation of the museum display for this group of Arab teachers stood out as easygoing, good-humored, and self-assured. Let me, then, turn to an examination of the way he handled this tour, taking into account that he had an ongoing relationship with this particular group of teachers, which may have made his task easier but also probably more consequential than tends to be the case in the kind of fleeting encounters between regular museum guides and their audiences that we have hitherto considered.

The guide opened the tour by stating that he had no intention to close his eyes to the problematics raised by the museum they were about to enter, which everybody seemed to understand as an allusion to the issue of Arab–Jewish relations. He framed his willingness to address this problematic as part of his search for what he called the golden path [shvil hazahav]. This opening reaffirmed his belief in the possibility of a meaningful museum encounter that can convey the Zionist perspective on Jewish settlement in the land of Israel for Arab visitors without ignoring their special positioning vis-à-vis that story. This optimistic note was followed by a warm-up story that manifested the essential solidarity that binds Arabs and Jews. The story was about a month-long trip he had recently taken to the United States with his wife. One day toward the end of the trip, as they were walking along a street in San Francisco, Raviv and his wife suddenly noticed a wonderful smell coming out of a small restaurant and were drawn to it. To their delight, they discovered that the restaurant was serving real humus spread [a popular Middle Eastern dish], which the wife, who was tired of American hamburgers, had been pining for. They got talking to the two guys who were running the place, and soon discovered that they were not Hispanics, as they had originally thought, but Palestinians who had originally come from the West Bank to find their luck in the United States. The guide concluded his story thus:

> I had such a good feeling, I felt at home, and I told him, "Look how strange it is, we're actually considered enemies...And it is just in meeting you that I feel at home, that I feel good." So he, out of politeness—and whoever knows Palestinian society knows that the answer was expected—he immediately said, "No, how come we're enemies." But we all know the reality, and that through politeness they try to wash it over is another story. So here's something that brings out a bit the problematics of the whole situation...
>
> Now, look, the Jewish settlement in the land of Israel and the Arabs in Israel are intertwined like Siamese twins. I say, if you want it or not, if you like it or not, their reality is such that there is integration [shiluv] between them, and this integration has many dimensions to it. We cannot touch upon all of its dimensions today, but will present some of them. This integration involved cooperation, mutual positive influence and also violence and extremism, as we all know, and this is really the basis for current events, that is, the situation today is related, actually derives from the historical turn of things... (Raviv, Yifat, 10.23.91)

The guide's opening story about the unexpected encounter in San Francisco set the stage for the theme of Arab–Jewish relations that would be woven into the whole tour, occupying a much more prominent place than it did in any of the other tours discussed so far. The narrative of Arab-Jewish past contacts is enveloped by a meta-narrative commentary on both the possibility and recognition of such contacts in the contemporary scene. The San Francisco encounter was facilitated by a shared culinary affinity and love for Middle Eastern food. Despite its amiable tone, however, this encounter harbored a recognition of the larger context of antagonistic relations between Arabs and Jews and indicated the basic mistrust the guide had experienced, fueled by the very familiarity with the Arab physical and social landscape that had made him feel so much at home in the first place. He somehow knew that the Palestinian's denial of enmity was a matter of politeness, based on his general knowledge of Arab ways, and did not apparently consider that this avowed bit of cultural knowledge might have implications for his relationship with his current audience. In openly communicating both his acknowledgment of political enmity and his sense of mistrust, he constructed himself as the open-minded and open-hearted native Israeli Jew, who is overwhelmed by a sensual love of the land of Israel, its sights and sounds and smells, but who is nobody's fool, either. For this guide, not only in this tour but also in the other tours I have recorded with him, the stories of intercultural contact and shared origins become the obvious vehicles for self-presentation and historical reflection. For example:

> ...All these tools here, all this agricultural agrotechnics at that period, the end of the 19th century in the land of Israel is identical, exactly, to biblical agriculture, i.e., agriculture we have been familiar with for 3,000 years. How do I know? Because the agricultural tools are the same, so there can't be a different agriculture if the tools are the same. In other words, the agricultural possibilities of the Arab farmer at the end of the 19th century were exactly the same as those of the farmers in the period of King Solomon, who is very popular in Arabic folklore, so let's mention him. Well, this is really a surprising thing, for 3,000 years a particular culture of agriculture is preserved without any move. The truth is that there's something of an error in this picture, there was movement, there was a shift and during the Byzantine era there was an enormous agricultural development. But with the Arabic conquest, the whole thing deteriorated, for some reason there was a considerable slide downward, they actually went backwards...
>
> Whoever knows the history of Islam knows that Islam in fact originally started out from a core group of merchants, right? Trade was very highly developed...And on the other hand, of course, there were the Bedouins, the nomadic herdsmen...It was a mercantile culture, certainly not an agriculturalist one. It wasn't their area of expertise at that time, and therefore they showed little understanding for agricultural needs...

Now, modern Arab society is very different from the agriculture-based Arab society, enclaves of which you can still see here and there. And I'm talking about mentality now. In the agricultural parts of traditional Arab society, one of the typical things was *hashlama* [the acceptance of things, alluding to what is popularly referred to as Arab fatalism]: "That's what we've got. That's enough for me." There was no desire to strive for more, to run ahead, and therefore they contented themselves with using these tools, and there was no breach of custom, there was no development. Of course, here and there were people with initiative but the general picture was that agriculture remained stagnant. Now, how do I know that these tools are the same as the ones they used in biblical times? Very simple, because I know the names. Look, it's a very nice thing, the tools enter into the folklore... (Raviv, Yifat 10.23.91)

This account is typical of the ones given by guides as they interpret the Traditional Agriculture Corner of the museum. Earlier examples of object narratives associated with this section of the museum have shown how it is interpreted to Jewish visitors (see chapters 3 and 4). As we see, a similar interpretive stance is taken by this guide when he interprets it to Arab visitors, appealing to both folklore and etymology in endowing the objects on display with an imaginary, biblical career. To these particular visitors, for whom the traditional agriculture corner may provide an occasion for animated personal reminiscing in response to the encounter with objects that have been collected in Arab villages—as I have observed several times, when visitors identified objects they remembered from their childhood—this strategy of biblical allusion amounted to an act of cultural appropriation, even of symbolic violence. Apparently bound by the rules of Arab politeness the guide had mentioned (see also Griefat & Katriel, 1989), Arab visitors rarely expressed their negative reactions openly, but when they did, their reaction was poignant, as in the aforementioned case of the confrontational encounter with Arab visitors described by Binyamin, and a couple of more muted encounters that I had occasion to witness myself.

Once when I asked a group of Arab teachers, who had told me that they felt the museum was telling their story more than the Jews' story—pointing to the many Arab-made objects found in the traditional agriculture corner—whether they would not prefer their museum to be located in an Arab village rather than a Jewish *kibbutz*, my question met with multiple evasions. Several teachers said it did not matter where the museum was; they assured me they were glad they could bring their school kids to see the implements that had until recently been in use in Arab villages but are now part of a vanishing tradition. In so saying, they not only reaffirmed their cultural ownership of the traditional agriculture corner of the museum, but also gently reminded me that contemporary Arabs are part of the modern world, not just vestiges of an agrarian past. They are very different from the traditional figure of the Arab that tends to be depicted as a timeless Other in Jewish settlement museum displays. One teacher suggested that a sepa-rate corner in the museum be devoted to the display of olive groves and olive oil industries, which have been central to traditional Arab agriculture and life in the area. The suggestion met with general approval by her colleagues, and I felt that if the museum were to follow it (which my queries suggest is unlikely to happen), this would be interpreted as a gesture of incorporation toward Arab visitors, enhancing their tentative sense of the museum space as an island of political neutrality, where Arabs and Jews can meet as children of the earth, producers and consumers of agricultural goods.

A comment by another teacher, however, brought the discussion back to reality. He waved my question aside, saying there are many more important things the Arab population needs—they would rather have proper medical services and schools before being given museums. His colleagues responded with chuckling sounds of approval, but at the same time, some of them were quick to check his protest with restraining, light-hearted calls of, "no politics here." At another time, similarly, when a grade-school child from a nearby Arab village openly showed his dissatisfaction with the claim that the valley had been an empty, swampy terrain before the arrival of the Jewish pioneers, he was hushed by his teacher, who said to him, "Keep quiet. The Palestine we know is not the Palestine of the Jews."

Here and there, however, explicit voices of contestation nevertheless sifted through the museum tours, as in an entry I found in the visitor book by an Arab teacher: "It's a pity the Arab contribution to the settlement of the land has not been highlighted sufficiently." Or in the muttering of an Arab school teacher, whose sarcastic comment encapsulated the problemat-ics of the tool display from the standpoint of Arab visitors, "The tools belong to father and grandfather, and the stories belong to Moshe and Chaim [both common Hebrew names]." In sharing my sense of this largely suppressed problematic with museum personnel, most of whom have struck me as thoughtful, creative, and open-minded people, I found that their response depended on their overall vision of the museum's role. The general attitude, it seems to me, is that settlement museums have been established to tell the story of the Jews, not of the Arabs, and that it is therefore legitimately told from the perspective of Zionist ideology. Even when conceding the role of the museum as an arena where contacts between Arabs and Jews could be fruitfully highlighted and explored, most museum professionals insisted that this was only a secondary matter, and that the primary focus should be on the story of the accomplishments associated with the Jewish nation-building mission. There is no argument with the aforementioned statement that the Palestine of the Jews and the Palestine of the Arabs represent two different geographies of the mind. Let the Arabs tell their version of the story, I was told again and again. Notably, in both tours and interviews, many of the guides emphasized differences between early pioneering settlement (*hityashvut*) and contemporary West Bank settlement (*hitnachalut*), glorifying the former while rejecting the latter as unacceptable political acts.

Thus, Raviv's interpretation of the museum to his Arab audience both reproduced representational strategies of cultural appropriation and objectification that were common in settlement museum discourse generally, and amplified them by providing a more elaborate version of the Arab–Jewish interdependence narrative. The vision of Arabs and Jews as Siamese twins does not go well with the attitude that distinguishes between their story of settlement history and ours, the Palestine we know and the one they know. Exploring points of contact and assuming the existence of parallel, incompatible tales are very different ways of narratively dealing with the problematics associated with Zionist settlement history. Although the contact theory was incorporated to some extent into most of the guided tours—both in terms of Arabs being viewed as embodying (Jewish) biblical agricultural lifeways and in terms of the story of mutually edifying agricultural learnings—it was only in Raviv's presentation that it became foregrounded to the point of excluding the possibility of invoking the parallel stories attitude.

At the same time, the point of view from which Raviv's story is narrated is totally that of the Jewish pioneer whose encounter with the Arab farmer gave him the exciting feeling of witnessing biblical landscapes and a true sense of homecoming. And the most impressive part about the story of settlement, as presented here, is the enormous leap forward the Jewish pioneers made in moving from the position of utterly inexperienced and incompetent farmers to that of agricultural experts who engineered unprecedented progress in cultivation methods and production rates. Raviv's story gains at least some of its authority from the repeatedly mentioned fact that he had firsthand familiarity with the agricultural tools on display, had himself worked with the different plows and other implements, and knew what it took to overcome the difficulties of becoming accustomed to this kind of labor. His story thus moves quite credibly between a highly effective dramatization of the pioneers' initial difficulties and the celebration of their ultimate triumphs, offering enthusiastic accounts of technological development interspersed with nods of recognition toward the values of continuity and tradition. Even though the pioneers' success is attributed to their initiative and entrepreneurial spirit, which stood in sharp contrast to the Arabs' proverbial fatalism and conservatism, it is also rooted in their romantic spirit and in their vision of a biblical revival. Some of these themes are illustrated in the following excerpt:

> ...At any rate I went through these phases of learning myself and I know, I can easily identify with this, I have used that plow quite a bit...Now look, there comes this Jew who knows nothing and has no idea, but he has one big dream, he can already envision himself cultivating the soil of the Holy Land, he is plowing and the furrows open up in the fields and he sows the seeds—and

those who sow in tears will reap in joy—he knows these expressions from the Bible, he knows lots of expressions associated with agricultural life in the land of Israel from the Bible, and he's full of enthusiasm, and he comes and looks at his neighbor who can already do everything, and it all seems very simple, he puts the harness on...and all of a sudden he doesn't know what to do [lengthy account of unsuccessful attempts to get the plowing going]....You should understand, the Jew arrived with this great dream of working the land of Israel, cultivating the fields and making the wilderness bloom, and going back to biblical days, etc. And suddenly he finds out that he can't even make one step, and so he feels a failure, and it doesn't feel just like a professional failure, "I'm not making it, how shall I learn, what am I doing here anyway? My dream is unrealistic, I can't fulfill it." And as you may know the worst thing that can happen to a person is to have his dream shattered...(Raviv, Yifat, 10.23.91)

The description of the profundity of the pioneers' initial disappointment and fears, which were fueled by their national dreams and what the guide referred to as their romanticism, served not only to underscore their eventual success but also to highlight the importance of the teachings and assistance they received from the Arab farmers who taught them how to work. Having become farmers, the Jews soon repaid those who had taught them by improving old tools and inventing new, more effective ones, even if they might sometimes be less malleable to human handling than the generations-old tools of the Arabs. By engaging in agricultural work, the pioneers then forged new links to the land of Israel through their intimate familiarity with its landscapes, fauna, and flora. This newfound sense of connection was intensified by its anchoring in the biblical texts to which they kept returning, but was no longer totally dependent on it.

This and similar accounts of the Jews' agricultural success, as compared to the Arabs' self-defeating conservatism in cultivation methods, clearly encode the Jews' point of view and are largely designed for Jewish ears. On this occasion, this rather colonialist version of the Zionist settlement story is mitigated at some points: At one point, the distinctive virtue of traditional tools is brought forth; at another point, referring to contemporary Palestinians' homegrown vegetables that helped them pull through the hardships entailed by the Palestinian uprising, the Intifada, the Arabs are commended for their ability to adapt themselves to difficult conditions. This is the other side of their conservative spirit of "we'll make do with what there is," and it is acknowledged as such. Also, several times the guide points out that the picture of the Arab as frozen in time does not apply to contemporary Arabs who have become full-fledged participants in the progressive drive for a better life. Finally, although the constant comparison between Arabs and Jews inevitably carries a judgmental tone, such an intention is explicitly rejected in favor of a quest for historical understanding:

The point is really to examine the issue from a historical perspective and not to give out grades. Who am I, standing here, what am I? What can I say for myself, how can I pass judgment? That's not the question…Well, I want to tell you two things about why things turned out that way in Jewish agriculture. What motivated them [the pioneers] was not just the economic issue. They felt that all the [Jewish] people were on their shoulders. They are holding up the whole nation, that is, the whole national question. That's what pushed them and gave them the intense feeling of fulfilling a dream. That's one thing. Secondly, what helped them a lot was that they had no tradition at all. You see, with the Arab *fallah* [*farmer*], his son comes and says to him, "Father, let's do it a little differently," so he says, "Come on, you want to teach the father how to make children? You want to teach the chicken how to lay eggs? Come on, leave me alone, why are you nagging me? My father worked like this, why do I need different things?" That's the blocking aspect of tradition. Then the son says the same to his own son, and so things don't move. With us, there was no such thing, there was no tradition, just because they didn't know they did all kinds of nonsense, but out of this nonsense good things came out, too. Well, this is another reason. And the third reason…the Arab *fallah* worked alone. At the beginning Jewish farmers worked the same way and develop-ment was indeed slower. In the second phase, farming became cooperative, the *kibbutz* and the *moshav* [cooperative settlement], this is undoubtedly what enabled all this [development], the togetherness, right? Poor people, a lot of poor people, when they get together can do a great thing. One poor person can't do anything…(Raviv, Yifat, 10.23.91)

In the foregoing excerpts, the guide presented a view of tradition as a constraining force and depicted the Jewish pioneers' lack of an agricultural heritage and their collectivist orientation as enabling conditions. In the next excerpt, he speaks to the role of the museum enterprise in promoting a personal view of the value of history, a knowledge that "I am part of history, I am connected to the past." He demonstrates the validity of these claims through a personal example that echoes the larger theme of Arab–Jewish contact he has expounded throughout:

In the introduction I talked about how the Arabs became integrated into the story of Jewish settlement in some ways that were nicer and some that were not. I presented this theme several times, and right here in this group I found a little proof for this in a way that touches me personally…Two of the guys here [refers to two of the Arab audience members] tell me that they are from Sandala [voices trying to correct his pronunciation, to no avail]. When we established a new settlement in the Gilboa in 1958 there were two farmers from Sandala [laughter at his pronunciation of the place's name]—that's how I talk, I've been saying it like that for 30 years, now you want to correct me?—there were two farmers, and note that I remember their names to this day, Amin and Abdallah, who helped us and taught us, for example how to grow watermelons. We were kids, just out of the army, what did we know?

And they helped, as neighbors they helped. And this guy says to me, "I am Abdallah's son." So what else can you want? Here, you see how things work...(Raviv, Yifat, 10.23.91)

Thus, in this personal experience story, the guide narratively implicates his audience in a web of mutuality patterned on the larger cultural theme of Arab–Jewish interdependence that ran through his interpretation from the very start. He chose this story as a closing narrative for the part of the tour dealing with agriculture in which the theme of mutual help in farming could be naturally foregrounded. As noted earlier, this recognition of the Arabs as participants in Jewish settlement history acknowledges their presence in the land, yet gives no voice or even indirect recognition to the Arabs' own experience of this apparently significant intercultural encounter. I felt that the guide's repeated refusal to accept the linguistic corrections volunteered by his audience for either the meaning or pronunciation of Arabic words and expressions unwittingly echoed this overall suppression of the native voice. At only one point, however, was such a corrective move inserted into the guide's flow of words in a way that signaled a shade of opposition on the part of an audience member. Explaining the medical implements used by the pioneers, the guide pointed to the cupping glasses adopted from traditional healing methods and said:

> Cupping glasses, yes?...There's a saying in Hebrew, when you want to tell someone, "Let it be, it can't help," they say that it will help "like cupping glasses to a dead person." That is, it doesn't help a living person so it certainly won't help a dead one. But you see, there are still people who use it and believe in it. It doesn't matter as long as it makes you feel better.
> [Visitor]: Don't say it doesn't help. It does help, and how! I know this, it helps, and you take out a bit of blood, too [assenting voices]. My uncle who used to work in Haifa, he had back pains, and what his wife cared most about was that he should go to work in the morning—for this she called in the guy who administered the cupping glasses. (Raviv, Yifat, 10.23.91)

Undeterred by this interruption, the guide continued to interpret the dining room display. Indeed, it was the segment of the tour devoted to the dining room, which was included in our instructional video, that triggered the argument concerning his lack of accommodation to his audience. It ran as follows:

> Allow me two more sentences in conclusion. Here was the center of life...Here was culture; here was the library; here were the musical instruments; here was the only radio there was. I still remember the radio, in the *moshav* [non-collective settlement] there was also the radio in one spot; I remember its shape, and there was one person who was responsible for it, and I remember on November 29 [1947] when everybody was standing around

that radio, listening to the report on the UN vote [ratifying the State of Israel], will we get it or not—sort of like they stand today watching the result of the lottery, will my number come out or not—they were standing there, the only radio, the only telephone, of course. That's what the arrangement was.... (Raviv, Yifat, 10.23.91)

The highly tense and dramatic scene of counting the results of the UN vote on November 29, 1947 that would determine whether the international community was prepared to accept Israel as a nation among nations is inscribed in Israeli collective memory as a pathos-filled juncture in Zionist history. Some of the people who viewed the video thought it was an unnecessarily provocative and exclusionary story to tell to an audience of adult Arabs for whom this piece of Zionist pathos might be particularly objectionable as it marked their defeat in the struggle over the control of the land of Israel/Palestine. The Arabs clearly had their own personal and collective memories of this juncture in prestate history and those who objected to the telling of this story felt that it went too far in silencing what was bound to be this audience's very different experience and recollection of the past. Others, as noted earlier, thought that narrating the story of the UN vote in this manner was quite appropriate, and regarded it as a good way of underwriting the fact that the museum was committed to telling the Zionist version of Jewish settlement in the land of Israel in a way that would highlight the Jews' historical experience. The vehemence with which both these positions were put forth and argued suggests that treading the golden path was not as easy as this guide had originally imagined, even as he recognized the complexity and many-sidedness of the problems involved.

The guide's final comments bring out both the candidness of his efforts and their limitations. Speaking as openly as he had promised, he pointed out the Jewish farmers' contribution to Israel's security efforts, both as leaders of the military battle against the Arabs and as creators of friendly links with the Arab population. He invoked the figure of the late Moshe Dayan, who was close to the Arab neighbors among whom he had grown up, spoke their language, and was considered by King Abdallah of Jordan to be "just like one of them." Yet at the same time, he was the most well-known warrior and general to have fought in the Israeli army. Indeed, the image of Moshe Dayan in this connection, as well as the guide's self-references to his own rootedness in the Israeli soil and his familiarity with Arabs whose language he could speak, point to the option of another kind of contact between Arabs and Jews. This possibility of contact is left implicit in the guide's narrative but is nevertheless there. It is the possibility that as Arabs become more like Jews—progress oriented and technologically sophisticated—Jews also become more like Arabs, having shed some of their European baggage and grown more attentive to local sights, sounds, and cultural ways.

This conciliatory note notwithstanding, the contact model associated with the figure of Moshe Dayan, which is based on a mutual recognition of rightful presence and a shared sense of place, is also one that denies the colonialist working of power and the pain of displacement. As I was listening to Raviv's exposition, I was reminded of a comment Binyamin had made as we were concluding an interview just two months before Raviv's guided tour was recorded (on August 23, 1991). Alluding to the already mentioned fact that the Yifat *kibbutz* and museum were located on the land of an Arab village that had been destroyed during the 1948 War, he pointed to the aged olive ɛɹove that painted the slope of the museum hill with the dazzling beauty of its gray-green leaves, and said with a tone that combined obvious emotion and a sense of resignation, "I never eat those olives. For me they are taboo. They are olives that they planted. How can I eat them?" It was a stone's throw from the place where Raviv later stood recounting his story of Arab–Jewish contact with such obvious relish, and with none of the troubled spirit to which Binyamin's privately communicated comment had given voice.

Clearly, museums are political instruments established by particular groups to give voice to their own versions of the past and not to those of other groups. But as the analyses presented in this chapter have illustrated, this storytelling project is not a straightforward affair. That both the performances of Ronen and Raviv (as excerpted in the video) appeared to some viewers unnecessarily provocative, to others condescending, and yet to others as verging on self-negation, suggests that the golden path Raviv believed he was walking and the strategies of linguistic accommodation that Ronen put so much faith in may have been more problematic than either of them had imagined. More often than not, Raviv's version of the museum story, despite its thematic focus on the history of Arab–Jewish contact, sounded more like a self-congratulatory story of Jewish ascendancy, and Ronen's obvious fascination with the world of orthodox Judaism actually led him to make statements that religious people could only find outrageous.

In fact, the hegemonic claims of the socialist Zionist narrative made by settlement museums are at the same time compelling and ambiguous in scope. Arab and orthodox Jewish visitors both represent groups that are socially located at the edges or out of the scope of socialist Zionist ideology, both potentially eroding its hegemony by putting forth alternative versions of Israel's recent history. This also appeared to be the case when visitors from Middle Eastern and North African backgrounds (Mizrahi Jews), who are considered marginal participants vis-à-vis the dominant version of the Ashkenazi-based pioneering enterprise, visited settlement museums. The story of Mizrahi Jews is constructed as a story of immigration, not of pioneering. The symbolic resonances attending the different linguistic references to newcomers to the land—as either pioneers or immigrants—could not be easily dismissed, just as references to Jewish religious roots and to the Palestinian narrative could be suppressed but not discarded.

Only on rare occasions were visitors openly invited to make their voices heard in any significant way. No such invitation was extended to the Mizrahi women or to the religious and Arab visitors described in this chapter. Of the visitor groups described here, the group of elderly *kibbutz* members, who were assumed to be like-minded participants in the pioneering enterprise, was the only one that was encouraged to join the guide in a rather controlled form of mutual reminiscing. Their lack of interest in so doing was expressed through physical disengagement rather than open challenge.

Oppositional Voices

The only sustained open resistance to the museum message that I encountered during my fieldwork occurred in the context of a pedagogical activity in the Yifat museum. Following a brief tour of the museum, school children who participate in this activity are invited to put on pioneers' clothes and simulate moments in the pioneers' lives. Although inviting children to become pioneers themselves was clearly a gesture of incorporation, it seems to me also to involve a more open-handed invitation to young visitors to give voice to their own views and reactions vis-à-vis the museum display. In this activity, after being briefly introduced to some of the main exhibits, the children are taken to the communal clothes cabin and are invited to dress up in the pioneers' clothing they find there. Large mirrors are placed near the cabin so they can dress up properly, an activity that involves much fun and laughter. Then they are divided into small groups of up to five children and are asked to invent a short skit that would represent some aspect of pioneering life. Each group works on its skit separately, and then they get together in the dining room or some other enclosed area and perform for the whole class, so that normally one gets up to six or seven skits per visit.

This activity provides children with an opportunity to express identification and involvement with the museum tale, but it also provides an opportunity to offer oppositional readings (Hall, 1980) of it that would probably not have been given an expressive outlet in the context of the museum tour if it were not for the activity. An example of such an oppositional reading that has stayed with me with particular force involved a visit of a fifth grade class of city children. Following a brief, very lively tour given by Yoni (a second-generation guide who is particularly effective in turning the museum tour into a playful experience for school children), and the dressing routine, the class was divided into five groups, each of which prepared its skit of pioneering life in different corners of the museum, and then congregated in the dining room to entertain and surprise each other with their creative responses to the place and its story. On that particular occasion, three out of the five groups came up with skits whose structure and message were very similar although they were prepared quite separately. The basic line of these skits ran as follows: Three kids march in, dressed in pioneer clothes, proudly holding agricultural tools in an upright position (as often seen in old photographs), and loudly singing pioneer songs. A few moments later, two other kids storm in from the other side of the room, holding agricultural tools as if they were electric guitars, singing contemporary rock songs at the top of their voices, completely drowning the sound of the pioneers' songs, and one of them cries out, "What do you want with these old songs?" The pioneers pretend to be startled, but a moment later they join the noisy rock singing, and all five finish, happily brandishing their tools to the sound of contemporary international rock music.

The message of these skits was quite clear: The children felt the museum story and what it stood for were outdated and irrelevant to their lives, concerns, and tastes. Not only did they not identify with the story, they also reinterpreted their position vis-à-vis the museum tale as one of generational strife in which they, with their raucous sounds of music, had the upper hand. The guide seemed to have sensed the serious challenge that fueled this playful performance, and the very moment the third group that put up a version of this skit finished its rock singing (which was joined by some of the peers in the audience), he dramatically called for attention and, turning to a picture that was hanging on the dining room's wall, he said, "Do you see that picture of a truck? It's the very green car on which the song, Our Car is Big and Green (a very well known kiddies' song), was written. Who knows that song?" He started singing it and immediately everyone joined in and the song was sung to its end with great relish. For a moment, it seemed that the sounds of yesteryear that bind the present generation to previous ones through the words and music that fill children's early educational experiences had the upper hand, that a Hebrew kindergarten song could be at least as binding as the generationally divisive sound of rock music. At the last minute, however, the tables were reversed once again: just as the public singing was dying out, the voices of two boys piped out from the end of the room, adding two more lines of their own to the tune of the traditional kiddies' song:

Baboker sigarya, ba'erev hashish,
(In the morning a cigarette, at night hashish)
Haoto shelanu mastul al hakvish.
(Our car runs high on the road).

With this final melodic gesture, the innocent song about the legendary truck that brings milk and eggs to the children of Israel was humorously incorporated into the contemporary drug scene that is at least part of the horizon of the world of youngsters in Israel today. I cannot say if one has to be able to sing these lines out to oneself to feel the bitter irony of this transformation as I felt it observing this scene, which made me realize how unexpectedly profound the gap can be between the museum guides and their audiences. And, moreover, how rarely the presumptions we make about the museum enterprise are allowed to be challenged as they were in the context of this activity, when children were momentarily, half-heartedly encouraged to offer their own readings of the museum scene.

Chapter 6

Contextualizing Settlement Museum Discourse

৪০∎ෆ৪

ON THE TEXTURE OF SETTLEMENT
MUSEUM NARRATION

Settlement museum narration can be said to involve a multilayered relationship between stories and objects. Essentially, these museums are constructed around the master-narrative of Israeli pioneering and it is the narrative logic of this tale that shapes the nature and the limits of the collecting and exhibiting practices that generate the display. In other words, museum making in this context has to do with *visualizing the story* of Zionist settlement. Museum guides then operate within the parameters set by the display, injecting narrative segments into their interpretive accounts at chosen junctures along the tour route. The objects serve as triggers and alibis for the act of narration, and through *narrating the objects* the tour guides concretize and usually multiply and reaffirm the meanings and values encoded in the master-narrative that grounds the museum project as a whole. The object stories are not linked together in an associative way, nor are they integrated in terms of an overarching narrative structure. They comprise evocative signs couched in an idiom of materiality whose power lies mainly in the narrative potential an object holds for a particular guide on given occasions. The evocative sense of presence attached to settlement museum artifacts has to do with the shared cultural symbolism related to the pioneering era that is propagated in the museum context as part of its intramural conversation, as well as with the guide's fund of personally meaningful stories.

Therefore, museum narrations are always both collaboratively constructed and individually inflected. In the storytelling context of the guided tour—as in the historical discourse of the Mexicano elders studied by Briggs

(1988)—the visual signs and key expressions associated with them provide the narrative backbone for the storytelling occasion. The signs that emerged as central to settlement museum narration include such terms and images as the hybrid plow, the sieve, the dining-room, the family tent, the *primus*, the tractor—to name but a few. These visual signs and the stories woven around them are utilized by tour guides in a modular and cumulative fashion as they construct the loosely structured museum text. Other means of verbal organization and dramatization are mobilized as well, enhancing the rhetorical effect of museum narration. These involve, as we have seen, the guides' autobiographical insertions, and their introduction of direct exchanges with audience members into the flow of talk. The latter engage listeners in brief question-and-answer sessions or in shared reminiscing. Another strategy involves citing pioneers' own testimonies or even role playing pioneers in bits of reconstructed, fictional exchanges. These citations may take the form of textual allusions inserted into the guide's oral performance—whether biblical stories or popular pioneering songs. The reproduction of written segments taken from pioneers' journals and diaries in selected locations on the museum walls or at selected moments in the unfolding of the tour was another such strategy. The textual references, whether oral or written, serve both to enliven the museum display and to appeal to the cultural authority of original texts. And all these strategies of citation and textualization mark the museum as a repository of not only the community's material culture but also of its linguistic heritage.

As we have seen, however, the most important interpretive strategy employed by the guides involved the insertion of narrative segments, which I have referred to as *embedded performances*. The framing of these performances marks a shift of key that is often announced by discursive means, through the use of such devices as, "Now listen to a nice story," or, "There's an interesting story about this plow here," or, "There's a story I have to tell you about this picture." Hymes (1981, pp. 79–141) referred to this kind of shift in framing as a "breakthrough into performance," arguing not only that performance is a distinctive form of communicative conduct in which a person assumes responsibility for presentation, but also that performance should be viewed as a graded phenomenon. Within such a framework, we can speak of a notion of "performative gradation" in terms of which the pole Hymes called "performance in full" marks the most authentic and authoritative performance that realizes "standards intrinsic to the tradition in which it occurs" (p. 84).

The end of a narrative insertion is often marked by shared laughter when humorous tales are involved, or by a moralizing coda when the tale is a pedagogical one (e.g., "and this should teach us that water is important and should not be wasted"). An interesting feature of settlement museum interpretation is that narrative segments addressed to audiences of children seem to represent the guides' notion of performances in full—they tended to be the most highly dramatized and elaborated narrations I observed, and included the use of impersonation and performed (fictive) conversational exchanges as part of the guide's spoken text. In fact, these performances in full are sometimes mobilized by tour guides in the form of self-citations inserted into the spoken text of guided tours addressed to adults, which are perceived not to permit the same level of dramatization or the inclusion of stories deemed childish. On these occasions, the stories are introduced by such comments as, "when kids come here I tell them the story about..." "kids are so eager to hear about this so I tell them." "Kids have no idea what it was like so I tell them the story of..." The use of such embedded performances in the form of allusions to performances addressing young audiences is a strategy of bypassing contextual constraints on repeatability.[1]

Other framing devices that involve openings and closings highlight the interest and value of the museum objects and the stories surrounding them. These metacommunicative devices underscore the preciousness, authenticity, or beauty of the items on display, and often give the museum narratives a personal inflection by emphasizing the speakers' investment in the museum stories and in the impact they can have on their audiences. Examples of such devices found in my data are, "There's an interesting story here about..." "You see this figure here in the picture, that's me, and there's something I really want to tell you about..." "It's such a nice story, I had to tell it to you..."

A distinctive rhetorical strategy that is frequently used by settlement museum guides to humorous effect involves the employment of deliberately anachronistic references—for example, referring to the horse-drawn plow as the pioneers' tractor, to a paper-made fan as their air conditioner, to an orange crate covered with a piece of jute cloth as their armchair, and so on. This linguistic usage highlights the technologically marked temporal distance of pioneering days even as it draws attention to the shared human needs that link past and present. Thus, both the use of linguistic expressions anchored in recognized idioms of the past and the humorous use of deliberately anachronistic references serve to identify and name the world depicted in the display as properly museum material, as intriguingly distant yet remarkably approachable—that is, as translatable.

Museum encounters can thus be viewed as complex communicative events in which language is used to protect and elevate the site and the objects it houses as well as to enhance visitors' identification with the site and its stories. This does not, however, imply that the guides' verbal performances always amplify the visual display. In fact, as we have seen, the verbal interpretation can also subvert the message encoded in the grammar of the display and render its overall meaning more complex. For example, the

---

[1]See Hymes' (1981) discussion of the dimension of repeatability of performances.

agricultural tools and machines are spatially arranged in linear fashion, encoding a chronological vision of progress by moving visitors from the hand-driven, primitive tools of yesteryear to the engine-propelled machines that supplanted them. The commentary accompanying the display, however, often interjects a note of nostalgia for the simple agricultural life that is no more, questioning the value of progress celebrated by the display itself. What we get is a much more nuanced and ambivalent message in which the spirit of progress and the spirit of nostalgia are simultaneously entertained.

Typically, most of the talking throughout the tour is done by the guide, whose control of the interaction signals her position as historical authority and ritual leader. Visitors' participation is generally restricted to the interjection of information questions, short replies to questions that are posed so as to advance the guide's story, and validating verbal and nonverbal responses in the form of back-channel cues. Yet this minimal and highly controlled participation is crucial to the construction of museum encounters as communicative events, offering validation that helps to regulate the degree of elaborateness the guide invests in each tour.

As official guardians of the past and its meanings, the guides cherish the museum stories as much as they cherish the objects in their guardianship. They share them with different audience groups differentially at their own discretion. However, there is always a promise of narrative abundance that cannot possibly be encapsulated in one tour. The guides point to it through repeated references to the shortness of the time, the many stories that remain untold, and so on. These comments also underscore the guide's role in selecting and actively constructing each performance afresh, often in response to visitors' directly expressed or implicitly assumed interests. The explicit lack of standardization in tour guides' performances clearly suggests that there is no definitive guided tour of the museum, but that all guided tours are, on principle, acceptable versions of the museum story (even though, obviously, not interchangeable ones). Each tour thus combines elements of ritual repetition and elements of a contingent, emergent performance.

This performative view of museum narration sheds new light on the role of the ubiquitous storytelling found in touristic contexts. Its most significant aspect, as Fine and Speer (1985) suggested, lies in the performative dimension of "the enactment of intense, dramatic stories which bind the hostess and tourist in an imaginative world" (p. 85). As was demonstrated in chapter 5 in discussing ethnic diversity, the secular/religious rift and the conflict between Arabs and Jews as issues that were foregrounded in particular museum encounters, the imaginative binding of settlement museum narrators and their audiences is not always easily achieved. In some of the cases of museum encounters, the ideological divisions associated with the Jewish settlement narrative defeated any hope of attaining a mutually reinforcing web of shared meanings and emotions between particular guides and particular audiences.

Although the guides are quite aware of the rhetorical burden they carry, they do not see themselves as inhabiting a culturally contested field. The guides tend to think of difficulties they face in conveying their message in didactic terms, not in ideological ones, but, as we have seen in chapter 4, their generational positioning vis-à-vis the museum's ideological message is a crucial factor in the ways they shape the museum tale.

The guides are constantly on the lookout for ways to make their message more palatable, entertaining, and emotionally appealing. If visitors are not drawn in, they tend to interpret this as a failure of presentational technique, not as an indication that the pioneering ethos and its messages may be rejected as outdated, irrelevant, or misconceived. Only on rare moments are any oppositional readings offered or allowed to come through. The spirit of friendly hospitality surrounding the museum tours discourages such moments from arising, usually quite successfully. The aforementioned rhetorical devices of elevation and enshrinement of the site also contribute to the diffusion of any subversive readings of the museum story. They combine with the lighthearted tone of jocular anecdotes told by the guides to produce a blend of appreciation, identification, and fellow feeling.

As noted, settlement museums are permeated with a spirit of nostalgia (Davis, 1979). Notably, different dimensions of nostalgia come into play in settlement museum interpretation: For some old-timer guides and elderly visitors, the museum encounter becomes an occasion for reminiscing, for expressing a yearning for a personally experienced past. For many of the guides and visitors, however, the Zionist narrative does not signal a personally lived past. Rather, for them it stands as a symbolically charged set of meanings and values, and the museum thus becomes a reflexive arena in which cultural meanings are both put on display and renegotiated, a site in which the dialectic of past and present is continually addressed in the form of explicit comparisons, implicit contrasts, claims to continuity, suggestions of causality, and so on.

At the same time, pioneering discourse itself is marked by a strong emphasis on the transformation of the landscape and the creation of a new social order. This gives it a future-oriented focus, so that in recreating the pioneering way of life in the context of heritage museums and sites, the future-oriented spirit of pioneering days is nostalgically invoked and preserved. This is a daunting task in intergenerational transmission, whose paradoxical flavor is undeniable: The museum provides a context for fixing and preserving the fleetingness of the pioneering moment, it seeks to revitalize a sense of the future through a past-oriented gesture of commemoration, and it works to enhance identification with the museum story even while accentuating its remoteness from present-day circumstances and the lives of most museum patrons.

Thus, my foregoing analysis has also sought to acknowledge the ambivalences, the paradoxical strains, and the contrary themes that were articulated in the ongoing construction of the museum narrative I have observed and recorded. Specifically, I dwelt on issues related to a distinctively Israeli version and the politics of nostalgia associated with the embattled cultural terrain in which settlement museum discourse is currently deployed. Rather than a story of family roots and childhood landscapes, it is a nostalgia of social feeling that is grounded in mythic moments and images of personal transformation and communal striving.

It is also a nostalgia that is precariously set within the Israeli cultural landscape and is met by multiple challenges from other cultural discourses. Thus, settlement museum discourse is now heard against the contemporary idiom of settlement associated with right-wing, religious settlers in the West Bank and the Gaza strip on the one hand, and against the increasingly prominent Palestinian interpretations of the Zionist enterprise on the other. It is heard against the growing centrality of ethnic voices in the Israeli sociocultural scene on the one hand, and of Holocaust memory and the search for Jewish (diasporic) roots in the symbolic construction of Jewish, Israeli identity on the other. It is heard as a nostalgic rejection of an individualistic, capitalistic orientation that has affected all walks of Israeli life, including the *kibbutz* movement. It is also heard as part of a complex cultural discourse about the past created by other heritage museums as well as other forms of cultural expression, including literary and artistic works, media productions, and school curricula. As I have shown in my discussion of settlement museums as potentially contested sites (chapter 5), this multivocal cultural conversation has shaped the open-ended texture of settlement museums encounters.

The open-endedness of the museum tale comes to the fore most clearly when it is considered within a broader cultural context. I conclude, therefore, by exploring some of the ways in which settlement museum discourse relates to other cultural arenas in which ways of speaking about the past are thematized. In the next section, I contextualize settlement museums by considering them within the framework of the Israeli heritage museum scene of which they are a part. In the one that follows, I broaden my scope so as to attend to the use of museums as cultural metaphors in some literary works concerned with pioneering heritage in Israel. I argue that these artistic expressions form part of the larger cultural context in relation to which the heritage idiom as it is cultivated in settlement museums must be heard. This double-layered contextualizing move helps me locate settlement museums within the Israeli heritage enterprise as a whole and within the uneasy cultural conversation that surrounds it.

THE ISRAELI HERITAGE MUSEUM SCENE

In Israel, some 2 million people are said to visit the prestate pioneering past annually in some 80 local historical museums and heritage sites now in operation. In particular, these visits have become an increasingly important dimension of experientially oriented educational programs sponsored by the public school system. The many small, local museums that have come to form a dynamic web of domestic tourism destinations are located in agricultural settlements (a good number of them in *kibbutzim*). As discussed throughout this study, they have become widely acknowledged institutional contexts for the display, narration, and celebration of the country's Zionist heritage and the pioneering values associated with it.

The planning and construction of more and more heritage museums is underway, an effort that combines a grass-roots preservationist movement and the institutional endorsement of the Society for Historic Preservation, local and regional authorities, or the Ministries of Culture and of Tourism. Newly established museums have become increasingly differentiated with regard to the geographical area and/or historical period they cover, partly in response to the growing competition among local museums over their "share of the visitors' market," as they themselves refer to it. Taken together, these heritage museums clearly present particular, complementary and repetitive versions of the master-narrative of prestate Zionism.

Like the museums established in pre-state years (Kol-Inbar, 1992), the many heritage museums established in the 1970s and 1980s are closely linked to the Israeli nation-building project. The establishment of these latter museums, however, is not directly continuous with the museum-making enterprise of prestate years. These museums differ in their focus on Zionist settlement rather than on biblical traces. They also find themselves in an increasingly pluralistic cultural field. At the point in Israeli history when these museums were established, the telling and retelling of the Zionist tale no longer played the same role it did in the pioneering days when it was originally spun. Indeed, the story of the utopian social and cultural revolution encapsulated in the notion of Israeli *halutzijut* (pioneering) no longer holds a privileged position in Israeli creation mythology. Therefore, these museums' efforts must now be seen as a gesture of social and cultural relegitimation on the part of that small although significant segment of Israeli-Jewish society (the elite groups of pioneers from Eastern and Central Europe and their descendants) for whom the official tale of Zionist settlement has served as a powerful self-defining and self-legitimating social discourse.[2]

---

[2]As noted by Firer (1985), history textbooks concerned with the pioneering era gave voice to the canonical version of the socialist-Zionist settlement story through the first two decades of statehood, but have undergone curricular revision in the years following the 1967 war (a turning point in Israeli history associated with the occupation of territories won during that war such as the West Bank, the Golan Heights, and the Sinai, and the settlement activities in them). Changes in ideological and political orientations involved a repositioning of the settlement ethos in relation to other fields of economic and social action such as urban and industrial development. It was signaled, inter alia, by such semantic switches as the shift from the earlier talk about *halutzim* (pioneers) to talk about *rishonim* (the first to arrive), a more generalized form of reference that does not privilege the story of early agricultural settlers over that of the many other newcomers who settled in towns and cities, or who initiated new fields of enterprise in later years.

Despite the far reaching changes in Israeli society since pioneering days, they do not seem to have touched the stories routinely told and heard in the settlement museums. Indeed, what was most striking to me about these stories was that they harked back to what was for me an utterly familiar, childhood version of the Zionist tale, uncomplicated by more recently experienced doubts and predicaments, unclouded by competing versions of the Israeli prestate saga. In other words, it is not the novelty of the contents of what the museums tell or show that I found intriguing but the very fact that so many museum enclaves have emerged in recent years in which a univocal version of the Israeli nation-building mythology is routinely reiterated in an unproblematic way. That these museums largely serve the domestic tourism market and remain curiously invisible to international tourists makes the question of their emergence all the more interesting.

The version of the past presented in settlement museums must however, be read against the larger background of the Israeli heritage museum landscape because they provide only one kind of culturally sanctioned context in which a particular version of the master-narrative of Jewish national revival in the land of Israel is inscribed and performed. Other versions appear in other types of heritage museums and cultural texts. Taken together they form a distinctive cultural system, a museumland if you will, that reiterates the basic, highly familiar storyline of the Zionist master-narrative of the Jews' return to the land of Israel. These museum tales make up a mutually supportive, if heterogeneous, narrative web whose various inflections tend to highlight different components of the Zionist tale. Consequently, visiting these different types of museums on different occasions both enriches and complicates visitors' sense of the scope and meaning of the Zionist master-narrative the museums jointly promote.

The impressive rise of museums devoted to recent (the past 100 years) Israeli history marks a partial shift from an earlier cultural focus on archaeological sites as educational and touristic destinations—notably those sites that serve as testimony to Jewish presence in the ancient land of Israel (Silberman, 1989). Clearly, the cultural concern with the preexilic, ancient Jewish traces found in archaeological digs has anchored a legitimizing discourse oriented to the repossession of the land. The pioneering story attempts to shift attention from the ancient relics found in the land to recent heroic acts of remaking it. Thus, by laminating a representational idiom of nation-building onto archaeological claims, the heritage enterprise now provides another layer of social legitimation that involves the reaffirmation of the Socialist-Zionist values of pioneering.

Two other types of heritage museums complement the pioneering narrative: museums of clandestine immigration and museums of military history. Clandestine immigration (ha'apala) museums—one of which is located in the port city of Haifa, the other in the nearby village of Atlit—commemorate the struggle for the immigration of refugees from Europe during the British blockade on the shores of Palestine between the years 1934 and 1948. These museums envision the land of Israel as a safe haven for persecuted Jews rather than a site of utopian fulfillment. They elaborate on the Zionist master-narrative by applying the idiom of heroic sacrifice to the journey component of the return-to-the-land-of-Israel story, highlighting the trials and tribulations of arrival in the ancient homeland.

The representational division of labor between settlement and clandestine immigration museums is echoed by the narrative places they occupy. The settlement story begins at the point of the pioneers' arrival in the land, just where the story of clandestine arrival of the newcomer–immigrants ends. This distinction replicates larger cultural distinctions between *halutzim* (pioneers) and *olim* (newcomer–immigrants), the first term referring to those who came in the earlier part of the century during prestate years out of free choice and an ideological commitment to participate in the Jewish nation-building project, the second to those who were uprooted from their homes in the Diaspora in later years and were driven to emigrate to the land of Israel, or to those who chose to do so in poststate years. [3]

The story of those who were not able to flee to Israel in time of need, which only hovers around the edges of the clandestine immigration museums, is most prominently inscribed in its own distinctive cultural spaces, in Holocaust museums such as *Yad Vashem* and *The Ghetto Fighters House.*

Notably, both pioneering settlement museums and clandestine immigration museums conclude their narrative mission with the establishment of the State of Israel. Both exclude from their heroic canons the story of the post-1948 mass immigration from North Africa and Middle Eastern countries, including the stories of the arrival of Mizrahi Jews and their creation of new agricultural settlements and towns in the late 1940s and through the 1950s. Even these settlement efforts, which have resulted in the establishment of many immigrant villages, are not spoken of as pioneering acts but as externally directed and regulated endeavors. Those whom Weingrod (1966) aptly called reluctant pioneers created planted communities (Cohen, 1970), not pioneering outposts. The stories relating to the beginnings of these communities are excluded from the heroic settlement canon. Moreover, as Schely-Newman (1991) suggested, these newcomers' own acts of self-narration foreground experiences of traumatic displacement rather than tales of heroic sacrifice and fulfillment. [4]

The heritage museum scene thus once again reproduces the differential symbolic treatment given to the history and culture of European and

---

[3]Compare Ram (1995a) for a discussion of these kinds of distinctions in the context of Israeli social science writing.

[4]The often traumatic encounter between new immigrants and old-timers in postindependence years (late 1940s and early 1950s) has begun to be seriously explored in historical research. See, for example, Ofer (1996) for a recent collection of essays devoted to this issue.

non-European newcomers to Israel as Dominguez (1986, 1990) argued in her work on the politics of heritage in Israel. As she pointed out, cultural representations of Mizrahi Jews are assigned to ethnographic museums and folkloric exhibits of Jewish communities in the Diaspora, including the composite portrait found in the Diaspora museum in Tel Aviv (Golden, 1996). In the contemporary Israeli museum scene, such representational practices reproduce deep-rooted societal divisions and exclusions in the society at large. They define Middle Eastern and North African Jews through the cultural shreds they brought with them from the Diaspora, not in terms of their experiences and place-making exploits after arrival. They are thus not depicted as "doers," as part of the activist and heroic texture of the Israeli nation-building saga, whether it takes the form of a struggle for immigration, the settling of the land, or involvement in military exploits as these are presented in the increasing number of museums devoted to Israeli military history, including the prestate undergrounds. They are located in different parts of the country and extend the tale of Zionist heroic devotion and sacrifice in the direction of combat heroism.

The establishment of the Old Yishuv Court Museum in the Jewish Quarter of the Old City of Jerusalem in 1976 was designed to enshrine yet another narrative version of the Land of Israel. This museum tells the story of the pre-Zionist presence of vibrant Jewish communities in Jerusalem of both Sephardi and Ashkenazi Jews. It is housed in the home of the Weingarten family, whose courtyard was a community institution from the 1930s until the fall of the Jewish quarter to the Jordanians in 1948. Following the 1967 War, when the Jewish quarter again came to be under Jewish rule, the family went back to its home, which it had occupied since 1812, and opened part of it as a museum devoted to the Old Yishuv, the pre-Zionist population of Jerusalem Jews.

Thus, the chronology charted by this museum clearly predates the pioneering era and suggests a very different periodization from the one proposed within the context of Zionist historiography. Not surprisingly, too, a good part of the museum is devoted to various aspects of Jewish religious life, a substantive domain completely absent from settlement museum displays (and at times, as we have seen, explicitly rejected in their narratives). Located in an urban setting, the Old Yishuv Court Museum concentrates on small industries, commerce, and craftsmanship, which were the forms of livelihood most common in the urban spaces that Jerusalem Jews typically populated. These were also precisely the occupations that the pioneering groups, who were engaged in settlement pursuits in the rural outposts of the Jezreel valley and the Galilee, considered irrelevant (if not detrimental) to the revival of Jewish life in the Land of Israel. The Old Yishuv, although right around the corner, was definitely not part of the new heroic story of the land of Israel in its Zionist version.

It is, indeed, a highly selective land of Israel that pioneering settlement museums depict. It is a land of Israel largely detached from its Arab inhabitants, whose image, when not invisible in the museum displays, provides either an idealized model of the native or an antithetical model against which the image of the heroic pioneer is measured. Thus, museumified Arabs appear in the guise of anthropology's timeless other (Fabian, 1983). They are ancient forefather figures whose primitive tools are given biblical names, to signify local tradition writ large. Settlement museums either omit or gloss over the history of Arab–Jewish conflict. And of course no mention is made of Palestinian views of the Zionist settlement project as part of a European colonialist venture and a direct threat to their own existence in the same stretch of land (e.g., Morris, 1989). The history of Arab–Jewish contact, when addressed, is told as a tale of long-standing cooperation and mutual learning with only passing references to conflict and security problems.

As this brief sketch of the Israeli heritage scene suggests, the Israeli pioneering tale, like its American counterpart (Bodnar, 1992), excludes from the patriotic pantheon of nation builders all those whose autobiographical and cultural profiles do not fit into the master-narrative of early pioneering. In the Israeli case, this symbolic exclusion applies to those who were in Palestine before the Zionists arrived (both Arabs and Jews), to the many European newcomers who chose to live in cities in prestate years, as well as to the many refugees from Europe and immigrants from Arab lands who arrived in Israel shortly before the establishment of the state and ever since. In a word, to most Israelis. Notably, however, what makes the status of the Israeli pioneering story so poignant and problematic as a foundation mythology is not only that it does not apply to all Israelis, but the very fact that it applies to some Israelis. It is relevant to the self-definition of the few who trace their cultural roots to the generations of early pioneers and who can effectively mobilize the symbols and values of the pioneering ethos and the social claims entailed by it.

Thus, the museums I have studied are imaginary sites that inscribe pioneer settlements as symbolically potent signs in a culturally compelling recreation of roots. They are fictionalized as places we have all come from (or might have, or should have). Truly houses of memory, they are inevitably also houses of forgetting. No memory is complete. Neither is forgetfulness. I would argue, somewhat provocatively, that the establishment of settlement museums as secular pilgrimage sites in the rural periphery of the country was matched by the emergence of saints' tombs (*kivrei tzadikim*) as centers of a folk–religious pilgrimage for Mizrahi Jews in other peripheral zones in Israel, especially in development towns largely populated by immigrants from Middle Eastern and North African countries and their descendants. The weaving of a culturally significant foundation mythology in pioneering terms has appealed mostly to the European-based (Ashkenazi) section of Israeli society as part of its search for cultural roots. The many newly established pilgrimages to saints' tombs have at the same time become a crucial part of an ethnic and folk–religious revival movement among Mizrahi Jews who flock to the graves of Saints who have either died in Israel or whose bones have been brought over from their North African places of origin (Ben-Ari & Bilu, 1987; Weingrod, 1990).

In both these cases, a particular segment of Israeli society has created new places and occasions for the performance and celebration of largely competing versions of Israeli identity and cultural experience. Both versions make counterassertions to the identity claims of the country's official cultural centers—Jerusalem with its aura of official orthodoxy on the one hand, and Tel Aviv as the heart of profane, cosmopolitan, mass culture on the other. The similarity, however, ends here. Although they share the functions of sacralizing the periphery and searching for particularized roots, as well as foregrounding an idiom of ritualized experience, these two types of modern Israeli pilgrimage obviously chart quite disparate, ethnically anchored geographies of meaning within the context of contemporary Israeli culture. At the same time, both Mizrahi and Ashkenazi Jews have started to make secular pilgrimages of another kind. They search for concrete traces of a dispossessed family past in the towns and villages of North Africa and Europe. Visits to sites of Jewish destruction in former Nazi camps are part of this trend. These various pilgrimage routes suggest that alongside the pioneering creation myth there are competing tales of origin and multiple forms of Israeli nostalgia.

As the next and final section shows, these nostalgic threads in Israeli culture have given rise to a new round of cultural responses. Even while settlement and other heritage museums continue to celebrate their version of Israel's foundation mythology, other voices are heard on the Israeli cultural scene that relentlessly question and even ridicule the pioneering mythology and the spirit of nostalgia the heritage industry has enshrined.

HERITAGE AS CULTURAL METAPHOR:
"CHILDREN, BEWARE OF MUSEUMS!"

By way of conclusion, I would like to locate the museum-making enterprise in the larger context of cultural production in contemporary Israel, and consider how settlement history, and the museums and sites that enshrine it, have become thematized in Israeli literature and theater. Interestingly, heritage museums have become a trope through which to mount a polemic against the kinds of cultural representations discussed in this study. Works of fiction offer counternarratives and contest the hegemonic voices amplified by the Israeli heritage industry. Located outside the Israeli museum scene, these subversive voices respond to it in significant ways, and a proper understanding of what heritage museums are about must take these voices into account, too.

In a review of literary works dealing with the Jezreel Valley and its settlement history as symbols of the pioneering ethos, Holzman (1993) discerned different phases in the depiction of the valley as a literary site. In the prepioneering settlement era, the valley did not occupy a central place in the literary landscape. When it was described, it either appeared as a site of biblical memories or as an alien and antagonistic space. Ever since the 1920s, when the myth of the pioneering project in the Jezreel Valley was spun, its landscape became a central symbol in literary writings, whether by authors who lived in the valley or by the many visitors who sang its praises. During the 1930s and 1940s, some authors born and raised in the region, for whom the valley and its landscapes were part of their mundane, taken-for-granted existence, have continued to idealize and celebrate the pioneering days whereas others were more realistic and somewhat critical. A more radically critical approach emerged in the 1950s and 1960s when second- and third-generation authors interrogated the earlier myths of settlement and cut the tale to human proportions. In the 1970s and 1980s, when so many settlement museums of the kind studied here were established, literary works took issue with current images of the pioneering past, interrogating their links to the present. Moreover, they also questioned the contemporary urge to celebrate the past by establishing heritage museums and sites.

The issues central to settlement museum discourse—the pioneering ethos and its enshrinement within a local preservation project—are prominent themes in a number of recent plays and novels by second-generation Israeli authors. These fictional treatments of the settlement museum enterprise serve as an intriguing counterpoint to the nostalgic version of pioneering history inscribed in the settlement museums themselves. Thus, rather than glorifying the pioneering past, these novels and plays focus significantly (if not solely) on the darker side of pioneering days in a decidedly antinostalgic mode. They deal with the hardships, jealousies, pettiness, and disappointments that actually poisoned the lives of the founding fathers. They present the pathos of nostalgic attempts to blur or even glorify these darker moments as pitiful.

The widely read novel *The Blue Mountain* (Shalev, 1991), which was originally published in Hebrew under the title of *Russian Novel*, is set in one of the early cooperative settlements in the Jezreel valley. Its author, Meir Shalev, who grew up in the area, provides a vivid account of the cultural problematic associated with pioneering heritage and its preservation. The novel is clearly multivocal, alternating between the author's fascination with the pioneering landscape that he invokes with unmatched vividness and his keen sense of disillusionment that takes its color from the personal and ideological crises in the lives of the novel's protagonists. The elderly schoolteacher of the village, whose enthusiasm for the history of the land of Israel as well as its fauna and flora have been so central to his students' education, looks back to his pioneering days with profound disappointment. He tells his former student:

> We may have dried the swamps, but the mud we discovered beneath them was far worse. Man's bond with the earth, man's union with Nature—is there anything more regressive and bestial? We raised a new generation of Jews who were no longer alienated and downtrodden, a generation of farmers linked to the land, a society of the grossest, most quarrelsome, most narrow-minded, most thick-skinned and thick-headed peasants! (p. 247)

And in a final note that negated the central pioneering symbol of the conquest of the land with all its patriarchal overtones, he conceded, "The earth cheated on us…She wasn't the virgin we thought she was" (p. 275).

Two central figures in this novel are grandsons of prominent members of the settlement's founding generation. Their devotion to the commemoration of their forefathers casts a bitter irony on the settlement enterprise as well as on mainstream preservation efforts of the kind that settlement museums undertake. Rather than developing the agricultural project of their parents and grandparents, both of these grandsons neglected the family farms they had inherited. One of them established a Pioneers' Graveyard on his property and made a great deal of money selling burial plots and services to members of the pioneering generation who had left the village (and often also the country) in the early days. They desired to be buried on the land they had failed to cultivate. Their final resting place was the place in which they could not bear to live.

The other grandson had been a pathetic farmer all his life but had developed an obsession with the pioneering past. Like other enthusiasts of pioneering days, he had spent many years collecting and preserving pioneering memorabilia, which he eventually housed in the small, local museum he had established. All that remained of the pioneering spirit was the much resented pioneers' graveyard and the Founders' Cabin, which the novel treats as the irrational and unproductive pursuit of a single man. Paradoxically but not surprisingly, both sites became tourist destinations for visitors who wanted to breathe in the aura of pioneering. They developed a life of their own, quite independent of the troubled village reality that surrounded them and that forms the heart of Shalev's novel.

The bitterness and disaffection that run through this novelistic account of pioneering days and their contemporary traces stand in sharp contrast to the elevation and enshrinement strategies found in settlement museums dealing with similar themes and issues. Moreover, the novel is no less a commentary on ways of speaking about the past as it is a commentary on the events and images of pioneering days. In it, museum making becomes a trope through which attachment to the myth-making agenda of history lovers is parodied, and representations of the past appear as lifeless and misleading traces masking a world that never was. This antinostalgic statement, however, is embedded within a novel so richly suffused with the sights, sounds, and smells of pioneering days that much of its subversive edge gives way to a sense of longing that attends culturally cherished images of the past.

A number of plays have also given voice to a similarly anti-nostalgic attitude toward the early years of settlement in the Jezreel valley. The well-received play by Jonathan Gefen, entitled *Sleep Valley* (also the title of a well-known Israeli lullaby), was staged by Beit Lessin Theater in the late 1980s (and was also broadcast by Israeli national television). Similarly, a television play by Moti Lerner entitled *The Loves of Bitaniya* was televisually enshrined as part of Independence Day programming in 1994. This latter play casts a dubious note on both the memory and the commemoration of pioneering days by weaving a fictional tale about the opening day of the (nonexistent) museum devoted to the history of Bitanyia, a no-longer-inhabited pioneering site overlooking the Lake of Galilee that has been mythologized in Israeli settlement ethos since the 1920s. As in Shalev's novel, Lerner's play depicts the museum-making enterprise as a vacuous and ineffective attempt to glorify a past whose traces still poison people's lives in the narrative present.

Perhaps the most blatantly antinostalgic attitude toward the collective past is found in a 1995 play by Shmuel Hasfari that was also produced by Beit Lessin Theater. Entitled *Hametz* (i.e., *Leavened Bread*, which is taboo during Passover), this successful play is set on the eve of Passover in 1973, the night in the Jewish calendar when the collective memory of the biblical story of Exodus is traditionally passed on from generation to generation. It is several months before the highly traumatic Yom Kippur War that broke out in October 1973. The play includes a state-wide chase after one of the characters, the self-described Zionist terrorist who goes from one heritage museum or site to another on motorcycle and sets them all on fire in a desperate gesture of rebellion against the tyranny of collective memory. Following his round of heritage terrorism, which draws a good deal of media attention and becomes a news item, he reaches his final destination, the top of the renowned site of Masada. There he makes a speech that contradicts the heroic message of this and other sites of memory:

> I don't want to be a hero. It's the end of the road. I'm on the top of the mountain. Soon the night will be over and the dream will be dashed. I'm not entering memory, I'm destroying memory. I don't want to tell my son "And tell your son" [*vehigadta lebincha*, a phrase from the Passover *Haggadah*], we are the desert generation that should die in the desert [reference to the story of Exodus], and the children, if they're not dead, if they're alive and ask questions—let them look at a tree, at a flower, at a bird, and get answers.

They should drink wine, eat pita bread with olive oil, and forget. Not "remember what they did to your father," not "remember" anything. Just like that, get up in the morning, go to school, learn arithmetic, play soccer, win a soccer game, not memory contests we play against ourselves. Children, beware of museums, beware of museums depicting the history of the nation. The teacher will say, this and that was like this and like that. And you, close your ears and start humming.... (Hasfari, 1995)

This provocative excerpt is the high point in the play itself. It was also included in a television report about the play that was part of a prime-time Friday night news broadcast. The heritage terrorist flamboyantly rejects the premises of the heritage enterprise and preservationist agenda associated with mainstream Israeli culture. He offers a personal, sensuous, present-oriented alternative to the dominant obsession with the collective past—its heroic and its sacrificial aspects—and their enshrinement in historical museums and sites.

Indeed, Israeli settlement museums are not culturally enclosed enclaves. Rather, they participate in an ongoing, ever-shifting cultural conversation that takes multiple forms and trajectories. For the many readers, theater-goers, and television viewers who have been exposed to antinostalgic and parodic portrayals of the pioneering past and the preservationist agenda of the heritage industry so startlingly epitomized in the Zionist terrorist's warning words, "Children, beware of museums!" no future visit to a settlement or other heritage museum can ever be the same.

* * *

As culturally sanctioned sites for telling and retelling the pioneering story, settlement museums are under ideological pressure to stabilize a privileged, once-hegemonic version of a particular past that is now under siege. What is at stake here is not just a matter of nostalgia. The discourse of settlement and its ramifications go to the very heart of Israel's most divisive political debates over control of the land and attachment to place. It is a debate that will eventually determine the future shape of the country and the possibility of peace in the region. It is therefore no wonder that settlement museums promote a version of the past that is cherished by those who have sponsored them. They are part of the cultural politics of contemporary Israel.

Thus, although the material display and the curatorial intentions that anchor the museum story exude an aura of continuity and stability, and although the representational practices employed in settlement museums are geared to the effacement of potential conflict, their story is told and retold in a culturally contested arena. The narrative of Jewish settlement, as well as the authorial voice of museum makers, must address a variety of audiences in a culturally and politically shifting environment. Both the persistence of the museums' storyline and its subtle inflections reveal how the museums position themselves within the larger cultural scene. No doubt, museums, as privileged houses of memory, have a story to tell. But in the final analysis, the meanings of the story that arise in actual museum encounters are forever in flux. Any account that seeks to capture these meanings as socioculturally constituted and situationally performed can therefore be no more than an open-ended report.

References

৪০ ▪ ○এ

Ames, M. (1992). *Cannibal tours and glass boxes: The anthropology of museums*. Vancouver: University of British Columbia Press.

Anderson, B. (1991). *Imagined communities: Reflections on the origin and spread of nationalism*. London: Verso.

Appadurai, A. (1981). The past as a scarce resource. *Man, 16*, 201–219.

Avitsur, S. (1986). *Mamtzi'im umeamtzim* [Inventors and adopters]. Jerusalem: Yad Ben–Zvi.

Azaryahu, M. (1993). From remains to relics: Authentic monuments in the Israeli landscape. *History & Memory, 5*(2), 82–103.

Azoulay, A. (1993). Al muzeonim lehistoria [With open doors: Museums of history in the Israeli public space]. *Theory & Criticism, 4*, 79–95.

Azoulay, A.. (1994). Museums and historical narratives in Israel's public space. In D. Sherman & I. Rogoff (Eds.), *Museum culture: History, discourses, spectacles* (pp. 85–109). London: Routledge.

Babcock, B. (1977). The story in the story: Metanarration in folk narrative. In R. Bauman (Ed.), *Verbal art as performance* (pp. 61–79). Prospect Heights, IL: Waveland Press.

Bakhtin, M. (1981). *The dialogic imagination*. Austin: University of Texas Press.

Bar-Gal, Y. (1993). *Moledet vegeografia bemea shnot chinuch Zioni* [Homeland and geography in a hundred years of Zionist education]. Tel Aviv: Am Oved.

Bar-Gal, Y., & Shamai, S. (1983). *Bitzot Emek Izrael: Aggadah umetzi'ut* [The Jezreel valley swamps—legend and reality]. *Kathedra, 27*, 163-179.

Bauman, R. (1977). *Verbal art as performance*. Prospect Heights, IL: Waveland Press.

Bauman, R. (1986). *Story, performance, and event: Contextual studies of oral narrative*. Cambridge, UK: Cambridge University Press.

Bauman, R., & Briggs, C. (1990). Poetics of performance as critical perspectives on language and social life. *Annual Review of Anthropology, 19*, 59-88.

Ben-Ari, E., & Bilu, Y. (1987). Saints' sanctuaries in Israeli development towns: On a mechanism of urban transformation. *Urban Anthropology, 16*(2), 243-272.

Ben-Avram, B., & Nir, H. (1995). *Iyunim ba'aliyah hashlishit: Dimui umzi'ut* [Studies in the third "aliyah": Image and reality]. Jerusalem: Yad Ben-Tzvi.

Ben-Yehuda, N. (1995). *The Masada myth*. Madison, WI: University of Wisconsin Press.

Bennett, T. (1988). The exhibitionary complex. *New Formations, 4*, 73-102.

Bernstein, D. (Ed.). (1992). *Pioneers and homemakers: Jewish women in pre-state Israel*. Albany: State University of New York Press.

Bodnar, J. (1992). *Remaking America: Public memory, commemoration and patriotism in the 20th century*. Princeton, NJ: Princeton University Press.

Booth, W. (1961). *The rhetoric of fiction*. Chicago: The University of Chicago Press.

Bourdieu, P. (1984). *Distinction: A social critique of the judgment of taste.* Cambridge, MA: Harvard University Press.

Briggs, C. (1988). *Competence in performance: The creativity of tradition in Mexicano verbal art.* Philadelphia: University of Pennsylvania Press.

Bronner, S. J. (1989). Object lessons: The work of ethnological museums and collections. In S. Bronner (Ed.), *Consuming visions: Accumulation and display of goods in America, 1880-1920* (pp. 217–254). New York: Norton.

Brow, J. (1990). Notes on community, hegemony, and the uses of the past. *Anthropological Quarterly, 63*(1), 1–6.

Brown, P., & Levinson, S. (1987). *Politeness: Universals in language usage.* Cambridge, UK: Cambridge University Press.

Bruner, E., & Gorfain, P. (1984). Dialogic narration and the paradoxes of Masada. In E. Bruner (Ed.), *Text, play & story: The construction & reconstruction of self & society.* Washington, DC: The American Ethnological Society.

Burke, K. (1969). *A rhetoric of motives.* Berkeley: University of California Press.

Cannizzo, J. (1991). Negotiated realities: Towards an ethnography of museums. In G. L. Pocius (Ed.), *Living in a material world: Approaches to material culture* (pp. 19–28). St John's, Canada: Institute of Social and Economic Research.

Chatman, S. (1978). *Story and discourse.* Ithaca, NY: Cornell University Press.

Clifford, J. (1988). *The predicament of culture: Twentieth century ethnography, literature and art.* Cambridge, MA: Harvard University Press.

Cohen, E. (1970). Development towns—the social dynamics of "planted" urban communities in Israel. In S. Eisenstadt, R. Bar-Yosef, & C. Adler (Eds.), *Integration and development in Israel* (pp. 587–617). Jerusalem: Israel University Press.

Cohen, E. (1985). The tourist guide: The origins, structure and dynamics of a role. *Annals of Tourism Research, 12,* 5–29.

Cohen, E. (1995a). Israel as a post-Zionist society. *Israel Affairs, 1*(3), 203–214.

Cohen, E. (1995b). The representation of Arabs and Jews on postcards in Israel. *History of Photography, 19*(3), 210–220.

Davis, F. (1979). *Yearning for yesterday: A sociology of nostalgia.* New York: The Free Press.

Diner, D. (1995). Cumulative contingency: Historicizing legitimacy in Israeli discourse. *History & Memory, 7*(1), 147–170.

Dominguez, V. (1986). The marketing of heritage. *American Ethnologist, 13*(3), 546–555.

Dominguez, V. (1989). *People as subject, people as object: Selfhood and peoplehood in contemporary Israel.* Madison: University of Wisconsin Press.

Dominguez, V. (1990). The politics of heritage in contemporary Israel. In R. G. Fox, (Ed.), *Nationalist ideologies and the production of national culture* (pp. 130–147). Washington, DC: American Ethnological Society.

Dorst, J. D. (1989). *The written suburb: An American site, an ethnographic dilemma.* Philadelphia: University of Pennsylvania Press.

Evens, T. M. S. (1995). *Two kinds of rationality: Kibbutz democracy and generational conflict.* Minneapolis: University of Minnesota Press.

Fabian, J. (1983). *Time and the other: How anthropology makes its object.* New York: Columbia University Press.

Falk, J., & Dierking, L. (1992) *The museum experience.* Washington, DC: Whalesback Books.

Fine, E., & Speer, J. (1985). Tour guide performances as sight sacralization. *Annals of Tourism Research, 12,* 73–95.

Fine, E., & Speer, J. (1992). *Performance, culture and identity.* New York: Praeger.

Firer, R. (1985). *Sochnim shel hachinuch hazioni* [The agents of Zionist education]. Tel Aviv: Hakibbutz Hameuchad.

Fogiel-Bijaoui, S. (1992). From revolution to motherhood: The case of women in the *kibbutz*, 1910–1948. In D. Bernstein, (Ed.), *Pioneers and home-makers* (pp. 211–233). Albany: State University of New York Press.

Gable, E., Handler, R., & Lawson, A. (1992). On the uses of relativism: Fact, Conjecture, and Black and White Histories at colonial Williamsburg. *American Ethnologist, 19*(4), 791–805.

Goffman, E. (1974). *Frame analysis: Essays on the organization of experience.* Cambridge, MA: Harvard University Press.

Golden, D. (1996). The museum of the Jewish Diaspora tells a story. In T. Selwyn, (Ed.), *The tourist image: Myth and mythmaking in tourism* (pp. 223–250). New York: Wiley.

Gover, O. (Ed.). (1993). *Chinuch bemuzeonim* [Education in museums]. Jerusalem: Ariel.

Griefat, Y., & Katriel, T. (1989). Life demands musayara: Communication and culture among Arabs in Israel. *International and Intercultural Communication Annual, 13,* 121–138.

Gurevitch, Z., & Aran, G. (1991). Al hamakom (antropologia Israelit) [On the place (Israeli anthropology)]. *Alpaim, 4,* 9–44.

Halbwachs, M. (1980). *The collective memory.* New York: Harper & Row.

Hall, S. (1980). Encoding/decoding. In S. Hall, D. Hobson, A. Lowe, & P. Willis (Eds.), *Culture, media, language* (pp. 128–138). London: Hutchinson.

Handelman, D. (1990). *Models and mirrors: Towards an anthropology of public events.* Cambridge, UK: Cambridge University Press.

Handelman, D. (1997). The presence of absence: The memorialism of national death in Israel. In E. Ben-Ari & Y. Bilu (Eds.), *Fabrications of land* (pp. 85–128). Albany: State University of New York Press.

Handler, R. (1988). *Nationalism and the politics of culture in Quebec.* Madison: University of Wisconsin Press.

Handler, R., & Saxton, W. (1988). Dyssimulation: Reflexivity, narrative, and the quest for authenticity in "Living History." *Cultural Anthropology, 3*(3), 242–260.

Hasfari, S. (1995). *Hametz* [Program, Beit Lesin Theater].

Hewson, R. (1987). *The heritage industry: Britain in a climate of decline.* London: Methuen.

Hobsbawm, E., & Ranger, T. (Eds.). (1984). *The invention of tradition.* Cambridge, UK: Cambridge University Press.

Holzman, A. (1993). Eretz kveda bechazon vetirosh: Emek Izrael basifrut ha'ivrit. [A country laden with vision and fruit: The Jezreel valley in Hebrew literature]. In M. Naor (Ed.), *The Jezreel valley 1900-1967. Idan* series 17 (pp. 205–227). Jerusalem: Yad Ben-Zvi.

Hooper-Greenhill, E. (1989). The museum in the disciplinary society. In S. M. Pearce (Ed.), *Museum studies in material culture* (pp. 61–72). London: Leicester University Press.

Hooper-Greenhill, E. (1992). *Museums and the shaping of knowledge.* London: Routledge.

Hooper-Greenhill, E. (Ed.). (1995). *Museum, media, message.* London: Routledge.

Horne, D. (1984). *The great museum: The re-presentation of history.* London: Pluto Press.

Hymes, D. (1962). The ethnography of speaking. In T. Gladwin & W. C. Sturtevant (Eds.), *Anthropology and human behavior* (pp. 13-53). Washington, DC: Anthropological Society of Washington.

Hymes, D. (1972). Models of the interaction of language and social life. In J. Gumperz & D. Hymes (Eds.), *Directions in sociolinguistics: The ethnography of communication* (pp. 35–71). New York: Holt, Rinehart & Winston.

Hymes, D. (1974). *Foundations in sociolinguistics: An ethnographic approach.* Philadelphia: University of Pennsylvania Press.

Hymes, D. (1981). *"In vain I tried to tell you": Essays in native American ethnopoetics.* Philadelphia: University of Pennsylvania Press.

Inbar, Y., & Schiller, E. (Eds.). (1990). *Muzeonim be-Israel* [Museums in Israel]. Jerusalem: Ariel Publications.

Jakobson, R. (1960). Closing statement: Linguistics and poetics. In T. Sebeok (Ed.), *Style in language* (pp. 350–377). New York: Wiley.

Johnson, R., McLennan, G., Schwartz, B., & Sutton, D. (Eds.). (1982). *Making histories: Studies in history-writing and politics.* London: Hutchinson & the Center for Contemporary Cultural Studies, University of Birmingham.

Kammen, M. (1991). *Mystic chords of memory.* New York: Vintage Books.

Karp, I., & Lavine, S. D. (Eds.).(1991). *Exhibiting cultures: The poetics and politics of museum display.* Washington, DC: Smithsonian Press.

Karp, I., Mullen Kraemer, C., & Lavine, S. D. (Eds.). (1992). *Museums and communities: The politics of public culture.* Washington, DC: Smithsonian Press.

Katriel, T. (1986). *Talking straight: "Dugri" speech in Israeli Sabra culture.* Cambridge, UK: Cambridge University Press.

Katriel, T. (1991). *Communal webs: Communication and culture in contemporary Israel.* Albany: State University of New York Press.

Katriel, T. (1993a). Remaking place: Cultural production in Israeli pioneer settlement museums. *History & Memory, 5* (2), 104–135.

Katriel, T. (1993b). Studying heritage museums as ideological and performative arenas. *Communication Monographs, 60*(1), 69–75.

Katriel, T. (1994a). Performing the past: Presentational styles in settlement museum interpretation. *Israel Social Science Research, 9*(1/2), 1–26.

Katriel, T. (1994b). Sites of memory: Discourses of the past in Israeli settlement museums. *The Quarterly Journal of Speech, 80*(1), 1–20.

Katriel, T. (1995). Trips and hiking as secular rituals in Israeli culture. *Jewish Folklore and Ethnology Review, 17*(1/2), 6–13.

Katriel, T. (in press). Pioneering women revisited: Representations of gender in some Israeli settlement museums. *Women's Studies International Forum.*

Katriel, T., & Shenhar, A. (1990). Tower and stockade: Dialogic narration in Israeli settlement ethos. *The Quarterly Journal of Speech, 76*(4), 359–380.

Katz, S. (1985). The Israeli teacher-guide: The emergence and perpetuation of a role. *Annals of Tourism Research, 12,* 49–72.

Kavanagh, G. (Ed.). (1991). *Museum languages: Objects and texts.* Leicester: Leicester University Press.

Kellerman, A. (1993). *Society and settlement: Jewish land of Israel in the twentieth century.* Albany: State University of New York Press.

Kellerman, A. (1996). Settlement myth and settlement activity: Interrelationships in Zionist land of Israel. *Transactions of the Institute of British Geographers, 20,* 363–378.

Keshet, S. (1995). *Hamachteret hanafshit: Al reshit haroman hakibutzi* [Underground soul: Ideological literature—The case of the kibbutz novel]. Tel Aviv: Hakibbutz Hameuchad.

Kimmerling, B. (1983). *Zionism and territory: The socio-territorial dimensions of Zionist politics.* Berkeley: University of California Press.

Kimmerling, B. (1995). Academic history caught in the cross-fire: The case of Israeli-Jewish historiography. *History & Memory, 7*(1), 41–65.

Kirshenblatt-Gimblett, B. (1991). Objects of ethnography. In I. Karp & S. D. Lavine (Eds.), *Exhibiting cultures: The poetics and politics of museum display* (pp. 386–443). Washington, DC: Smithsonian Press.

Kol-Inbar, Y. (1992). *Toldot hamuzeonim ba'aretz ad kum hamdina kebitui lachazon hazioni* [The history of museums in Israel until the establishment of the state as an expression of Zionist vision]. Unpublished master's thesis, Department of Art History, The Hebrew University of Jerusalem.

Leon, W., & Rosenzweig, R. (1989). *History museums in the United States: A critical assessment.* Urbana & Chicago: University of Illinois Press.

Leshem, N. (1991). *Shirat hadeshe* [Song of the grass] Efal: Yad Tabenkin.

Liebman, C., & Don-Yehia, E. (1983). Civil religion in Israel: Traditional Judaism and political culture in the Jewish state. Berkeley: University of California Press.

Lowenthal, D. (1982). The pioneer landscape. Great Plains Quarterly, Winter, 5–19.

Lowenthal, D. (1985). The past is a foreign country. Cambridge: Cambridge University Press.

Lowenthal, D. (1989). Pioneer museums. In W. Leon & R. Rosenzweig (Eds.), History museums in the United States (pp. 115–127). Urbana & Chicago: University of Illinois Press.

Lumley, R. (Ed.). (1988). The museum time machine: Putting cultures on display. London: Routledge.

MacCannell, D. (1989). The tourist: A new theory of the leisure class. New York: Schocken Books.

Macdonald, S., & Silverstone, R. (1990). Rewriting the museums' fictions: Taxonomies, stories and readers. Cultural Studies, 4(2), 4–19.

Maier, C. S. (1988). The unmasterable past: History, Holocaust, and the German national identity. Cambridge, MA: Harvard University Press.

Middleton, D., & Edwards, D. (Eds.). (1990). Collective remembering. London: Sage.

Morris, B. (1989). The birth of the Palestinian refugee problem, 1947-1949. Cambridge, UK: Cambridge University Press.

Myerhoff, B. (1979). Number our days. New York: Simon & Schuster.

Myerhoff, B. (1992). Remembered lives: The work of ritual, storytelling, and growing old. Ann Arbor: The University of Michigan Press.

Naor, M. (Ed.). (1993). Emek Izrael 1900–1967 [The Jezreel valley 1900–1967]. (Idan series 17). Jerusalem: Yad Ben-Zvi.

Nora, P. (1989). Between memory and history: Les Lieux de Memoire [The sites of memory]. Representations, 26, 7–25.

Ofer, D. (Ed.). (1996). Bein olim levatikim [Israel in the Great Wave of Immigration 1948–1953]. Jerusalem: Yad Izhak Ben-Zvi.

Oring, E. (1981). Israeli humor. Albany: State University of New York Press.

Pappe, I. (1995). Critique and agenda: The post-Zionist scholars in Israel. History & Memory, 7(1), 66–90.

Pearce, S. (Ed.). (1990). Objects of knowledge. London: The Athlone Press.

Pearce, S. (1994). Interpreting objects and collections. London: Routledge.

Penslar, D. J. (1995). Innovation and revisionism in Israeli historiography. History & Memory, 7(1), 125–146.

Price, R., & Price, S. (1995). Executing culture: Musee, museo, museum. American Anthropologist, 97(1), 97–109.

Ram, U. (1995a). The changing agenda of Israeli sociology. Albany: State University of New York Press.

Ram, U. (1995b). Zionist historiography and the invention of modern Jewish nationhood: The case of Ben-Zion Dinur. History & Memory, 7(1), 91–124.

Rosaldo, R. (1989) Imperialist nostalgia. Representations, 26, 107-122.

Rosovsky, N., & Ungerleider-Mayerson, J. (1989). The museums of Israel. Tel-Aviv: Steimatzky.

Schechner, R. (1985). Between theater and anthropology. Philadelphia: University of Pennsylvania Press.

Schely-Newman, E. (1991). Self and community in historical narratives. Unpublished doctoral dissertation, University of Chicago.

Segev, T. (1986). 1949—the first Israelis. New York: The Free Press.

Segev, T. (1991). Hamilion hashvi': Haisraelim vehashoa [The seventh million: The Israelis and the Holocaust]. Jerusalem: Keter Publications.

Shafir, G. (1989). Land, labor and the origins of the Israeli-Palestinian conflict 1882–1914. Cambridge, UK: Cambridge University Press.

Shalev, M. (1991). *The blue mountain.* New York: Harper Collins.

Shapira, A. (1995). Politics and collective memory: The debate over the "New Historians" in Israel. *History & Memory, 7*(1), 9–40.

Shokeid, M. (1995). *A gay synagogue in New York.* New York: Columbia University Press.

Shuman, A. (1986). *Storytelling rights: The uses of oral and written texts by urban adolescents.* Cambridge, UK: Cambridge University Press.

Silberman, N. A. (1989). *Between past and present: Archaeology, ideology, and nationalism in the modern Middle East.* New York: Doubleday.

Silverstein, M. (1976). Shifters, linguistic categories and cultural description. In K. Basso & H. Selby (Eds.), *Meaning in anthropology* (pp. 11–55). Albuquerque: University of New Mexico Press.

Snow, S. E. (1993). *Performing the pilgrims: A study of ethnohistorical role-playing at Plimoth plantation.* Jackson: University Press of Mississippi.

Sternhell, Z. (1995). *Binyan uma o tikun chevra?* [Nation-building or a new society?] Tel-Aviv: Am Oved.

Stewart, S. (1993). *On longing: Narratives of the miniature, the gigantic, the souvenir, the collection.* Durham, NC & London: Duke University Press.

Stone, P., & Molyneaux, B. (1994). *The presented past: Heritage museums and education.* London: Routledge.

Talmon-Garber, Y. (1970). *Yachid vechevra bakibbutz* [The kibbutz: Sociological studies]. Jerusalem: The Magnes Press.

Thompson, M. (1979). *Rubbish theory.* New York: Oxford University Press.

Tilden, F. (1957). *Interpreting our heritage.* Chapel Hill: The University of North Carolina Press.

Tsur, M. (1981). *Kan al pnei ha'adama* [Here on the face of the earth]. Tel Aviv: Hakibbutz Hameuchad.

Tsur, M. (1995). *Hatishma koli* [A call for dialogue]. Tel-Aviv: Am Oved.

Ufaz, G. (1986). *Zikat hakibbutz limkorot hayahadut bemachshevet "Chug shdemot"* [The ties of the Kibbutz to Jewish sources as expressed in the thought of the "Shdemot Circle"]. Unpublished doctoral dissertation, Tel-Aviv University.

Vergo, P. (Ed.). (1989). *The new museology.* London: Reaktion Books.

Wallace, M. (1981). Visiting the past: History museums in the United States. *Radical History Review, 25,* 63–96.

Weingrod, A. (1966). *Reluctant pioneers.* Ithaca, NY: Cornell University Press.

Weingrod, A. (1990). *The saint of Beersheba.* Albany: State University of New York Press.

Zafrir, S. (1992). *Bchinat hashimush be'erkat hadracha hamvuseset al sirtonim behachsharat madrichim bechinuch muzeonim* [Development and assessment of film-based materials for museum guides]. Unpublished master's thesis, School of Education, University of Haifa.

Zemer, A. (Ed.). (1993). *Etnografia yehudit bamuzeon* [Jewish ethnography in the museum]. Publication of the Israeli chapter of ICOM.

Zerubavel, Y. (1995). *Recovered roots: Collective memory and the making of Israeli national tradition.* Chicago: Chicago University Press.

Author Index

୫ଓଔ

Subject Index

ഔൠ